OXFORD

D0361723

take off in
Spanish

Rosa María Martín

OXFORD
UNIVERSITY PRESS

OXFORD

UNIVERSITY PRESS

Great Clarendon Street, Oxford OX2 6DP

Oxford University Press is a department of the University of Oxford.
It furthers the University's objective of excellence in research, scholarship,
and education by publishing worldwide in

Oxford New York

Auckland Cape Town Dar es Salaam Hong Kong Karachi
Kuala Lumpur Madrid Melbourne Mexico City Nairobi
New Delhi Shanghai Taipei Toronto

With offices in

Argentina Austria Brazil Chile Czech Republic France Greece
Guatemala Hungary Italy Japan Poland Portugal Singapore
South Korea Switzerland Thailand Turkey Ukraine Vietnam

Oxford is a registered trade mark of Oxford University Press
in the UK and in certain other countries

Published in the United States
by Oxford University Press Inc., New York

British Library Cataloguing in Publication Data

Data available

Library of Congress Cataloging in Publication Data

Data available

ISBN 978–0–19–953432–6 (Book and CDs)
ISBN 978–0–19–860991–9 (Coursebook)

This coursebook is only available as a component of Take Off In Spanish

1

Commissioning, development, and project management: Tracy Traynor
Project management (2nd edition): Natalie Pomier
Audio production: Gerald Ramshaw; Daniel Pageon, Actors World Production Ltd
Music: David Stoll
Design: Keith Shaw
Editorial: Brigitte Lee
Teaching consultant: Jenny Ollerenshaw

Printed in China through Phoenix Offset

Contents

Introduction

Oxford Take Off In Spanish is designed to help the beginner develop the basic language skills necessary to communicate in Spanish in most everyday situations. It is intended for learners working by themselves, providing all the information and support necessary for successful language learning.

How to use the course
The book and the recording are closely integrated, as the emphasis is on speaking and listening. The recording contains step-by-step instructions on how to work through the units. The presenter will tell you when to use the recording on its own, when to use the book, and when and how to use the two together. The book provides support in the form of transcriptions of the recording material, translations of new vocabulary, and grammar explanations. You'll find this icon ⓐ in the book when you need to listen to the recording.

1 (recording/book) Read the unit objectives on the first page telling you what you will learn in the unit, and then begin by listening to the **dialogue** on the recording. You may not understand everything the first time you hear it, but try to resist the temptation to look at the transcript in the book. The first activity on the recording will

help you develop your listening skills by suggesting things to concentrate on and listen out for. You'll be given the opportunity to repeat some of the key sentences and phrases from the dialogue before you hear it a second time. You may need to refer to the vocabulary list (book) before completing the second activity (book). Listen to the dialogue as many times as you like, but as far as possible try not to refer to the dialogue transcript (book).

2 (book) Once you have listened to all the new language, take some time to work through the **transcript, Vocabulary, Language Building,** and **activities** in the book to help you understand how it works.

3 (recording) Then it's time to practise speaking: first **Pronunciation practice** and then the **Your turn** activity. You will be given all the instructions and cues you need by the presenter on the recording. The first few times you do this you may need to refer back to the vocabulary and language building sections in the book, but aim to do it without the book after that.

4 (book) The fourth learning section, **Culture,** concentrates on reading practice. Try reading it first without referring to the

vocabulary list to see how much you can already understand, making guesses about any words or phrases you are not sure of. The activities which accompany the text will help you develop reading comprehension skills.

5 (recording/book) For the final learning section, return to the recording to listen to the **Story**. This section gives you the opportunity to have some fun with the language and hear the characters in the story use the language you have just learnt in different situations. The aim is to give you the confidence to cope with authentic Spanish. There are activities in the book to help you.

6 (book) Return to the book, and work through the activities in the **Test** section to see how well you can remember and use the language you have covered in the unit. This is best done as a written exercise. Add up the final score and, if it is not as high as you had hoped, try going back and reviewing some of the sections.

7 (recording/book) As a final review, turn to the **Summary** on the last page of the unit. This will test your understanding of the new situations, vocabulary, and grammar introduced in the unit. Use the book to prepare your answers, either by writing them down or speaking aloud, then return to the recording to test yourself. You will be given

prompts in English on the recording, so you can do this test without the book.

8 (book) At the very end of each unit you will find some suggestions for **revision** and ideas for further practice.

Each unit builds on the work of the preceding units, so it's very important to learn the vocabulary and structures from each unit before you move on. There are review sections after units 3, 7, 10, and 14 for you to test yourself on the material learnt so far.

Other support features
If you want a more detailed grammar explanation than those given in the Language Building sections, you will find a *Grammar Summary* at the end of the book. For a definition of the grammar terms used in the course, see the *Glossary of Grammatical Terms* on page 245.

The *Answers* section at the end of the book will give you the answers to all the book activities. Some activities require you to give information about yourself, so you may also need to check some vocabulary in a dictionary.

At the end of the book you'll find a comprehensive Spanish–English Vocabulary.

At the end of the book you'll find a comprehensive Spanish–English Vocabulary.

For additional practice, your *Take Off In Spanish* pack contains an extra CD or cassette you can listen to while on the go without having to refer to the coursebook. You will also find a travel dictionary and phrasebook that easily slips into your handbag or pocket when you travel around.

Introduction

More and more people are choosing to learn Spanish and it is easy to see why. Spanish is spoken by almost 400 million people as their first language. It is one of the easier languages to start learning as it is derived from Latin and so a lot of vocabulary will be recognizable to the English speaker. The pronunciation of Spanish is also consistent and relatively straightforward for the English-speaking learner.

Throughout the Middle Ages a variety of Spanish dialects were spoken in Spain. The dialect of Castile, or Castilian Spanish, eventually became recognized as the official language in the 13th century and it is Castilian Spanish which is taught in this course. Although the majority of words in Spanish come from Latin, many come from other sources which reflect Spain's rich and colourful history: Greek, Basque, and Celtic from the pre-Latin times, Arabic from the Muslim occupation, French from the 11th century pilgrimages to Santiago de Compostela in northwestern Spain, Italian from the 15th and 16th centuries, American Indian languages from colonial times, to name but a few. Presiding over the Spanish language is the Real Academia de la Lengua Española, which makes the rules for what is and is not acceptable and reviews and ratifies modifications and changes.

Learning to communicate in another language may be challenging, but it is also a very rewarding and enriching experience. Most Spanish speakers you come across will be impressed by your attempts and very encouraging. We have made this course as varied and entertaining as possible, and we hope you enjoy it.

Pronunciation

To achieve good pronunciation, there is no substitute for listening carefully to the recording and, if possible, to Spanish native speakers, and trying to reproduce the sounds you hear. Here are a few guidelines for you to keep in mind when doing so. You will find this section most useful if you listen to the Pronunciation section on the recording as you read it.

Pronunciation

Vowels

Vowels in Spanish are pronounced consistently and they are always short.

Written as	Phonetic symbol	English approximation	Example
a	/a/	*between* cat *and* arm	casa, padre
e	/e/	let	leche, tren
i	/i/	kit	fin, distinto
o	/o/	lost	coche, honrado
u	/u/	good	uno, fruta
u + e	/we/	wet	bueno
i + e	/je/	yet	tiene
e + i	/ei/	wait	aceite
i + u	/ju/	you	ciudad

Consonants

Most consonants are pronounced as in English. The exceptions are:

Written as	Phonetic symbol	English approximation	Example
v	/b/	bed	vacaciones, viejo
z	/θ/	think	zumo, zapato
c + i/e	/θ/	think	cine, centro
h		*not pronounced*	hermano, helado
j	/x/	*Scottish* loch	jamón, jota
g + i/e	/x/	*Scottish* loch	gente, gigante
ñ	/ɲ/	onion	niño, piña
r beginning of word and after l, n, s	/rr/	*rolled*	rojo, sonrisa
between vowels	/r/	*softer*	pero, caro
rr	/rr/	*rolled*	perro, carro

Combinations

qu	/k/	k [u *not pronounced*]	queso, quiero
ll	/ʝ/	million	llave, calle
gu + i/e	/g/	hard g [u *not pronounced*]	guerra, guitarra
gu + a	/gw/	hard g [u *pronounced*]	guapo

Stress

Words in Spanish are stressed as follows:
- word ending in a vowel or **n** or **s** – on the penultimate syllable
  - casa, quieren, comes
- word ending in any other consonant – on last syllable
  - hablar, salud
- irregular stress shown by an accent
  - película

Starting out
En camino

OBJECTIVES

In this unit you'll learn how to:

- ✓ greet people
- ✓ meet people and give your name
- ✓ ask for a drink and something to eat

And cover the following grammar and language:

- ✓ masculine and feminine nouns
- ✓ formal and informal ways of saying 'you'
- ✓ the verb ser ('to be')
- ✓ question forms
- ✓ polite requests using **quiero** ('I'd like'), **para mí** ('for me'), and **por favor** ('please')

LEARNING SPANISH 1

Spanish is relatively easy to learn, especially at the beginning. Many words are similar to their English equivalents, which means you can build up vocabulary quickly. Spanish is also comparatively easy for English speakers to pronounce.

You can go far with just a little language, so even when you are not sure how to form a correct, complete sentence, try using the words you do know. Don't worry about getting things wrong. Even with some errors, people will still be able to understand you. The more confidence you gain in actually communicating, the more fluent you'll become.

Finally, it's important to work through each unit at your own pace, listening to the recording several times if necessary before going on.

Now start the recording for Unit 1.

Saludos

 **ACTIVITY 1** is on the recording.

ACTIVITY 2

Match the person with the correct time of day.

1	Señor González	a	night
2	Juan	b	morning
3	Señora Martín	c	afternoon

DIALOGUE 1

○ ¡Hola! Buenos días, señor Pérez.
■ Buenos días, señora Martín. ¿Cómo está usted?
○ Bien, gracias. ¿Y usted?
■ Muy bien, gracias. Adiós.

■ Buenas tardes, señorita García.
○ Buenas tardes, señor González. ¿Qué tal está?
■ Bien, gracias.

○ Hola, buenas noches, Juan. ¿Qué tal?
■ Bien, gracias. ¿Y tú?
○ ¡Muy bien!

VOCABULARY

¡hola!	hello
buenos días	good morning
el señor (Sr.)	Mr
la señora (Sra.)	Mrs, Ms
¿cómo está usted?	how are you? [*formal*]
bien	fine
gracias	thank you
y	and
usted	you [*formal*]
muy bien	very well
adiós	goodbye
buenas tardes	good afternoon/evening
la señorita (Srta.)	Miss
buenas noches	goodnight
¿qué?	what?
¿qué tal?	how are things?
tú	you [*informal*]

If you are uncertain about any of the grammatical terms used in the **Language Building** *sections, see the Glossary of Grammatical Terms on page 245.*

✓ Señor, señora

In Spanish, all nouns have a gender: they are either masculine (**señor, amigo**) or feminine (**señora, amiga**). The gender of the noun determines the form of other words used with it, such as the definite article ('the') and the indefinite article ('a'):

un/el amigo	a/the (male) friend
una/la amiga	a/the (female) friend

As a general rule, most nouns ending in **-o** are masculine and most nouns ending in **-a** are feminine. There are some exceptions: for these and words that don't end in **-o** or **-a**, it's best to learn the gender as you go along.

✓ Formal and informal ways of saying 'you'

There are two ways of addressing people in Spanish, depending on the level of formality.

usted is used in formal situations – to people such as waiters or shop assistants, in business contexts, or when talking to older people; **tú** is used more informally, with younger people and people you know well.

In Spain, the use of **tú** is becoming more common, especially among younger people. However, sometimes it's difficult even for a Spaniard to know which form to use. If in doubt, use **usted** unless you are invited to use **tú** by the Spanish person you're speaking to. It's always better to err on the side of caution than to risk giving offence.

✓ Exclamations and questions

Spanish exclamations and questions begin and end with an exclamation or question mark; these are inverted at the beginning (**¡Hola! ¿Cómo está usted?**). In questions, the word order is usually the same as in English.

ACTIVITY 3

tú or **usted**? Choose the correct form for these people.

1 a bank employee
2 your Spanish friend
3 a shop assistant
4 the teenage son of your Spanish friend
5 the father of your Spanish friend

🎧 Now do activities 4 and 5 on the recording.

¡Mucho gusto!

ACTIVITY 6 is on the recording.

ACTIVITY 7

For all true/false activities, correct the statements which are false.

1 The conversations take place in the afternoon.   T/F
2 Sr. González has met Sra. Yuste before.   T/F
3 Sr. González knows Sr. Gómez.   T/F
4 Sr. Gómez asks Sra. Yuste how she is.   T/F

DIALOGUE 2

○ ¿Es usted la señora Yuste?
■ Sí, soy la señora Yuste.
○ Buenos días, yo soy el señor González. Mucho gusto.
■ Encantada.

○ ¡Señor Gómez! ¡Buenos días, señor Gómez!
▼ ¡Señor González! Buenos días! ¿Qué tal está?
○ Muy bien, gracias. Ésta es la señora Yuste. Éste es el señor Gómez.
▼ Encantado, señora … Perdone, ¿cómo se llama?
○ Yuste, me llamo Carmen Yuste.
▼ Mucho gusto, señora Yuste.

VOCABULARY	
mucho gusto	pleased to meet you [*literally* much pleasure]
(él/ella; usted) es	(he/she/it) is; (you) are [*formal*]
sí	yes
(yo) soy	(I) am
encantada	pleased to meet you [*said by a woman*]
ésta	this [*fem.*]
éste	this [*masc.*]
encantado	pleased to meet you [*said by a man*]
perdone	excuse me
¿cómo se llama?	what's your name?
me llamo …	my name is …

⊘ *ser* ('to be')

In Spanish there are two verbs 'to be' – **estar** and **ser**. They are used in different ways: **ser** is used to describe a permanent state; **estar** will be covered in Unit 2.

(yo) **soy**	I am	(nosotros/as) **somos**	we are
(tú) **eres**	you are [*informal*]	(vosotros/as) **sois**	you are [*informal pl.*]
(él/ella) **es**	he/she/it is	(ellos/as) **son**	they are
(usted) **es**	you are [*formal*]	(ustedes) **son**	you are [*formal pl.*]

Note that the formal words for 'you' (**usted/ustedes**) take the third person singular/plural form of the verb respectively, i.e. **usted es /ustedes son**.

The subject pronoun (**yo**, **tú**, etc.) is usually omitted. It is used mainly for emphasis or to avoid confusion.

> **Soy** la señora Yuste. I'm Sra. Yuste.
> **Yo soy** el señor González. I'm Sr. González.

The subject pronouns **nosotros** ('we'), **vosotros** ('you'), and **ellos** ('they') refer to an exclusively masculine group or a mixed group (e.g. a group of men and women); **nosotras**, **vosotras**, and **ellas** refer to an exclusively feminine group.

⊘ Introductions

To introduce someone, you use **éste** for a man and **ésta** for a woman.

> **Éste** es el señor Pérez. **Ésta** es la señorita Gil. This is Sr. Pérez. This is Srta. Gil.

⊘ *Encantado/encantada* and *mucho gusto*

encantado changes form depending on who says it. A man says **encantado**, but a woman says **encantada**. This follows the rule of -**o** as a masculine ending and -**a** as a feminine ending. However, **mucho gusto** doesn't change form, whether it's spoken by a man or a woman.

ACTIVITY 8

Match the Spanish with the correct English translation.

1 ¿Es usted la señora Yuste?   a I'm Sra. Yuste.
2 Yo soy la señora Yuste.   b This is Sra. Yuste.
3 Ésta es la señora Yuste.   c Are you Sra. Yuste?

🎧 Now do activities 9 and 10 on the recording.

1.3 At the café
En la cafetería

 **ACTIVITY 11** is on the recording.

ACTIVITY 12

What did María and Juan order?

María: to drink _____   Juan: to drink _____
      to eat _____   to eat _____

DIALOGUE 3

- ■ Buenas tardes, ¿qué van a tomar?
- ○ Quiero un café con leche, por favor.
- ■ ¿Y usted, señora?
- ▼ Yo quiero un zumo de naranja.
- ■ Muy bien, un café con leche y un zumo de naranja.

- ■ ¿Algo más? ¿Quieren una tapa?
- ○ Sí, para mí un bocadillo de queso, por favor.
- ■ ¿Algo más?
- ▼ Nada más, gracias.
- ■ Aquí tienen, un café con leche, un zumo de naranja y un bocadillo. ¿El bocadillo es para usted, señor?
- ○ Sí, gracias.

VOCABULARY	
¿qué van a tomar?	what would you like to have? [*formal*] [*literally* what are you going to have?]
quiero …	I'd like … [*literally* I want]
un café con leche	a coffee with milk
por favor	please
un zumo (de naranja)	an (orange) juice
¿algo más?	anything else?
una tapa	a bar snack
para	for
para mí	for me
un bocadillo (de queso)	a (cheese) baguette-style sandwich
nada más	nothing else
aquí	here
aquí tienen	here you are [*literally* here you have]

⊘ Asking for something to eat or drink

To ask for something to eat or drink in Spanish, you can use the following expressions.

Quiero una cerveza. I'd like a beer.
Para mí un café sólo, **por favor.** A black coffee for me, please.

Or simply:

Un helado, **por favor.** An ice-cream, please.
Un pastel, **por favor.** A cake, please.

⊘ *un zumo de .../un bocadillo de ...*

To say what kind of fruit juice or sandwich you want, you use **de** ('of') as a link word.

un zumo **de manzana** an apple juice [*literally* a juice of apple]
un bocadillo **de queso** – a cheese sandwich
un zumo **de piña** a pineapple juice

ACTIVITY 13

You're in a café in Spain ordering drinks and a snack for yourself and a friend. How would you ask for:

1 a ham sandwich and a cheese sandwich?
2 an apple juice and a coffee?

ACTIVITY 14

Match the Spanish with the correct English translation.

1 nada más	a for you
2 para usted	b I'd like a sandwich, please
3 ¿algo más?	c for me
4 un zumo de naranja, por favor	d nothing else
5 quiero un bocadillo, por favor	e anything else?
6 para mí	f an orange juice, please

 Now do activities 15 and 16 on the recording.

7

Los bares y las cafeterías

Much of Spanish social and business life takes place in the bar (**el bar**) and the café (**la cafetería**), where people go to meet friends, read the newspaper, have informal business meetings, or to take a break during working hours. Bars and cafés are open all day and often until quite late at night. You can have a coffee (**un café**), a beer (**una cerveza**), or a soft drink (**un refresco**), as well as a snack (**una tapa**). Many bars also operate as restaurants, serving full meals.

The main meal of the day is lunch, taken around 2–3 p.m. Spaniards also have mid-morning coffee and often fit in an aperitif of **tapas** and a drink (a beer, wine, or soft drink) around midday. They may also eat **un sándwich**, **un bocadillo** (a sandwich made with a baguette), or a variety of other snacks. City bars are usually busy, business is brisk, and the service efficient.

You can order your drink at the bar or sit at a table and wait to be served by the waiter (**el camarero**) or waitress (**la camarera**). White coffee or coffee with milk (**café con leche**) is commonly drunk mid-morning. For black coffee, ask for **un café sólo**. Many Spaniards like something in between – black coffee with just a little milk – called **un cortado**, literally 'a cut coffee'. Order first and ask for the bill (**la cuenta**) when you wish to pay. It is common also to leave a small tip (**una propina**) as you leave.

ACTIVITY 17

Here's a menu showing drinks and snacks from the Bar Rioja. Can you identify what they are and sort them into food and drink items? Reading them aloud may help you to recognize what they are.

Using the menu, how would you order a drink and food for the following people? There may be more than one item on the menu that's appropriate. Use **quiero**, **para mí**, and **por favor** in your orders.

María – would like a dessert and a hot drink: she doesn't like tea or milk.
Juan – would like a fizzy soft drink and is a vegetarian.
Miguel – would like a hot milky drink and some pasta.

CULTURE

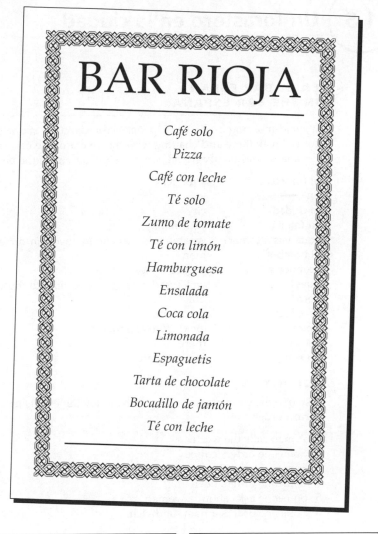

BAR RIOJA

Café solo

Pizza

Café con leche

Té solo

Zumo de tomate

Té con limón

Hamburguesa

Ensalada

Coca cola

Limonada

Espaguetis

Tarta de chocolate

Bocadillo de jamón

Té con leche

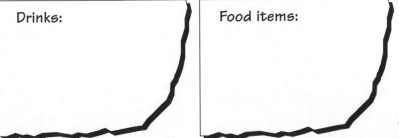

Drinks:

Food items:

EN EL BAR ESPAÑA
IN THE BAR ESPAÑA

It's mid-morning in the Bar España. María García is taking her coffee break there and chatting with the owner of the bar, Sr. España, an old family friend, when a stranger enters the bar.

el forastero	stranger
en	in
la ciudad	city
su familia	your family
¿qué vas a tomar?	what would you like to have? [*informal*]
el hombre	man
¿conoce a ... ?	do you know ... ?
pues	well [*used when thinking how to reply*]
pero	but
esta foto	this photo
¡mire!	look! [*formal imperative*]
allí	there
no está	she isn't here

ACTIVITY 18

Listen to the conversation and put the following events in the correct order.

1 A man calls the waiter.
2 Someone orders coffee.
3 Someone asks about the waiter's family.
4 Someone orders beer.
5 Someone asks about a woman.
6 Someone orders a ham sandwich.

ACTIVITY 19

Who says what? Choose between Sr. España (E), María García (M), and the stranger (S).

1 How are you [*formal*]?   E/M/S
2 How are things?   E/M/S
3 Do you know the woman in this photo?   E/M/S
4 This is Srta. García.   E/M/S
5 Nothing else.   E/M/S

STORY TRANSCRIPT

Sr. España	Hola, buenos días, María.
María	Hola, buenos días, señor España, ¿cómo está usted?
Sr. España	Muy bien. ¿Y tú? ¿Qué tal?
María	Bien ... bien, gracias. ¿Y qué tal su familia?
Sr. España	Bien, gracias. ¿Qué vas a tomar?
María	Un café con leche, por favor.
Sr. España	¿Algo más?
María	Sí, quiero ... un bocadillo de jamón.
Forastero	Buenos días. ¡Por favor!
Sr. España	Sí, señor, ¿qué va a tomar?
Forastero	Una cerveza, por favor.
Sr. España	¿Algo más, señor?
Forastero	No, nada más, gracias. Por favor, ¿conoce a la señorita de esta foto?
Sr. España	Pues ... Sí. Ésta es María ... ¡María García! ... Pero ... esta foto ... esta foto ...
Forastero	¿La ... señorita ... García?
Sr. España	Sí, ésta es la señorita García ... Mire ... está aquí en el bar ... allí, allí ... ¡María! ¡María! ... ¡Ah! No está.

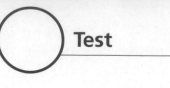

Test

Now it's time to test your progress in Unit 1.

1 Match the words and phrases to their Spanish translations.

1	Good morning	a	Buenas tardes
2	Pleased to meet you	b	Ésta es …
3	Thank you	c	Muy bien, gracias
4	This is …	d	Buenas noches
5	Good afternoon	e	¿Cómo está?
6	Goodnight	f	Encantado
7	How are you?	g	Bien, gracias
8	Very well, thank you	h	Gracias
9	Well/Fine, thank you	i	Buenos días

`9`

2 How would you ask for these things in a café or a bar?
(Score 2 points for a correct answer, 1 point if you make
one error.)

1 A white coffee and a bar snack.
2 A cheese sandwich and a beer.
3 A tomato juice and a salad.
4 A black coffee and a ham sandwich.

`8`

3 Raymond Castle has to go to the airport to meet a Spanish
business colleague, Francisco Santillana. They haven't met
before and Sr. Santillana doesn't speak English. Complete
their conversation below.

Castle   ¿1_____ _____ el Sr. Santillana? Yo 2___ el Sr.
            Castle.
Santillana Sí, soy yo. (shaking hands) ¡3_____!
Castle   (shaking hands) ¡4_____ _____!
Santillana ¿5_____ _____?
Castle   6_____, gracias.

`9`

Answers to the activities are in the Answer section on page 213.

4 How would you say the following in Spanish? (2 points for each correct answer, 1 point if you make one error.)

   1 Are you Sra. Martín?
   2 How are you?
   3 Good morning!
   4 This is Sra. Martín.
   5 I'd like a white coffee.

10

5 Take the part of the customer in the following dialogue. (Deduct 1 point for each error.)

Camarero	¿Qué va a tomar?	
Cliente	(Order a lemon tea.)	(3 points)
Camarero	¿Algo más?	
Cliente	(Say yes and order a ham sandwich and a salad.)	(4 points)
Camarero	¿Algo más?	
Cliente	(Say nothing more and thanks.)	(3 points)

10

6 Write the Spanish for each of the following words, using the correct form of the definite article **el** or **la**.

Example: Mr **el señor**

   1 Mrs
   2 Miss
   3 waiter
   4 waitress
   5 male friend

5

 **TOTAL SCORE** **51**

If you scored less than 41, look at the Language Building sections again before completing the Summary on page 14.

Summary 1

 Now try this final test, summarizing the main points covered in this unit.

How would you:
1 greet someone in the morning? in the afternoon or early evening? at night?
2 ask a business acquaintance how he is?
3 ask a friend how she is?
4 say you're very well, thanks?
5 introduce Sra. Martín?
6 say 'pleased to meet you'?
7 order a white coffee and an orange juice?
8 say 'thank you'?

REVISION

Before moving on to Unit 2, play Unit 1 through again and compare what you can say and understand now with what you knew when you started. Make a note of any vocabulary you still feel unsure of.

Remember that it will also be useful revision to come back and listen to Unit 1 again after working through the next few units, in order to reinforce what you've learned here.

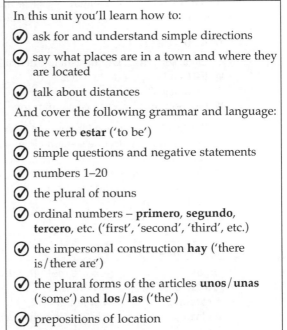

2

Out and about
En la ciudad

OBJECTIVES

In this unit you'll learn how to:

- ✓ ask for and understand simple directions
- ✓ say what places are in a town and where they are located
- ✓ talk about distances

And cover the following grammar and language:

- ✓ the verb **estar** ('to be')
- ✓ simple questions and negative statements
- ✓ numbers 1–20
- ✓ the plural of nouns
- ✓ ordinal numbers – **primero**, **segundo**, **tercero**, etc. ('first', 'second', 'third', etc.)
- ✓ the impersonal construction **hay** ('there is/there are')
- ✓ the plural forms of the articles **unos/unas** ('some') and **los/las** ('the')
- ✓ prepositions of location

LEARNING SPANISH 2

Don't try to do too much at once. You will learn more effectively if you study for half an hour or so at regular intervals. It also helps if you can learn with someone else. If you can persuade a friend or family member to study with you, it will give you an extra impetus to keep working. Agree times to meet and goals for the week, and test each other regularly.

Now start the recording for Unit 2.

🔊 **ACTIVITY 1** is on the recording.

ACTIVITY 2

Match the places with the correct location and distance.

the cathedral   in a square   15 minutes away
Goya's house   in a village   5 minutes away

DIALOGUE 1

○ Oiga, señorita. ¿Dónde está la catedral, por favor?
■ Está en la plaza de España.
○ ¿Está lejos?
■ No, está muy cerca, a cinco minutos.

○ Por favor, ¿dónde está la casa de Goya?
■ Está en un pueblo que se llama Fuendetodos.
○ ¿Está lejos?
■ No, no está lejos; en coche a quince minutos. Está a veinte kilómetros de la ciudad, al sur.
○ ¿Está en el mapa?
■ Sí, mire … Aquí.

| VOCABULARY |

¡oiga!	excuse me! [*literally* hear me; *formal*]
¿dónde está … ?	where is … ?
la catedral	cathedral
la plaza	square [*in a town/village*]
lejos	far
muy cerca	very near
a cinco minutos	five minutes away [*literally* at five minutes]
la casa	house
el pueblo	town, village
que se llama	which is called
en coche	by car [*literally* in car]
a quince minutos	15 minutes away
a veinte kilómetros	20 kilometres away
de la ciudad	from the city [*literally* of the city]
al sur	to the south
el mapa	map

✓ *estar* ('to be')

There are two verbs meaning 'to be' – **ser** (see Unit 1) and **estar**. One use of **estar** is to state where someone or something is located: **está en la plaza** ('it's in the square'). Other uses are covered in Units 5, 7, and 9.

(yo) **estoy**	I am	(nosotros/as) **estamos**	we are
(tú) **estás**	you are	(vosotros/as) **estáis**	you are
(él/ella; usted) **está**	he/she/it is; you are	(ellos/as; ustedes) **están**	they are; you are

In words with an irregular stress pattern, an accent is used to indicate a stressed vowel.

✓ Forming simple questions and negative statements

A simple statement is made into a question by a change in intonation: the voice rises at the end of the sentence instead of falling.

> **¿Está lejos? No, no está lejos.** Is it far? No, it isn't far.

To form a negative statement, add **no** before the verb: <u>no</u> **está lejos.**

✓ Numbers from 0 to 20

0	**cero**					
1	**uno/una**	6	**seis**	11	**once**	16	**dieciséis**
2	**dos**	7	**siete**	12	**doce**	17	**diecisiete**
3	**tres**	8	**ocho**	13	**trece**	18	**dieciocho**
4	**cuatro**	9	**nueve**	14	**catorce**	19	**diecinueve**
5	**cinco**	10	**diez**	15	**quince**	20	**veinte**

uno drops the **-o** when it occurs before a noun: **un kilómetro** ('one kilometre'); **una** doesn't change: **está a una hora** ('it's an hour away').

✓ The articles in the plural

	singular		plural	
	masculine	*feminine*	*masculine*	*feminine*
a/an/some	**un**	**una**	**unos**	**unas**
the	**el**	**la**	**los**	**las**

✓ The plural of nouns

To make a noun ending in **-o** or **-a** plural, simply add **s**: **el kilo → los kilos**, **la casa → las casas**. Nouns ending in **-l**, **-n**, or **-s** add **-es** to form the plural. If the last syllable is accented in the singular, the accent is dropped in the plural: **el melón → los melones** ('melons'); **el inglés → los ingleses** ('Englishmen').

 Now do activities 3 and 4 on the recording.

2.2 In the street

En la calle

ACTIVITY 5 is on the recording.

ACTIVITY 6

1	Calle Molina is a long walk.	T/F
2	Calle Miguel Servet is at the end of avenida Goya on the right.	T/F
3	The house is the third house on the right.	T/F
4	It's next to a bank.	T/F

DIALOGUE 2

○ ¿Dónde está la calle Molina, por favor?

■ La calle Molina … está lejos. La tercera calle a la izquierda, todo recto hasta el final y la segunda a la derecha.

○ ¿Puede repetir, por favor?

■ La tercera a la izquierda, todo recto hasta el final de la calle y la segunda calle a la derecha.

○ ¡Taxi! A la calle Miguel Servet, por favor. Está cerca de la avenida Goya.

■ Sí, señor. … ¿Está aquí?

○ No. Es todo recto, al final de la avenida a la izquierda. El número diecinueve.

■ ¿Aquí?

○ Es el tercer portal a la izquierda. Al lado del banco.

VOCABULARY	
la calle	street
a la izquierda	on the left
(todo) recto	straight on
a la derecha	on the right
hasta	until
el final	end
¿puede repetir?	can you repeat that?
la avenida	avenue
vale	OK
el número	number
es	it is [*from* ser]
el portal	doorway
al lado de	next to
el banco	bank

✓ Directions

In directions, the words for 'left' and 'right' are always given in the feminine form: **la izquierda, la derecha**. To say something is on the left or on the right, you use the preposition **a** [*literally* 'at', 'to']:

a la izquierda   on the left   **a** la derecha   on the right

When **a** is followed by the masculine definite article **el**, the words combine to become **al**, but when **a** is followed by the feminine definite article **la**, the words do not change:

a + el → al	**al** final	to the end
a + la is unchanged	**a la** derecha	on the right

The preposition **de** ('of', 'from') also follows this pattern:

de + el → del	al lado **del** banco	next to the bank
de + la is unchanged	**de la** ciudad	from the city

✓ Ordinal numbers

In directions involving streets, ordinal numbers ('first', 'second', 'third', etc.) are given in the feminine form because **la calle** is feminine.

la primera (calle) a la derecha   the first (street) on the right
la segunda (calle) a la izquierda   the second (street) on the left

The masculine form is **el primero, el segundo, el tercero**, etc. Note that the **-o** is dropped for **primero** and **tercero** when they are used in front of a masculine noun.

el primero	the first	**el primer equipo**	the first team
el segundo	the second	**el segundo tren**	the second train
el tercero	the third	**el tercer edificio**	the third building

A full list of ordinal numbers is given in the Grammar Summary on page 230.

ACTIVITY 7

Match the Spanish with the correct English translation.

1 Todo recto hasta el final, la segunda a la derecha.
    a It's the first street on the right.

2 Es la tercera calle a la izquierda.
    b It's the third house on the right.

3 Es la primera calle a la derecha.
    c It's the third street on the left.

4 Es el tercer portal a la derecha.
    d Straight on to the end, the second on the right.

 Now do activities 8 and 9 on the recording.

19

At the tourist information office
En la oficina de turismo

ACTIVITY 10 is on the recording.

ACTIVITY 11

The hotel is E: what are the other buildings?

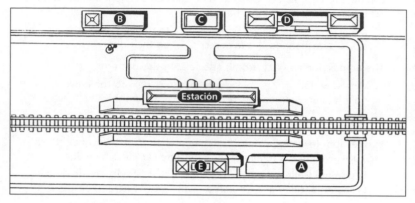

DIALOGUE 3

○ Por favor, ¿hay un hotel por aquí?
■ Sí, hay un hotel detrás de la estación, El Hotel Oriente.
○ Gracias. ¿Hay un supermercado por aquí?
■ Sí, hay un supermercado al lado del Hotel Oriente.
○ ¿Y, dónde está el restaurante Las Vegas?
■ Está al lado del banco, enfrente de la estación, entre el banco y el hospital.

VOCABULARY	
la oficina de turismo	tourist information office
¿hay … ?	is there … ?
por aquí	around here
hay …	there is …
detrás de	behind
la estación	station
el supermercado	supermarket
el restaurante	restaurant
enfrente de	opposite
entre	between
el hospital	hospital

✓ *hay* ('there is/there are')

hay is the impersonal form of the verb **haber** ('to have') and is used to mean 'there is/there are'. Its form does not change.

Hay un restaurante cerca de aquí. There is a restaurant near here.
¿**Hay** bares en esta calle? Are there (any) bars in this street?
No **hay** un hospital por aquí. There isn't a hospital around here.

✓ Prepositions and prepositional phrase of location

Prepositions are words which are used to indicate where something is in relation to something else. Remember that **de + el → del**.

Hay un hotel **al lado de** la estación. There is a hotel next to the station.
Hay un supermercado **enfrente del** hotel. There is a supermarket opposite the hotel.
Hay un hotel **detrás de** la estación. There is a hotel behind the station.
Hay una parada de autobús **delante del** museo. There is a bus stop in front of the museum.
Hay un aparcamiento **debajo del** hotel. There is car park underneath the hotel.
Hay una oficina **encima del** bar. There is an office above the bar.

ACTIVITY 12

Match the Spanish with the English translation.

1	al lado de ...	a	opposite
2	enfrente de ...	b	the station
3	por aquí	c	between
4	delante de	d	around here
5	detrás de	e	next to
6	entre	f	behind
7	¿hay ... ?	g	in front of
8	la estación	h	is there ... ?

ACTIVITY 13

You're in the tourist information office and want to find out where things are.

1 How would you ask if the following facilities are nearby?
   a a bank   b a hotel   c a supermarket
2 You know there is a station and a restaurant.
   How do you ask where they are?

(🎧) Now do activities 14 and 15 on the recording.

2.4) A stroll in Zaragoza
Un paseo en Zaragoza

Spain has a vibrant culture and many Spanish cities have a wealth of monuments (**monumentos**) and other important and interesting buildings (**edificios importantes e interesantes**) worth visiting. Read the following text about Zaragoza, a historic city in the north of Spain, and follow the guide on the map.

Un paseo para una mañana de domingo
Zaragoza está en el norte de España. Es una ciudad histórica con murallas romanas. Hay muchos monumentos y edificios importantes e interesantes en Zaragoza. Mire el mapa y siga las direcciones.

1 La Seo es una catedral del siglo trece.
2 Siga recto por la Plaza del Pilar. A la derecha está la Basílica del Pilar de los siglos diecisiete y dieciocho.
3 A la izquierda está la calle Alfonso, una calle muy importante. Siga recto y tome la sexta calle a la derecha. Al final está el museo Pablo Gargallo en el palacio de los Argillo.
4 Al final de la calle Alfonso está la calle Coso. A la derecha está el Palacio de Sástago del siglo dieciséis.
5 Enfrente está el Casino Mercantil, un edificio modernista del siglo veinte.

en el norte	in the north
el paseo	stroll
la mañana	morning
el domingo	Sunday
una ciudad histórica	a historic city
con	with
las murallas romanas	Roman walls
muchos monumentos	many monuments
seguir (sigo)	to follow
¡siga!	follow/carry on [*formal imperative*]
el siglo	century
por	along
tomar	to take
¡tome!	take [*formal imperative*]
el palacio	palace

ACTIVITY 16

Look at the map again. Can you find the monuments
mentioned in the text? Write down their names and the
century each of them dates from, if it is given.

1 La Seo: 13th century

2 _____

3 _____

4 _____

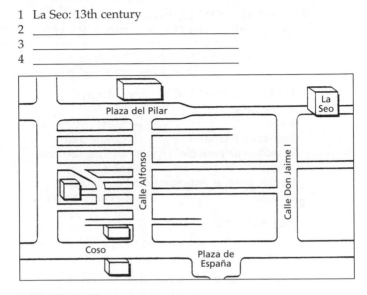

ACTIVITY 17

Using the map, give directions in Spanish.

1 You are at the Basílica del Pilar.
¿Dónde está el Palacio de Sástago?
2 You are at the Museo Pablo Gargallo.
¿Dónde está la Basílica del Pilar?
3 You are at the Basílica del Pilar.
¿Dónde está La Seo?

ACTIVITY 18

Now look at the instructions below. Which building are you
being directed to?

1 You are at the Museo Pablo Gargallo.
Siga recto, la segunda a la izquierda al final.
2 You are at the Basílica del Pilar.
Todo recto al final de la calle Alfonso. A la izquierda. Está a
la izquierda.
3 You are at the Palacio de Sástago.
La primera a la derecha. La segunda a la izquierda, al final
de la calle.

23

2.5 Un forastero en la ciudad

¿HAY UN HOTEL POR AQUÍ?
IS THERE A HOTEL AROUND HERE?

María has left the Bar España. The stranger is talking with Sr. España, who gives him some directions. Where is he going?

la biblioteca municipal	local library
en autobús	by bus
a ver	let's see
conozco a (María)	I know (María)
la sección de periódicos	newspaper section
¡silencio!	silence!
los documentos antiguos	old documents
de nada	not at all, it's a pleasure

ACTIVITY 19

Listen to the recording again and put the events in the correct order.

1 The stranger asks where there is a hotel.
2 The stranger asks where the newspaper section is.
3 Sr. España tells the stranger his name.
4 Sr. España tells the stranger where there is a hotel.
5 The librarian tells the stranger to keep quiet.
6 The stranger asks Sr. España where the local library is.

ACTIVITY 20

Which of these statements is true (**verdadero**) and which is false (**falso**)?

1 El hotel está lejos. V/F
2 El hotel está enfrente de la estación. V/F
3 La biblioteca está lejos. V/F
4 El hotel está cerca de la casa de María. V/F
5 En la biblioteca hay periódicos antiguos. V/F

ACTIVITY 21

Can you find the Spanish for these questions in the story transcript? Write the questions down and then give the answers in Spanish.

1 Are there any old newspapers?
2 What's it called?
3 Is there a newspaper section?
4 Is there a hotel round here?
5 Where's the public library?
6 You know María, don't you?
7 Where is it?
8 Here?

STORY TRANSCRIPT

Forastero	Por favor, señor …
Sr. España	Señor España. Me llamo Juan España.
Forastero	¿Hay un hotel por aquí?
Sr. España	Sí, señor. Hay un hotel muy cerca, está enfrente de la estación.
Forastero	¿Cómo se llama?
Sr. España	Se llama Hotel de la Estación. Está a cinco minutos. Siga esta calle todo recto y tome la segunda a la izquierda. El hotel está allí.
Forastero	Muchas gracias. Oiga … señor … España …
Sr. España	Sí, señor.
Forastero	¿Dónde está la biblioteca municipal?
Sr. España	Pues … a ver … ¡está lejos! A quince o veinte minutos en autobús. Hay una parada al lado del bar. Está cerca de la casa de María, la señorita de la foto. Usted conoce a María, ¿no?
Forastero	No, a María no, pero conozco a … Bueno, perdone, adiós.

En la biblioteca

Forastero	Por favor, ¿hay una sección de periódicos?
Mujer	Sí, hay.
Forastero	¿Dónde está?
Mujer	Está aquí, a la derecha … Silencio, por favor.
Forastero	Perdone. ¿Hay periódicos antiguos?
Mujer	Sí. Hay periódicos y documentos muy antiguos allí, a la izquierda.
Forastero	Gracias. ¿Aquí?
Mujer	Sí, aquí, enfrente de la oficina.
Forastero	Muchas gracias.
Mujer	De nada.

Test

Now it's time to test your progress in Unit 2.

1 Match these words and phrases to their Spanish translations.

1	Is there a bank round here?	a	Está muy cerca.
2	Is it far?	b	¿Dónde está el banco?
3	It's next to the bank.	c	No hay bancos por aquí.
4	Where is the bank?	d	Está detrás del banco.
5	There aren't any banks around here.	e	Está al lado del banco.
6	It's opposite the bank.	f	Está enfrente del banco.
7	It's behind the bank.	g	¿Hay un banco por aquí?
8	It's very near.	h	¿Está lejos?

8

2 How would you give these directions in Spanish? (Score 2 points for each correct answer and 1 point if you make one error.)

1 Second on the right and all the way to the end of the street.
2 Third street on the left and it's on the right.
3 All the way to the end of the street, left, and it's on the left.
4 First on the right, second on the left, and it's on the right.

8

3 Raymond Castle is in Spain on business. He needs to buy some things and to visit a bank, so he asks the hotel receptionist for information. Fill in the blanks in the conversation.

Raymond   Por 1_____. ¿2_____ un supermercado por 3_____ ?
Recepcionista   Sí, señor. Siga todo recto, al 4_____ de la calle. La 5_____ a la izquierda.
Raymond   Gracias. Y ¿6_____ hay un banco?
Recepcionista   Hay un banco al 7_____ del supermercado.
Raymond   ¿8_____ lejos?
Recepcionista   No, no. Está 9_____ cinco minutos.

9

4 Write down the following numbers in Spanish.

1	16	3	7	5	13	7	11	9	5
2	17	4	20	6	3	8	12	10	8

10

5 Complete the following dialogue. Deduct 1 point for each error.

A: ¿Dónde está el museo?
B: Say it's in the Plaza de España.

_____ (2 points)

A: ¿Está muy lejos?
B: Say it's five minutes away on the bus.

_____ (4 points)

A: ¿Qué número?
B: Say number fourteen.

_____ (1 point)

A: ¿Dónde está la parada?
B: Say it's the first street on the left.

_____ (3 points)

10

6 Write the plural forms of these words.

1 la casa
2 el melón
3 el pastel
4 el tomate
5 la plaza

5

TOTAL SCORE **50**

If you scored less than 40, look at the Language Building sections again before completing the Summary on page 28.

Summary 2

Now try this final test, summarizing the main points covered in this unit.

How would you:
1 ask if there is a museum in the area?
2 ask where the bank is?
3 ask where avenida Goya is?
4 say that the cathedral is ten minutes away?
5 say that Bilbao is in the north of Spain?
6 say it's the second street on the left?
7 tell someone to go straight on to the end of the street?
8 say that the hotel is opposite the station?

REVISION

Before moving on to Unit 3, play Unit 2 through again and listen out for the three main question forms introduced in this unit: ¿hay ... ? and ¿dónde hay ... ?/¿dónde está ... ? Imagine you're on holiday and want to find out about various facilities: practise how you would ask what there is and where to find it, using these phrases and the vocabulary you have learned in the unit.

Shopping
De compras

OBJECTIVES

In this unit you'll learn how to:

✓ ask for items when shopping for food

✓ ask prices

✓ ask for items at the post office

And cover the following grammar and language:

✓ the formal imperative

✓ numbers up to 1,000

✓ more polite requests using **querer** ('to want')

✓ adjectives

✓ the direct object pronoun **lo/la/los/las**
('him', 'her', 'it', 'them')

LEARNING SPANISH 3

When you're attempting an activity, always try listening to the recordings several times before looking at the transcript in your book. When you first listen, it may feel as though you haven't understood very much, but try doing the activities anyway. The activities are structured to help you to understand the dialogues and to work out what's happening for yourself. Write down some kind of answer, and don't look at the answer key until you've had a go, even if you consider it only to be a guess. Guesswork is an important strategy in learning a new language and you'll probably be pleasantly surprised at how often you're right.

Now start the recording for Unit 3.

3.1 In the shop
En la tienda

ACTIVITY 1 is on the recording.

ACTIVITY 2

Match the product with the correct quantity.

A potatoes / onions / tomatoes / cheese / oil / wine
B a kilo / two bottles / two kilos / a litre / half a kilo /
100 grams

DIALOGUE 1

○ ¿Qué desea?
■ Quiero un kilo de patatas.
○ Un kilo de patatas. ¿Algo más?
■ Sí. Quiero dos kilos de cebollas y medio kilo de tomates.
○ Muy bien. ¿Algo más?
■ Nada más, gracias.

○ ¿Qué quería?
■ Cien gramos de queso.
○ ¿Algo más?
■ Sí, deme un litro de aceite, por favor.
○ ¿Quiere algo más?
■ Ummm, sí. Dos botellas de vino.
○ Aquí tiene.
■ Muchas gracias.

VOCABULARY

¿qué desea?	what would you like?
un kilo	a kilo
la patata	potato
la cebolla	onion
medio kilo	half a kilo
el tomate	tomato
¿qué quería?	what would you like?
cien gramos	100 grams
deme …	could I have … ? [*literally* give me …]
un litro	a litre
el aceite	oil
la botella	bottle
el vino	wine

✓ The formal imperative

The formal imperative is used in many everyday transactions, such as asking for things in shops and giving directions. Learn these useful phrases by heart. There will be more on the imperative in Units 13 and 14.

Deme un paquete de patatas fritas. Could you give me a packet of crisps? (from **dar**, 'to give')
Deme una lata de sardinas. Could you give me a tin of sardines?
Oiga, por favor. Excuse me, please. (from **oír**, 'to hear')
Siga ... Follow .../Carry on ... (from **seguir**, 'to follow')
Mire ... Look ... (from **mirar**, 'to look')
Tome ... Take ... (from **tomar**, 'to take')

✓ Weights and measures

Grams or kilos are used for weights and litres for liquid.

Quiero **cien gramos de** queso. I'd like 100 grams of cheese.
Deme **dos kilos de** zanahorias. Could you give me two kilos of carrots?
Quiero **un litro de** leche. I'd like a litre of milk.

Note that the indefinite article is used for **un cuarto** ('a quarter'), but not with **medio** ('half'). The word **kilo** can be included or omitted.

Quiero **un cuarto de** jamón. I'd like a quarter of ham.
Deme **medio kilo de** queso. Could you give me half a kilo of cheese?

✓ Numbers: 20 to 1000

20	veinte	50	cincuenta	80	ochenta
30	treinta	60	sesenta	90	noventa
40	cuarenta	70	setenta		

100	cien	500	quinientos/as	900	novecientos/as
200	doscientos/as	600	seiscientos/as	1.000	mil
300	trescientos/as	700	setecientos/as		
400	cuatrocientos/as	800	ochocientos/as		

There is no word for 'and' in numbers over 100: **ciento noventa** – 190. Note how **cien** changes to **ciento** when followed by another number.

ACTIVITY 3

Match the item with the correct container/quantity.

A tomates / cebollas / queso / zumo de naranja / patatas fritas / aceite
B paquete / cien gramos / botella / kilo / lata / litro

(🎧) Now do activities 4 and 5 on the recording.

At the post office

En la oficina de Correos

ACTIVITY 6 is on the recording.

ACTIVITY 7

1	A postcard costs five hundred cents.	T/F
2	The first customer buys five postcards.	T/F
3	He buys a small envelope.	T/F
4	It costs ninety-five céntimos to send the parcel.	T/F
5	The second customer buys stamps for a parcel.	T/F

DIALOGUE 2

○ ¿Cuánto vale una postal, por favor?
■ Setenta céntimos.
○ Deme cinco postales, por favor.
■ Son tres euros cincuenta. ¿Algo más?
○ Sí. Un sobre grande, por favor. ¿Cuánto es?
■ Treinta y cinco céntimos.

○ Oiga, quiero mandar este paquete a Inglaterra.
■ Un momento … a ver … noventa y cinco céntimos.
○ ¿Y una carta para el Reino Unido?
■ Cincuenta céntimos.
○ ¿Y una postal?
■ Cuaranta céntimos.
○ Gracias. Deme sellos para el paquete, cinco postales y una carta.

VOCABULARY

¿cuánto vale?	how much is it? [how much is it worth?]
la postal	postcard
el céntimo	cent (of a euro)
el euro	euro
el sobre	envelope
grande	large
¿cuánto es?	how much is it?
mandar	to send
el paquete	parcel
el Reino Unido	UK
un momento	one moment
la carta	letter
el sello	(postage) stamp

✓ More on numbers

The word **y** ('and') is used to link numbers above 30. In the numbers
16–19 and 21–29, **y** changes to **i** and the two numbers form one word:

16 **dieciséis**	37 **treinta y siete**	73 **setenta y tres**
24 **veinticuatro**	44 **cuarenta y cuatro**	86 **ochenta y seis**
25 **veinticinco**	55 **cincuenta y cinco**	99 **noventa y nueve**
31 **treinta y uno**	62 **sesenta y dos**	

The words for the hundreds actually change ending depending on the
gender of what they refer to.

Quinientas casas. 500 houses.

This is because the hundreds function like adjectives (see section 3.3).

✓ Asking how much something costs

These are three different ways of asking how much something costs:

¿Cuánto es? How much is it (altogether)?
¿Cuánto vale? How much is it?/How much do I owe you?
¿Cuánto cuesta? How much does it cost (altogether)?

Note that **¿cuánto vale?** and **¿cuánto cuesta?** take a verb in the plural
when they are used for more than one thing:

¿Cuánto cuestan /¿Cuánto valen los sellos? How much are the stamps?

The verb **ser** is used in response to the question **¿cuánto es?**

¿Cuánto es? **Son** ochenta y cinco céntimos.
How much is it? It is [*literally* they are] 85 cents.

The plural form (**son**) is used because it refers to the number of cents.

ACTIVITY 8

Without looking at Dialogue 2, fill in the blanks, using words
from the list below.

para/son/grande/más/cuánto/cuesta/deme/mandar

- Un sobre 1_____, por favor.
- ○ ¿Algo 2_____?
- Sí. ¿Cuánto 3_____ un sello 4_____ Inglaterra?
- ○ Cincuenta céntimos.
- 5_____ cinco sellos por favor. ¿6_____ es?
- ○ 7_____ dos euros cincuenta.
- Quiero 8_____ este paquete a Inglaterra.

Now do activities 9 and 10 on the recording.

En la frutería

ACTIVITY 11 is on the recording.

ACTIVITY 12

1 What costs €1.60?
2 What costs €1.80?
3 What costs €3?
4 What weighs 3 kilos?

DIALOGUE 3

○ ¿Qué quería?
■ Un melón.
○ ¿Lo quiere grande o pequeño?
■ Lo quiero grande, por favor. ¿Cuánto es?
○ Un euro sesenta. ¿Algo más?
■ Sí. ¿Tiene piñas?
○ Sí, las tengo muy baratas, a un euro ochenta. Dos por tres euros. Mire, estas dos son muy buenas. ¿Las quiere?
■ Sí, sí, las quiero. Ummm ... ¿Cuánto vale la sandía?
○ A un euro cincuenta, el kilo. Ésta pesa tres kilos. ¿La quiere?
■ No, no, la quiero pequeña. Ésta.
○ Tenga. ¿Algo más?
■ Nada más, gracias.

VOCABULARY	
la frutería	fruiterer's
el melón	melon
lo/la	it
pequeño	small
¿tiene ... ?	do you have ... ?
la piña	pineapple
los/las	them
tengo ...	I have ...
barato	cheap
bueno	good
la sandía	watermelon
pesar	to weigh
tenga	here you are [*literally* have; *formal imperative*]

✓ Adjectives

Adjectives agree in number (singular or plural) and gender (masculine or feminine) with the noun they describe. They usually come after the noun:

	masculine	*feminine*
singular	un melón **pequeño**	una manzana **pequeña**
plural	dos melones **pequeños**	cuatro manzanas **pequeñas**

There is more on adjectives in Units 4, 5, and 9.

✓ More on introductions

To introduce a group of people, you use **éstos** for men and **éstas** for women. For a mixed group you use **éstos**:

Éstos son mis hermanos. These are my brothers.
Éstas son mis hermanas. These are my sisters.

✓ Direct object pronouns *lo/la* ('him', 'her', 'it'), *los/las* ('them')

The direct object of a verb is the noun, pronoun, or phrase which is directly affected by the action of the verb. In Spanish, the form of the direct object pronouns for 'it' and 'them' is affected by gender as well as number:

	sing.	*pl.*
masc.	**lo**	**los**
fem.	**la**	**las**

Do you want ...	¿Quiere ...	
the melon?	**el melón**?	sí, **lo** quiero
the meat?	**la carne**?	sí, **la** quiero
the tomatoes?	**los tomates**?	no, no **los** quiero
the strawberries?	**las fresas**?	sí, **las** quiero

Note that they come before the verb. There is more on direct object pronouns in 4.2

ACTIVITY 13

Ask for the following items using **quiero** and the correct form of the direct object pronoun **lo**, **la**, **los**, or **las**.

Example: Cheese. **El queso. Lo quiero.**

1 A packet of crisps.
2 A can of sardines.
3 A litre of oil.
4 Two bottles of wine.
5 Ham.
6 Stamps.

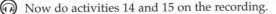 Now do activities 14 and 15 on the recording.

Los mercados españoles

CULTURE

ACTIVITY 16

Study the list of different kinds of shops below. What can you buy in each shop? Read the text and write the Spanish for what you can buy next to the appropriate shop. Then find out from the vocabulary list what the products are in English if you don't already know them.

la carnicería   la pastelería
la frutería   la panadería
la verdulería   la pescadería
la charcutería

ACTIVITY 17

Read the text again and complete the crossword without looking at the vocabulary list.

En España, hay muchos supermercados. Pero los mercados también son importantes. El mercado es una tradición española muy antigua. En muchos de los mercados españoles hay tiendas pequeñas que se llaman puestos. Hay muchas clases de puestos. En la carnicería hay carne, como salchichas, cordero, y cerdo. En la frutería hay fruta: naranjas, fresas, melones, etc. En la verdulería hay verdura, como patatas, cebollas o zanahorias. En la charcutería hay productos españoles muy típicos, como jamón serrano y chorizo. En las pastelerías y panaderías hay pasteles, galletas y pan. En la pescadería hay muchas clases de pescado como sardinas y merluza. Y en los puestos de comestibles hay sal, azúcar, o aceite.

el mercado	market
también	also
el puesto	market stall
la carnicería	butcher's
la salchicha	sausage
el cordero	lamb
el cerdo	pork
la fruta	fruit
la verdulería	greengrocer's
la verdura	vegetables
la charcutería	delicatessen
el jamón serrano	cured ham

el chorizo	*spicy sausage*
la pastelería	cake and pastry shop
la panadería	baker's
la galleta	biscuit
el pan	bread
la pescadería	fishmonger's
el pescado	fish
la merluza	hake
el puesto de comestibles	grocer's
la sal	salt
el azúcar	sugar

Across

1 You can buy these in 2 across.
2 The name of the shop where you buy meat.
3 The name for a market stall.
4 You'd find this at the grocer's.
5 This is used to fry things and to put on salads.
6 This is sweet and can be bought in the same stall as 4 across.

Down

1 You buy this in 5 down.
2 This is a kind of fish.
3 An alcoholic drink.
4 Meat from a young sheep.
5 The place where you can buy 1 down and 6 down.
6 You buy this in 5 down or a cake shop.

MARÍA EN EL MERCADO
MARÍA AT THE MARKET

María leaves home to go to the market. Although she doesn't see him, the stranger from the bar is waiting outside her house. He follows her as she goes into the fishmonger's.

el vendedor	stallholder
los calamares	squid
el dinero	money
¿Me conoce?	Do you know me?
creo que sí	I think so
la cartera	wallet
¡qué hombre tan raro!	what a strange man!
el empleado/la empleada	employee
quiero mandar esta carta certificada	I'd like to send this as a registered letter

ACTIVITY 18

Listen to the recording and answer the following questions in English.

1 Who buys some fish?
2 Who drops some money?
3 Who picks up the money?
4 Who drops the wallet?
5 Who knows who?
6 Who wants to send a letter?

ACTIVITY 19

Who says the following: María (M), the stranger (S), the fishmonger (F), or the post office employee (P)?

1 Quiero un kilo de sardinas.   M/S/F/P
2 ¿Quiere algo más?   M/S/F/P
3 ¿Me conoce?   M/S/F/P
4 ¡Qué hombre tan raro!   M/S/F/P
5 Quiero mandar esta carta certificada. M/S/F/P
6 Es un euro veinticinco.   M/S/F/P

ACTIVITY 20

Here are the answers to some of the questions in the dialogue. What are the questions?

1 Muy bien, gracias.
2 Quiero un kilo de sardinas y medio kilo de calamares.
3 No gracias.
4 Creo que sí.
5 Es un euro veinticinco.

STORY TRANSCRIPT

María	Hola, buenos días, señor José.
Vendedor	Buenos días, señorita María. ¿Qué tal?
María	Muy bien, gracias.
Vendedor	¿Qué quería?
María	Quiero un kilo de sardinas y medio kilo de calamares.
Vendedor	Aquí tiene. Son dos euros cincuenta. ¿Quiere algo más?
María	No gracias. Oh, el dinero …
Forastero	Aquí tiene, señorita …
María	Oh, muchas gracias …
Forastero	De nada, señorita … María.
María	Oh … ¿Me conoce? Señor …
Forastero	Creo que sí … sí … Adiós, señorita María …
María	¡Oiga, señor! ¡Oiga … un momento! ¿Esta cartera …?
Vendedor	¡Qué hombre tan raro!
María	Adiós, señor José.
Vendedor	¡Señorita, señorita … el pescado!
María	¡Ah! Sí. Perdone. Gracias.

En correos

Forastero	Por favor … quiero mandar esta carta certificada. ¿Cuánto cuesta el sello?
Empleada	A ver … Es un euro veinticinco.
Forastero	Muy bien, … un momento … ¡La cartera! ¿Dónde está la cartera? Un momento … un momento, por favor.
Empleada	¡Señor! ¡Oiga señor! ¡Es un euro veinticinco!

Test

Now it's time to test your progress in Unit 3.

1 Match the words and phrases to their Spanish translations.

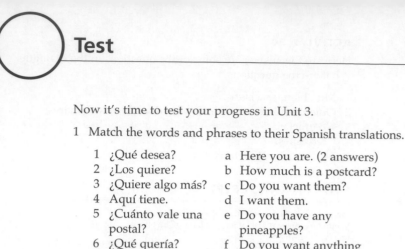

1	¿Qué desea?	a	Here you are. (2 answers)
2	¿Los quiere?	b	How much is a postcard?
3	¿Quiere algo más?	c	Do you want them?
4	Aquí tiene.	d	I want them.
5	¿Cuánto vale una postal?	e	Do you have any pineapples?
6	¿Qué quería?	f	Do you want anything else? (2 answers)
7	¿Tiene piñas?	g	What would you like? (2 answers)
8	Las quiero.		
9	¿Algo más?		
10	Tenga.		

`10`

2 How would you ask for these things in Spanish? (Score 2 points for every correct answer and 1 point if you make a mistake.) Start your request with **Quiero ...**

1 Two kilos of potatoes and half a kilo of onions.
2 A litre of wine and a can of oil.
3 100 grams of ham and 200 grams of cheese.
4 Two packets of crisps and a box of biscuits.
5 Four postcards and five stamps for the UK.

`10`

3 Give the Spanish for these numbers.

1	18	3	35	5	100	7	500	9	440
2	27	4	59	6	250	8	370	10	99

`10`

4 In which shops would you buy the following food items? Give your answers in English and Spanish.

1 jamón   6 sardinas
2 queso   7 sal
3 carne   8 melones
4 fresas   9 pasteles
5 zanahorias   10 pan

10

5 Take the part of the customer in the following dialogue with a shop assistant (**dependienta**).

Cliente: (Ask how much the watermelons are.)
_____

Dependienta: Valen un euro cincuenta. ¿Cuántas quiere?
Cliente: (Ask for two.)
_____

Dependienta: ¿Las quiere grandes?
Cliente: (Say no, you want small ones.)
_____

Dependienta: ¿Algo más?
Cliente: (Say you don't want anything else.)
_____

(Ask for the price.)
_____

10

6 Complete the following sentences using the appropriate formal imperative.

1 _____ un paquete de patatas fritas, por favor.
2 _____ , por favor.
3 _____ esta calle hasta el final.
4 _____ la tercera calle a la izquierda.
5 ¡_____ estas naranjas! Son buenas.

5

TOTAL SCORE 55

If you scored less than 45, look at the Language Building sections again before completing the Summary on page 42.

Summary 3

 Now try this final test, summarizing the main points covered in this unit.

How would you:
1 say you want half a kilo of strawberries?
2 say you want a packet of crisps?
3 say you want a litre of milk?
4 say you don't want anything else?
5 say you want two bottles of wine?
6 ask how much a stamp for the UK costs?
7 say that something costs 2 euros 50?
8 say you want five envelopes?
9 say 'here you are' as you hand your money over to the assistant?

REVISION

Before moving on to the first Review, play this unit through again and check that you know the food vocabulary. A good way of remembering the items is to make a shopping list in Spanish. Classify each food item into categories such as vegetables, fish, meat, and so on. Then practise writing down in Spanish which shops you'd go to in order to buy each item. If you don't know the word for what you need, look it up in your dictionary.

Review 1

VOCABULARY

1 Look at the Spanish expressions below and group them
according to what they mean. Which ones are for:

   a greeting people?   c asking how someone is?
   b saying goodbye?   d saying how you are?

   1 ¿Qué tal?   5 Adiós.
   2 Buenos días.   6 Buenas tardes.
   3 ¿Cómo está usted?   7 Muy bien.
   4 Bien, gracias.   8 Buenas noches.

2 Match the phrases on the left with those on the right to
complete the food and drink items.

un café   de queso
un té   de naranja
un zumo   con limón
un bocadillo de chocolate
una tarta   con leche

3 Follow each plan and choose the right directions from a–e.

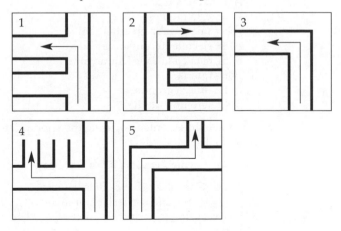

*Answers to the activities can be found in the Answer section
on page 213.*

a Todo recto hasta el final y la primera a la izquierda.
b La primera a la izquierda y la segunda a la derecha.
c La segunda a la izquierda.
d Todo recto hasta el final, la primera a la derecha y la primera a la izquierda.
e La tercera a la derecha.

4 Possible or impossible? Put a tick or a cross next to each phrase.

1 Una lata de tomates.   4 Un paquete de patatas fritas.
2 Un litro de zanahorias. 5 Cien gramos de leche.
3 Un kilo de queso.

GRAMMAR AND USAGE

5 Choose the best response to each of the following questions.

1 ¿Cómo está usted?
  A Muy bien, gracias.
  B Mucho gusto.
2 ¿Es usted la señora Martínez?
  A Sí, es la señora Martínez.
  B Sí, soy la señora Martínez.
3 ¿Dónde está el museo?
  A Está en la plaza.
  B Sí, está muy cerca.
4 ¿Hay una parada en esta calle?
  A Sí, delante del supermercado.
  B Sí, está en la calle Domínguez.
5 ¿Qué quería?
  A La quiero grande.
  B Quiero una sandía.

6 Complete these sentences, using the appropriate words from the list.

está / las / deme / cuesta / a / de / al / hay

1 ¡Señor González! Buenos días. ¿Cómo _____ usted?
2 _____ un café con leche, por favor.
3 La casa está _____ diez kilómetros _____ la ciudad _____ norte.
4 _____ un hotel detrás de la estación.
5 ¿Cuánto _____ un sello para Inglaterra?
6 Tengo dos naranjas. ¿_____ quiere?

7 Choose the most appropriate word to complete the sentences.

1 Quiero un sello (**para/de**) el Reino Unido.
2 El hospital está detrás (**del/de la**) banco.
3 (**Es/Está**) la tercera casa a la izquierda.
4 Yo (**soy/es**) el señor González.
5 El bocadillo (**es/está**) para usted.

🎧 LISTENING

8 Your Spanish business colleague has left a message on your answerphone giving you instructions about how to get to his house this evening. Listen to the message and answer the questions in English.

1 How long does it take to get to your friend's house from the Plaza de las Flores?
2 Which direction do you turn at the end of the Avenida de la Independencia?
3 What number is the house?
4 What is next to the house?
5 What is in front of the house?

9 Listen to this conversation in a shop. There are five differences between what you hear and the transcript here. Underline the differences.

A: ¿Qué quería?
B: ¿Tiene latas de sardinas?
A: Sí. ¿Cuántas quiere?
B: ¿Las tiene grandes?
A: No. Las tengo pequeñas. ¿Las quiere pequeñas?
B: Sí. Quiero cinco.
A: Aquí tiene. ¿Algo más?
B: Sí. Deme dos kilos de naranjas.
A: ¿Algo más?
B: Sí. ¿Cuánto valen las sandías?
A: Dos euros treinta. ¿Quiere una?
B: Deme dos.
A: ¿Algo más?
B: Nada más. ¿Cuánto es?
A: Son ocho euros sesenta.

10 Practise saying each of these names, and then listen to the recording to check your pronunciation.

1 Señor Pérez   3 Señorita María García
2 Señora Martín   4 Señor Juan Gómez

11 You're in Seville on business. Complete the conversation you have with a Spanish colleague.

Juan Gómez: Buenas tardes. Me llamo Juan Gómez.
You: (Say you're pleased to meet him and tell him
             your name.)

_____.

Juan Gómez: ¿Cómo está usted?
You: (Tell him you're well and ask how he is.)

_____.

Juan Gómez: Bien. ¿Quiere un café?
You: (Say yes. Ask if there's a bar in the area.)

_____.

Juan Gómez: Sí, hay uno al final de la calle.
In the bar
Juan Gómez: Usted es de Manchester. ¿Dónde está?
You: (Tell him that it's in the north of England.)

_____.

Juan Gómez: ¿Está cerca de Londres?
You: (Tell him no, it's 300 kilometres from London.)

_____

12 You're going to hear some questions on the recording. The questions will be about the following topics, but in a different order. You'll be asked about:

– your name
– how you are feeling
– if you'd like tea or coffee
– if your house is in a city
– where your home town is
– how much it costs to send a card to Spain
– if there is a museum in your city

Use this list to prepare what you're going to say, then test yourself using the recording.

▷ ▷ ▷ ▷ ▷ ▷ ▷ ▷ ▷ ▷ ▷ ▷ ▷ ▷ ▷

Personal information
Información personal

OBJECTIVES

In this unit you'll learn how to:

- ✓ say where you live and where you're from
- ✓ say what job you do
- ✓ give your address and telephone number
- ✓ spell your name and address

And cover the following grammar and language:

- ✓ the present tense of regular verbs ending in -ar, -er, and -ir
- ✓ the verb ser ('to be') for nationalities and professions
- ✓ nouns and adjectives of nationality
- ✓ nouns of profession
- ✓ revision of numbers

LEARNING SPANISH 4

A wide vocabulary is the key to successful language learning, but don't try to learn too much at once. It's best to study frequently, for short periods of time. Take six or seven items of vocabulary as a maximum and learn them. Put them into sentences to fix them in your mind, then come back to them later. Much of the vocabulary in this book is presented by topic – for example, buildings in a town, methods of transport. Learning vocabulary in this way is usually very effective.

It is important to get a good Spanish–English dictionary to support your learning. While you may feel you don't need a large dictionary at this stage, make sure it is comprehensive enough to illustrate the word in use in sample phrases.

🔊 Now start the recording for Unit 4.

¿De dónde es usted?

ACTIVITY 1 is on the recording.

ACTIVITY 2

	¿De dónde es?	¿Dónde vive?
Pepe García Margarita Herrero Jorge Martínez El hermano de Pepe García		

DIALOGUE 1

- ■ ¡Hola! Buenas tardes. Soy Pepe García.
- ○ Encantada. Margarita Herrero. Y éste es el señor Jorge Martínez.
- ■ Mucho gusto.
- ▼ Encantado.
- ■ ¿Ustedes no son españoles?
- ▼ No, yo soy argentino y Margarita es de México.
- ■ ¡Ah! Hay muchos mexicanos en mi trabajo. Y mi hermano trabaja en México. ¿Ustedes viven en España?
- ▼ Yo vivo en España. Margarita vive en México.
- ■ ¿Dónde vive usted?
- ▼ Yo vivo en Barcelona.
- ■ ¡Yo también! ¡Qué casualidad! Cenamos juntos y hablamos.

| VOCABULARY |

¿de dónde es?	where are you from?
vivir	to live
argentino	Argentinian
México	Mexico
mexicano	Mexican
el trabajo	job
el hermano	brother
trabajar	to work
¡qué casualidad!	what a coincidence!
cenar	to have dinner
juntos/as	together
hablar	to talk, speak

✓ The present tense of regular verbs: -ar verbs

There are three different types of regular Spanish verbs. Their infinitives end in **-ar** (e.g. **trabajar**, 'to work'), **-er** (e.g. **comer**, 'to eat, to have lunch'), or **-ir** (e.g. **vivir**, 'to live').

All the verbs in each regular group have the same endings in the present tense, which are added to the stem of the verb (**trabaj-, viv-, com-**). The endings for regular **-ar** verbs are as follows:

trabaj**o**	trabaj**amos**
trabaj**as**	trabaj**áis**
trabaj**a**	trabaj**an**

Other **-ar** verbs: **llamar** ('to call'), **viajar** ('to travel'), **cenar** ('to have dinner'), **estudiar** ('to study'). For **-ir** and **-er** verbs see pages 51 and 53.

✓ Nationalities

Words describing nationality usually change ending according to whether a man or woman is being described, although there are a few exceptions: **estadounidense** ('American'), **canadiense** ('Canadian'). Nationalities do not begin with a capital letter and can be used either as an adjective or noun: **un irlandés** ('an Irishman'), **es irlandés** ('he's Irish').

Country	El país	[masc. sing.]	[fem. sing.]
France	Francia	francés	francesa
Germany	Alemania	alemán	alemana
Spain	España	español	española

In the plural, **-s** is added to all feminine forms and to masculine forms ending in **-o** in the singular. Other masculine forms take the ending **-es**.

Mis padres son **españoles**. My parents are Spanish.
Las mujeres son **escocesas**. The women are Scottish.

ACTIVITY 3

Complete the story with the correct form of the verbs in brackets. New vocabulary: **a veces** ('sometimes').

Mi hermano y yo (1 **estar**) en Barcelona. La casa (2 **estar**) en el centro de la ciudad. Yo (3 **trabajar**) y mi hermano (4 **estudiar**) en la universidad. A veces nosotros (5 **viajar**) a Madrid. Mis padres (6 **estar**) allí. A veces nosotros (7 **cenar**) en un restaurante cerca de mi trabajo. (8 **Hablar**) de la universidad y del trabajo.

 Now do activities 4 and 5 on the recording.

¿Quién es quién?

🎧 **ACTIVITY 6** is on the recording.

ACTIVITY 7

1 What is Rosita Blasco's profession?
2 What is the name of the accountant?
3 Who is the head of personnel?
4 Where is Señorita Vázquez?
5 Who is a neighbour of Rosita?
6 How many drivers are there?

DIALOGUE 2

■ Buenos días a ustedes. Les presento a la señorita Rosita Blasco, la nueva secretaria bilingüe de la empresa.
○ Buenos días.
■ Ésta es Carmen Soto. Carmen es contable en la empresa. Y, éste es Javier Montero, jefe de personal, y a su lado está Ana Vázquez, representante de ventas.
○ Ana me conoce. Vivimos en la misma calle.
■ ¡Qué casualidad! Bueno ... Pepe Espinosa es diseñador y a su lado está Sara Gil, ingeniera. Pepe Salas y Jaime Vargas son los conductores.
○ Encantada de conocerles.

VOCABULARY	

¿quién?	who?
les presento	I'd like to introduce you to [*literally* I present to you]
la empresa	company, firm
nuevo	new
el secretario/la secretaria	secretary
bilingüe	bilingual
el/la contable	accountant
el jefe/la jefa (de personal)	head (of personnel)
el/la representante de ventas	sales representative
mismo	same
el diseñador/la diseñadora	designer
el ingeniero/la ingeniera	engineer
el conductor/la conductora	driver
encantada de conocerles	I'm very pleased to meet you

✓ The present tense of regular verbs: -ir verbs

Endings for regular -ir verbs in the present tense are as follows:

vivir ('to live')

viv**o**	viv**imos**
viv**es**	viv**ís**
viv**e**	viv**en**

Other regular -ir verbs: **escribir** ('to write'), **permitir** ('to permit'), **salir** ('to leave'/'to go out'), **conducir** ('to drive'). Note that **salir** and **conducir** add a consonant in the first person singular form – **salgo, condu<u>z</u>co** – but the rest of the verb is regular.

✓ Preposition *a* with people

In Spanish, when the object of the verb is a person, the preposition **a** must be used.

> Le presento **a los empleados**. I'd like to introduce you to the staff.
> Conozco **al empresario**. I know the company director.

✓ Direct object pronouns 2

The direct object pronouns **me** ('me'), **te** ('you'), **nos** ('us'), and **os** ('you') are used in the same way as **lo/la/los/las** (see 3.3).

> Ana **me** conoce. Ana knows me.
> **Os** llamamos todos los domingos. We call you [*plural*] every Sunday.

✓ Describing professions

Note that the article is not used when you say what someone's job is:
Miguel es profesor ('Miguel is a teacher').

ACTIVITY 8

Complete the story by supplying the correct form of the verbs.

A veces mi hermano y yo (1 **escribir**) a mis padres en Madrid. A veces, ellos (2 **llamar**) por teléfono. (3 **Hablar**) de la familia, de mi trabajo y de los estudios de mi hermano. Tengo un coche pero no (4 **conducir**) a mi trabajo. Yo (5 **salir**) de casa a las ocho y mi hermano (6 **salir**) a las nueve. Los amigos (7 **vivir**) cerca de nuestra casa y (8 **salir**) juntos.

 Now do activities 9 and 10 on the recording.

How do you spell it?
¿Cómo se escribe?

ACTIVITY 11 is on the recording.

ACTIVITY 12

1 Which floor does María live on?	1st/2nd/3rd
2 In which year was she born?	1955/1965/1975
3 What is her phone number?	329 5568/
	329 5678/
	329 5579
4 On which day in February was she born?	11/12/13
5 What is the number of her home?	16/17/18

DIALOGUE 3

○ ¿Su apellido, por favor?
■ Barrull.
○ ¿Cómo se escribe?
■ B-A-R-R-U-L-L.
○ ¿Su nombre?
■ María.
○ Su dirección, por favor.
■ Calle Mayor, diecisiete, tercero D; Bilbao.
○ ¿Fecha de nacimiento?
■ El doce de febrero, de mil novecientos setenta y cinco.
○ Necesito su número de teléfono también.
■ Tres dos nueve … Cincuenta y cinco, sesenta y ocho.

VOCABULARY	
el apellido	surname
¿cómo se escribe?	how do you spell it?
el nombre	(first) name
la dirección	address
la fecha de nacimiento	date of birth
febrero	February
necesitar	to need
el número de teléfono	telephone number

✓ The present tense of regular verbs: -er verbs

comer ('to eat')　　como　　comemos
　　　　　　　　　comes　　coméis
　　　　　　　　　come　　comen

Other examples of regular -er verbs are: **responder** ('to respond'), **leer** ('to read'), **correr** ('to run'), **ver** ('to see, to watch'), **creer** ('to believe'), **prometer** ('to promise').

✓ The alphabet

Note that there is one letter which does not appear in the English alphabet: ñ (eñe – pronounced 'enyeh'). Until the early 1990s, ch and ll were also considered separate letters in Spanish, appearing in dictionaries after C and L respectively. They now appear as part of the C and L entries. Check your dictionary to see if you have an old or a new version.

✓ Addresses and telephone numbers

Spanish addresses start with the street name, followed by the number:

Calle Mayor, diecisiete 17 High Street

Most Spaniards who live in the city live in flats. Their addresses include the street number, the floor on which they live, and the 'door', usually indicated by a letter. In this example, 3° is short for **tercer piso**:

Avenida San José 20, 3° D 20 San José Avenue, 3rd floor, door D

Spanish telephone numbers can be given in two ways:

12 34 56　　doce, treinta y cuatro, cincuenta y seis
623 4567　　seis, dos, tres … cuarenta y cinco, sesenta y siete

Note that groups of even numbers are given in pairs, for example 4567 is usually given as '45, 67' (**cuarenta y cinco, sesenta y siete**), not as in English '4-5-6-7'.

ACTIVITY 13

Write down the numbers in words.

1　2468583
2　Calle Monzón, 26
3　00 44 91 238 9963
4　Avenida de la Independencia, 35
5　0181 245 5428
6　Paseo de Goya, 153

Now do activities 14 and 15 on the recording.

A country of many cultures

Un país de muchas culturas

ACTIVITY 16

Read the questions about the languages of Spain and refer to the map. Do you know any of the answers to these questions? Now read the text and use the information to answer the questions in English and Spanish.

1 How many official languages are there in Spain?
2 What are they?
3 From which language do most of them originate?
4 How many variants of Catalan are referred to in the text?
5 Where are they spoken?
6 Which language do experts know least about?
7 What is another name for Spanish?

Hoy España es un país de muchas culturas, tradiciones e idiomas. En la constitución hay cuatro lenguas oficiales: el castellano o español, el catalán, el gallego y el euskera o vasco. El catalán, el gallego y el castellano tienen su origen en el latín. Pero el euskera o vasco es una lengua completamente diferente. No conocemos el origen de esta lengua. También hay otras lenguas y dialectos. Por ejemplo, en Mallorca, hablan el mallorquín y en Valencia el valenciano. Son variantes del catalán. Mire en el mapa las zonas lingüísticas.

hoy	today
el idioma	language
la lengua	language
otro	other

ACTIVITY 17

Complete these sentences without looking at the text, if you can. Then read through the text to check your answers.

1 España es un país de muchas _____.
2 Hay cuatro lenguas _____.
3 El catalán, el gallego y el castellano tienen su _____ en el latín.
4 El euskera o vasco es completamente _____.
5 El mallorquín y el valenciano son variantes del _____.

ACTIVITY 18

Look at these words in Catalan. They are quite similar to some Castilian words we have already studied. Find the Catalan word that matches each English description. Then write the Spanish equivalent.

English	Catalan	Spanish
a verb	el banc	_____
a family member	adéu	_____
a word for goodbye	la ciutat	_____
a vegetable	el pare	_____
a number	el tomàquet	_____
a drink	vint-i-quatre	_____
a building	café amb llet	_____
a large town	treballar	_____

4.5 Un forastero en la ciudad

UN VIEJO AMIGO
AN OLD FRIEND

Después de la escena en el mercado, el forastero vuelve al bar
España y empieza a hablar con el señor España.

After the scene in the market, the stranger returns to Bar
España and strikes up a conversation with Sr. España.

viejo	old
la compañía	company, firm
la tarjeta	(business) card
bonito	nice, pretty
mucho	much, a great deal
la oficina de seguros	insurance firm
creer	to believe
la esquina	the corner
llamar (por teléfono)	to call [*on the telephone*]
cuando	when
llámeme cuando venga María	call me when María comes

ACTIVITY 19

¿Verdadero o falso?

1 Jorge habla mucho con el señor España.   V/F
2 El señor España conoce a María muy bien. V/F
3 Jorge no conoce a María.   V/F
4 Jorge es del sur de España.   V/F
5 No tiene tarjeta.   V/F
6 María trabaja en una tienda.   V/F
7 Trabaja en el centro de la ciudad.   V/F
8 Vive cerca del bar España.   V/F

ACTIVITY 20

Complete these questions taken from the dialogue and then
match them with the answers.

1 ¿Qué tal _____?
2 Usted conoce a María, ¿_____?
3 ¿De _____ es usted?
4 ¿____ ____ trabaja María?
5 ¿Vive _____?

a Bueno, vive cerca de aquí.
b Soy del sur de España.
c Trabaja en una oficina de seguros en el centro.
d Muy bien, gracias.
e Sí, la conozco muy bien.

ACTIVITY 21

Who …

1 … works in a bar?
2 … works as a salesperson?
3 … works in an office?
4 … works in the centre of town?
5 … lives in the south of Spain?
6 … is staying in a hotel?
7 … visits the bar regularly for coffee?
8 … lives near the bar?

STORY TRANSCRIPT

Jorge	¡Buenas tardes!
Sr. España	Buenas tardes, señor. ¿Qué tal está?
Jorge	Muy bien gracias, ¿y usted?
Sr. España	Muy bien.
Jorge	Usted conoce a María, ¿verdad?
Sr. España	Sí, la conozco muy bien.
Jorge	Yo soy un viejo amigo de la familia. Me llamo Jorge Jimeno.
Sr. España	Pero ella no le conoce a usted.
Jorge	Sí, sí, me conoce. Soy amigo de la familia.
Sr. España	¿De dónde es usted?
Jorge	Soy de Granada. Soy representante de ventas de una compañía. Mire usted … aquí tiene mi tarjeta.
Sr. España	Gracias. Granada es una ciudad muy bonita, ¿verdad?
Jorge	Sí, muy bonita.
Sr. España	¿Usted viaja mucho en su trabajo?
Jorge	Sí, mucho. Sr. España … ¿María trabaja?
Sr. España	Sí, trabaja.
Jorge	¿En qué trabaja?
Sr. España	Creo que trabaja en una oficina de seguros en el centro … en la plaza de la Independencia.
Jorge	¿Y vive cerca?
Sr. España	Bueno …
Jorge	Sr. España, soy amigo de la familia.
Sr. España	Bueno, vive cerca de aquí … en la calle Ancha … en la esquina.
Jorge	Mire, señor, estoy en este hotel. Aquí está el número de teléfono. Llámeme cuando venga María.
Sr. España	Sí, señor. Ella toma café aquí.

Test

Now it's time to test your progress in Unit 4.

1 Introduce these people to a friend, giving their nationality. (Score 2 points for each question, 1 point if you make one mistake.)

Example: Señor Giménez/Argentina. **Éste es el** señor Giménez. Es **argentino**.

1 Señora Campos/España.
2 Jorge Ballesteros/México.
3 Señorita Tomás/Argentina.
4 Madame Deschamps/Francia.
5 Dieter Müller/Alemania.
6 Peter Jones and Barry Wright/Inglaterra.

| 12 |

2 Complete this short biography by supplying the verbs in the correct form. (Score 1 point for each correct answer.)

Me (1 llamar) Francisca y (2 ser) de España. (3 vivir) en Londres en Inglaterra con mi hermano. (4 Trabajar) juntos en una empresa internacional. Yo (5 trabajar) en la oficina, (6 ser) secretaria bilingüe, y mi hermano (7 ser) conductor. Cuando (8 estar) juntos en la oficina (9 comer) juntos. Nosotros (10 vivir) en un apartamento en el norte de Londres.

| 10 |

3 Write down in Spanish what these people do for a living.

1 El señor Rodríguez _____. (teacher)
2 La señorita Martín _____. (student)
3 El señor Ortega y la señora Sánchez _____. (engineers)
4 La señora Serrano y la señorita Moreno _____. (secretaries)
5 El señor Carrasco _____. (receptionist)

| 5 |

4   Write down these addresses and telephone numbers in words. (Score 2 points for each correct answer, 1 point if you make one mistake.)

1   Calle Santa Engracia 25. Tel: 91 533 1237.
2   Avenida Diagonal 143. Tel: 93 418 95 58.
3   Paseo de la Independencia 76. Tel: 96 348 68 94.
4   Carretera Cariñena 97, 3° G. Tel: 976 29 92 78
5   Plaza España 15. Tel: 92 456 3284.

10

5   Complete your side of the conversation below. (Deduct 1 point for each mistake.)

You: (Introduce yourself to Sr. Giménez.)   (2 points)
Sr. G: Mucho gusto. ¿En qué trabaja usted?
You: (Tell him you are a sales representative.)   (2 points)
Sr. G: ¡Ah! Yo también. Pero usted no es
        español/a, ¿verdad?
You: No. (Tell him your nationality but that
        you live and work in Madrid.)   (2 points)
Sr. G: Yo vivo en Madrid también. ¿En qué calle
        vive?
You: (Tell him you live in a street called
        Castellana.)   (1 point)
Sr. G: ¿Qué número?
You: (Tell him number 17.)   (1 point)
Sr. G: ¡Mi hermano vive en el número veinte!

8

6   Complete the sentences using the appropriate verb with the correct endings.

conoc-/llam-/viv-/trabaj-/com-

1   (Nosotros) _____ en un banco.
2   ¿(Vosotros) _____ en un restaurante?
3   (Yo) _____ en una plaza.
4   Mis padres _____ por teléfono.
5   Él no _____ a María.

5

TOTAL SCORE   **50**

If you scored less than 40, look at the Language Building sections again before completing the Summary on page 60.

Summary 4

 Now try this final test, summarizing the main points covered in this unit.

How would you:
1 say this is Sra. Martínez?
2 ask someone you have just met if he is Argentinian?
3 say you live in Barcelona?
4 ask some colleagues if they work in France?
5 say 'we eat in a restaurant'?
6 say you're a teacher?
7 ask some men if they're drivers?
8 say you know María?
9 say they live at 86 Rosas Street?
10 say your telephone number is 318 6583?

REVISION

Think of the jobs that your family and friends do, and practise answering the question **¿en qué trabaja?** by saying what their professions are. Use your dictionary to find out what the jobs are in Spanish, and how they change according to gender and number. This is a useful method of extending your vocabulary of jobs and professions.

You can adopt the same approach for addresses and telephone numbers. Practise saying the addresses and telephone numbers of friends and family in Spanish. Notice telephone numbers wherever you go and practise saying them in Spanish as well. Remember, practice makes perfect. You'll soon be saying numbers without thinking about it.

Home and family
La casa y la familia

OBJECTIVES

In this unit you will learn how to:

✓ talk about your family

✓ give ages

✓ describe different parts of the house

✓ talk about different kinds of accommodation

✓ give dates

And cover the following grammar and language:

✓ the verb **tener** ('to have')

✓ possessive adjectives **mi**, **tu**, **su**, etc. ('my', 'your', 'his/her', etc.)

✓ position of adjectives

✓ prepositions **de**, **para**, **por**

LEARNING SPANISH 5

Buy a notebook and divide it into alphabetical sections. Every time you learn a new item of vocabulary, write it in the correct section. You may also want to reproduce the same vocabulary in another part of the book, this time by topic, as recommended in Unit 4.

It's often useful to put the item of vocabulary into a sample sentence. This will help you to remember it. Take your notebook with you wherever you go, or you could make a recording of new vocabulary to listen to in the car or bath. If you practise regularly, you can learn a great deal of vocabulary in a short time. If you're not sure of the pronunciation of a word, include a pronunciation guide.

Now start the recording for Unit 5.

¿Está usted casada?

ACTIVITY 1 is on the recording.

ACTIVITY 2

Fill in the details of Pepe and Margarita's families.

Oscar es _____ de Margarita. Margarita es _____ de Oscar. Pablo es _____ de Margarita. El padre de Pepe es _____ de Carmen. Carmen es _____ de José.

DIALOGUE 1

- ■ ¿Está usted casada?
- ○ Sí. Estoy casada. Mi marido se llama Oscar.
- ■ ¿Tiene hijos?
- ○ Sí, tenemos tres hijos. ¿Y usted?
- ■ Sí, yo también estoy casado. Tengo dos hijos.
- ○ Mire; aquí tengo una foto. ¡Les hacemos muchas fotos! Éste es mi hijo, Pablo, y ésta es su hermana, Patricia. Y ésta es la pequeña, María José.
- ■ Ah, sí. ¡Qué guapa!
- ○ ¿Cuántos años tienen sus hijos?
- ■ Mi hija, Carmen, tiene doce y mi hijo, José, tiene ocho.
- ○ Mi hijo tiene diez años, Patricia tiene ocho y María José tiene cinco. Me escriben todos los días.

VOCABULARY	
casado	married
el marido	husband
tener (tengo)	to have
el hijo	son
la hija	daughter
los hijos/los niños	children
la mujer	woman, wife
la hermana	sister
¡qué guapa!	how pretty, beautiful!
el padre	father
hacer fotos	to take photographs
¿cuántos años tienen?	how old are they? [*literally* how many years do they have?]

✓ *tener* ('to have')

tener ('to have') is also used to give a person's age. It is irregular:

tengo	**tenemos**
tienes	**tenéis**
tiene	**tienen**

Tengo dos hermanos. I have two brothers.
Tiene quince años. He/She is 15. [*literally* He/She has 15 years.]

✓ *¿cuánto ... ?* ('How many ... ?')

¿cuánto? is an adjective, which means that it changes ending to agree with the noun it refers to:

¿**Cuántos hermanos** tiene? How many brothers have you got?
¿**Cuánta gente hay**? How many people are there?

✓ Indirect object pronouns

Indirect object pronouns are used to replace nouns which are indirectly affected by the action of the verb: **me, te, le, nos, os, les.** Like direct object pronouns, they come before the verb.

¡**Les** hacemos muchas fotos! We take lots of photographs of them.
Me escriben todos los días. They write to me every day.

✓ Possessive adjectives: *mi, tu, su, nuestro, vuestro*

In Spanish, the possessive adjectives ('my', 'your', 'his', etc.) take a different form depending on the gender and number of the noun described. For mixed groups, the masculine form is used.

mi hermano my brother	**mis hermanos** my brothers and sisters
tu padre your father	**tus padres** your parents
su hijo your/his/her/their son	**sus hijos** your/his/her/their children
nuestro abuelo our grandfather	**nuestros abuelos** our grandparents
vuestro tío your uncle	**vuestros tíos** your aunts and uncles

---

ACTIVITY 3

Choose the correct form of **cuántos / cuántas** for a–c and the correct possessive adjective for d–f.

a ¿_____ hermanos tienes?
b ¿_____ abuelos tienes?
c ¿_____ mujeres hay?
d Tengo un hermano. ____ hermano se llama Pedro.
e Pedro tiene un abuelo. ____ abuelo se llama Alberto.
f ¡Hola María! ¿Es ésta ____ hermana?

Ⓐ Now do activities 4 and 5 on the recording.

5.2 Do you live in an apartment?
¿Vive usted en un apartamento?

ACTIVITY 6 is on the recording.

ACTIVITY 7

¿Pepe o Margarita? ¿Quién …

1 vive en un apartamento?
2 vive en un piso viejo?
3 vive en el décimo piso?
4 tiene una cocina pequeña?
5 tiene una casa en el pueblo?
6 tiene un baño muy grande?

DIALOGUE 2

- ¿Vive usted en el centro de la ciudad?
- Sí. Vivo en un apartamento. También tenemos un apartamento en la playa.
- Tenemos un piso en el centro y una casa en el pueblo. ¿Cómo es su apartamento?
- Es grande y moderno. Está en el décimo piso. Hay una entrada ancha. Tiene un salón, un comedor y una cocina y tres dormitorios. La cocina es pequeña …
- Mi piso no es grande. Está en el centro de la ciudad y es viejo. Está en el tercer piso. La cocina es estrecha. La casa del pueblo es grande y vieja. Tiene un baño muy grande. Es de mi madre.

VOCABULARY

el apartamento	apartment
la playa	beach
el piso	flat, apartment, floor (of a building)
¿cómo es … ?	what's … like? [*literally* how is … ?]
moderno	modern
décimo	tenth
la entrada	entrance hall
ancho	wide
el salón	lounge
el comedor	dining room
la cocina	kitchen
el dormitorio	bedroom
estrecho	narrow
el (cuarto de) baño	bathroom

✓ ¿Cómo es … ?

¿cómo es … ? is used to ask people to describe something, such as their house, or to describe someone's appearance or character (see Unit 9).

¿**Cómo es** el apartamento? What's the apartment like?
¿**Cómo es**? What's it/he/she like?

As these are permanent characteristics, the verb **ser** is used. Note the use of **estar** in the following example to enquire how someone is feeling (a temporary state):

¿**Cómo está**? How are you?; How is he/she?

✓ Position of adjectives

Adjectives agree in gender and number with the noun they describe and normally follow the noun:

un apartamento **viejo** an old apartment
una vista **bonita** a pretty view
una entrada **ancha** a wide hallway
una habitación **pequeña** a small room

A few adjectives precede the noun: see Grammar Summary, page 226.

✓ Preposition *de*

de is used to show possession (the equivalent of the English 's). Note that the word order is different from English.

la madre **de** Juan Juan's mother [*literally* the mother of Juan]
La casa es **de** mi madre. The house is my mother's.

ACTIVITY 8

Complete the sentences with the appropriate adjective from the list, making sure you use the correct form.

moderno/pequeño/bonito/ancho/antiguo

1 El chico tiene dos años. Es muy _____.
2 El hotel tiene dos años. Es muy _____.
3 Las vistas del hotel son _____.
4 La avenida en el centro de la ciudad es _____.
5 El centro de la ciudad tiene mucha historia; tiene muchos edificios _____.

🎧 Now do activities 9 and 10 on the recording.

5.3 I'd like a room

Quiero una habitación

ACTIVITY 11 is on the recording.

ACTIVITY 12

1	La habitación es para tres personas.	V/F
2	La habitación es para dos noches.	V/F
3	La habitación cuesta 70 euros por noche.	V/F
4	Hoy es el trece de julio.	V/F
5	La habitación está en el tercer piso.	V/F

DIALOGUE 3

■ Buenos días. Quiero una habitación, por favor.
○ Sí, señor. ¿Para cuántas personas?
■ Una doble, para dos personas. Y tenemos un niño de dos años.
○ De acuerdo. ¿Para cuántas noches la quiere?
■ Para tres noches.
○ Deme el pasaporte, por favor. Gracias.
■ ¿Cuánto es por noche?
○ Setenta euros por noche.
   A ver, una habitación para tres noches, para el trece, cartorce y quince de julio. Es la número doscientos treinta y cinco. Está en el segundo piso. ¿Tiene equipaje?
■ Sí. Está en el coche. ¿Puedo pagar con tarjeta de crédito?
○ Sí, señor.

VOCABULARY

para	for
la persona	person
una (habitación) doble	a double (room)
el niño/la niña	little boy/girl
de dos años	aged two [*literally* of two years]
de acuerdo	fine [*literally* agreed]
la noche	night
el pasaporte	passport
por noche	per night
julio	July
el equipaje	luggage
poder (puedo)	to be able to
pagar	to pay
la tarjeta de crédito	credit card

✓ *por* and *para*

These two prepositions are frequently confused by learners of Spanish: both can be translated 'for', but which is used depends on the situation. They correspond to a range of different prepositions in English.

para is used to describe a purpose, intention, or destination.

> La medicina es **para** la tos. The medicine is for your cough.
> El regalo es **para** mi madre. The gift is for my mother.
> Este tren es **para** Madrid. This train is for Madrid.

por is used to describe cause or motive.

> No podemos ir **por** el mal tiempo. We can't go because of the bad weather.
> Hace mucho **por** la compañía. He does a lot for the company.

por can also be used to describe movement through, time during, approximate location, or means by which something is done.

> ¿Hay un banco **por** aquí? Is there a bank around here?
> Vamos **por** el parque y **por** la avenida. We'll go through the park and along the avenue.
> Le mandé un mensaje **por** fax. I sent him a message by fax.

por is also used to describe rate or ratio.

> Son sesenta euros **por** noche. It costs 60 euros a night.

✓ Dates: *las fechas*

enero	January	**mayo**	May	**septiembre**	September
febrero	February	**junio**	June	**octubre**	October
marzo	March	**julio**	July	**noviembre**	November
abril	April	**agosto**	August	**diciembre**	December

Unlike English, the months in Spanish do not take a capital letter. With the exception of the first, dates are given as cardinal numbers:

> **el uno/el primero de** mayo 1st May
> **el veinte de** agosto 20th August

ACTIVITY 13

What are these dates? Write them in full in Spanish.

a 31-3   b 3-6   c 10-11   d 12-12   e 23-5   f 5-9

🎧 Now do activities 14 and 15 on the recording.

En venta

Many Spanish people buy second homes, usually **apartamentos** or **chalets**, on or near the coast. They either rent out their properties to other people during the year, or stay there themselves during the summer holidays, and sometimes at weekends too.

ACTIVITY 16

You're looking for somewhere to buy on the Costa Brava, near Barcelona on the east coast of Spain. Salou and Cambrils are two holiday towns within a few kilometres of each other.

Read the newspaper advertisements below, then decide which ones match your requirements in a–h. Here's what you're looking for:

a something just for you but with a pool if possible.
b somewhere with more than one bathroom because you have a young family.
c a fairly cheap flat just for you.
d an unfurnished apartment with two bedrooms near the beach but also near the centre of town.
e somewhere with a separate garage and a separate kitchen.
f somewhere with a good view of the sea.
g somewhere just for you with a garden and maybe a pool.
h somewhere in a quiet area for the whole family.

céntrico	central
el salón-estar	living room
los muebles	furniture
amueblado	furnished
primera línea	right next to the beach [*literally* first line (of buildings)]
la oportunidad	bargain
perfecto estado	perfect condition
el lavadero	washing room
rentabilidad alquiler	profitable for renting
el aseo	toilet
la calefacción	central heating
la parcela	plot (of land)
el euro	euro

CULTURE

1

SALOU:

Apartamento céntrico, muy cerca de la playa, 2 dormitorios, salón-estar, comedor, cocina y terraza. Sin muebles. Precio: 48.100€ Ref 852

2

SALOU:

Apartamento 3 dormitorios, cocina independiente, amueblado, gran terraza, garaje independiente. Precio 52.900€

3

CAMBRILS:

Apartamento situado en primerísima línea, maravillosas vistas al mar, edificio de calidad y de tres plantas, tres dormitorios, salón-estar, comedor, cocina, baño, terraza, amueblado, plaza de parking incluida. 107.000€

4

SALOU:

Apartamento 1 habitación, salón-comedor, cocina, baño, terraza. 33.100€

5

CAMBRILS:

Golf Sant-Jordi. Apartamento primera línea playa, 1 habitación, piscina. 40.900€

6

CAMBRILS:

Oportunidad, piso de tres dormitorios, gran terraza y solarium, en perfecto estado, zona muy tranquila. Precio 51.100€ Ref 454

7

CAMBRILS:

Apartamento cerca del mar, una habitación, cocina equipada, lavadero, jardín y piscina. Rentabilidad alquiler. Precio 38.500€

8

CAMBRILS:

Chalet individual, en urbanización muy tranquila, 3 dormitorios y un estudio, dos baños, un aseo, calefacción, garaje, solarium, parcela de 600m^2. Precio 141.200€ Ref 441

5.5 Un forastero en la ciudad

JORGE CAMBIA DE HOTEL
JORGE CHANGES HOTEL

Jorge está en la biblioteca con los periodicos. Luego, cambia su hotel. No quiere una habitación tranquila. Quiere una habitación con vista a la calle. ¿Por qué?

Jorge is in the library with the newspapers. Then he changes his hotel. He doesn't want a quiet room – he wants a room with a view of the street. Why?

luego	then, afterwards
¿por qué?	why?
la información	information
sobre	about
la fotocopia	photocopy
el artículo	(newspaper) article
la llave	key
cambiar	to change
el parque	park
atrás	behind
la vista	view
bonito	nice, pretty
tranquilo	quiet, peaceful
el ruido	noise
el tráfico	traffic
no importa	it's not important

ACTIVITY 17

Answer the following questions in English.

1 What is Jorge looking for in the library?
2 What does he ask the librarian?
3 What reason does he give for leaving the first hotel?
4 Why does the receptionist at the new hotel offer him the first room?
5 Why doesn't he accept this room?
6 What is perfect about the second room?

Put these phrases in the order you hear them.

1 Es una habitación muy tranquila.
2 Ésa es la casa de María.
3 Un amigo está en otro hotel.
4 Quiero una fotocopia de este artículo.
5 Aquí está la información sobre María y la familia.

ACTIVITY 19

¿Verdadero o falso?

1 En el artículo hay una foto de la familia de María. V / F
2 Hay un amigo de Jorge Jimeno en el hotel Corona. V / F
3 Quiere una habitación para una noche.   V / F
4 Jorge Jimeno está en la habitación 220.   V / F
5 La habitación tiene una vista muy bonita.   V / F
6 La casa de María está enfrente del hotel.   V / F
7 María no está en la calle.   V / F

STORY TRANSCRIPT

Jorge	A ver … sí … aquí está la información sobre María y la familia. Y también hay una foto de toda la familia. Por favor, quiero una fotocopia de este artículo.
Mujer	Sí, señor. Pase por aquí.
…	
Recepcionista	Buenos días, señor.
Jorge	Buenos días. Un amigo está en otro hotel cerca de aquí. Me cambio de hotel.
Recepcionista	Muy bien. ¿Tiene usted la llave?
Jorge	Sí, aquí tiene.
Recepcionista	¿Cómo se llama el hotel?
Jorge	Hotel Corona.
…	
Jorge	Buenos días. Quiero una habitación, por favor.
Recepcionista	¿Para cuántas noches?
Jorge	Dos o tres.
Recepcionista	Bueno … la habitación número 211. Aquí tiene la llave.
Jorge	¿Esta habitación da a la calle?
Recepcionista	No, señor. Da al parque, atrás. Es una habitación muy tranquila con una vista muy bonita.
Jorge	No, necesito una habitación con vista a la calle. Es muy importante.
Recepcionista	De acuerdo. Pero hay ruido del tráfico.
Jorge	No importa.
Recepcionista	Pues la habitación número doscientos veinte está libre. ¿La quiere?
Jorge	Sí, gracias.
…	
Jorge	A ver. Sí. Ésa es la casa de María. Está enfrente. Esta habitación es perfecta. Y allí está María en la calle.

Now it's time to test your progress in Unit 5.

1 Write down in Spanish the following information about your family. (Score 2 points for each correct answer, 1 point if you make one mistake.)

  1 Say you have three brothers and one sister.
  2 Say you have two children, a boy aged eight and a girl aged six.
  3 Say your father is sixty and your mother is fifty-eight.
  4 Say you are married and your wife's/husband's name is Josefina/José.

| | 8 |

2 Match the sentences 1–5 with a suitable response from a–e.

  1 Ésta es una foto de mi casa.
  2 Usted está casada, ¿verdad?
  3 ¿Cuántos años tiene su hijo?
  4 ¿Cuántos hijos tiene usted?
  5 Ésta es la pequeña, María.

  a Tiene ocho.
  b Tengo dos.
  c ¡Qué guapa!
  d Sí, mi marido se llama Oscar.
  e ¡Es grande!

| | 5 |

3 Study the family tree and complete the sentences.

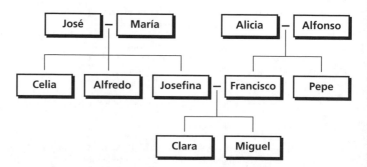

1 José es _____ de Clara y Miguel.
2 Alfredo es _____ de Clara y Miguel.
3 Miguel es _____ de Clara.
4 Miguel es _____ de Francisco.
5 Clara es _____ de Miguel.
6 Francisco es _____ de Clara.
7 Josefina es _____ de Miguel.
8 Alicia es _____ de Clara.

| 8 |

4 Fill the gaps with either **por** or **para**.

1 Estas manzanas son ___ mi madre.
2 ¿Cuánto cuesta la habitación ___ noche?
3 Mi padre trabaja ___ la noche.
4 Siga ___ esta calle hasta el final.
5 ___ mí, la sopa.
6 Llamo a mi amigo ___ teléfono.

| 6 |

5 You're booking a hotel room in Spain. Write your
requirements in Spanish. (2 points for each correct answer,
1 point if you make one mistake.)

1 A double room for three nights.
2 You want the room on 14th February.
3 Ask how much it costs.
4 Ask if the room is on the third floor.
5 Say you have luggage.

| 10 |

6 Write these dates in full in Spanish.

1 23-6   2 13-2   3 19-9   4 30-7   5 1-5

| 5 |

TOTAL SCORE | 42 |

If you scored less than 32, look at the Language Building
sections again before completing the Summary on page 74.

Summary 5

Now try this final test, summarizing the main points covered in this unit.

How would you:
  1 ask someone if she's married?
  2 say you have three children?
  3 say about a little girl 'how pretty'?
  4 say she's three years old?
  5 say María is José's sister?
  6 ask how old María is?
  7 ask someone what her flat's like?
  8 say it's a big flat in the centre of the city?
  9 say it has a beautiful view?
  10 say you'd like a double room for three nights?

REVISION

Draw your own family tree and make sentences about the various relationships. Then construct sentences giving the ages of the various members of your family.

Now practise saying where your house is and what it's like. How many rooms are there and what are they? You can use your dictionary to add to the vocabulary you have already learned in this unit.

Practise dates, making sure you know the names of the days and months. Every day say what date it is. Pick out key dates in your family calendar (for example, birthdays) and practise saying them in Spanish.

6

What time is it?
¿Qué hora es?

OBJECTIVES

In this unit you'll learn how to:

✓ ask and tell the time

✓ ask and say what time shops and other facilities open and close

✓ ask and say what time events start and finish

✓ talk about working hours and daily routines

✓ talk about the days of the week

And cover the following grammar and language:

✓ time expressions **de ... a** and **desde ... hasta** ('from ... until')

✓ reflexive verbs

✓ radical-changing verbs

LEARNING SPANISH 6

Confidence is so important when speaking a language. A good way of overcoming any inhibitions you may feel is to practise saying the words and sentences you learn on your own when no one can hear you. Exaggerate the pronunciation and enjoy yourself. If you get the opportunity, through film or with Spanish speakers, listen carefully to how they speak and try to reproduce their speaking style with your own voice. Use a tape recorder to record yourself speaking and play it back as often as you like. Little by little you will gain confidence when you are speaking with other people.

Now start the recording for Unit 6.

75

What's your timetable?

¿Qué horario tienes?

ⓐ **ACTIVITY 1** is on the recording.

ACTIVITY 2

Which is the odd one out in each group?

1	Jobs:	a shop assistant	c	sales representative
		b office worker	d	accountant
2	Workplace:	a insurance office	c	furniture shop
		b electrical appliances shop	d	sales office
3	Finish work:	a 6 p.m.	c	8.15 p.m.
		b 5 p.m.	d	8 p.m.
4	For lunch:	a 1 1/2 hours	c	2 hours
		b 3 hours	d	2 1/2 hours

DIALOGUE 1

■ ¿Qué haces? ¿Trabajas?

○ Sí, trabajo en una tienda de electrodomésticos. Soy dependiente. ¿Y tú?

■ Yo trabajo en una compañía de seguros, en una oficina.

○ ¿Qué horario tienes?

■ Trabajo de nueve a seis. Tengo una hora a mediodía para comer, a la una y media.

○ Yo trabajo de nueve a una y de cuatro a ocho. Tengo tres horas a mediodía para comer.

■ ¿En qué trabaja usted?

▼ Soy representante de ventas de una compañía de muebles.

■ ¿Qué horario tiene?

▼ Mi horario es de nueve a una y media y por la tarde de cuatro a ocho y cuarto.

■ ¿Viaja mucho?

▼ Sí. Viajo mucho. Cuando viajo, no tengo horario.

VOCABULARY

hacer (hago)	to do
la tienda de electrodomésticos	electrical appliance shop
el dependiente/la dependienta	shop assistant
el horario	timetable
el mediodía	midday

⊘ Telling the time

In Spanish, times are given using the verb **ser**:

¿Qué hora **es**? What time is it?   **Son** las cuatro. It's four o'clock.

The definite article and the verb are both used in the plural – **son las cuatro** – except for **es la una** ('it's one o'clock'). The 24-hour clock is used mainly at stations and airports: **las catorce horas** ('14.00'), **las catorce treinta** ('14.30').

For half hours add **y media**. To give times with quarter hours, you use **cuarto** ('quarter') with **y** ('and') or **menos** ('less'):

Son las ocho **y media**. It's half past eight.
las once **y cuarto** a quarter past eleven [*literally* eleven and quarter]
las doce **menos cuarto** a quarter to twelve [*literally* twelve less quarter]

y and **menos** are also used with minutes:

las ocho **y** diez ten past eight   las nueve **menos** cinco five to nine

To specify what time something happens the preposition **a** is used:

a las ocho de la mañana   at eight o'clock in [*literally* of] the morning
a las ocho de la tarde   at eight o'clock in the evening
a las once de la noche   at eleven o'clock at night
a medianoche/a mediodía   at (around) midnight/at (around) midday

⊘ de ... a ('from ... to'), desde ... hasta ('from ... until')

There are two ways of saying what hours you work or when a shop is open: these are interchangeable.

Trabajo **de** nueve **a** seis. I work from nine until six.
Trabajo **desde** las nueve **hasta** las seis. I work from nine until six.

The definite article is dropped with **de ... a**, but kept with **desde ... hasta**.

ACTIVITY 3

1 Give the Spanish for the following times.
   a 10 o'clock   b 11.30   c 3 o'clock   d 6.30

2 What do you do? Use **Soy ...** or **Trabajo en ...**
   a sales representative   c head of personnel
   b furniture company   d grocer's shop

3 Write down these hours using **de ... a** or **desde ... hasta**.
   a from 10 to 1 and from 4 to 7   c from 9 to 1 and 4 to 8
   b from 9 until 5   d from 2 until 10 o'clock

🎧 Now do activities 4 and 5 on the recording.

6.2 What time do you get up?
¿A qué hora te levantas?

ACTIVITY 6 is on the recording.

ACTIVITY 7

What time does Bernardo …

1 get up?
2 leave home in the morning?
3 start work in the morning?
4 finish work in the evening?
5 have supper?
6 go to bed?

DIALOGUE 2

- ¿A qué hora te levantas?
- Me levanto a las siete de la mañana.
- ¿A qué hora sales de casa?
- Desayuno a las siete y media y salgo de mi casa a las ocho. Llego a mi trabajo a las ocho y media.
- ¿Trabajas hasta la una?
- Sí. A mediodía voy a casa para comer con la familia. Después tomamos café y hablamos. Descanso, veo la tele, leo el periódico …
- ¿A qué hora vuelves a trabajar?
- Por la tarde trabajo de cuatro y media a ocho. Vuelvo a casa y ceno a las nueve y media.
- ¿Y a qué hora te acuestas?
- A las once y media o a las doce menos cuarto.

VOCABULARY

levantarse	to get up
durante	during
desayunar	to have breakfast
llegar	to arrive
ir	to go
voy	I go
después	afterwards
descansar	to relax
la tele	television
volver (vuelvo)	to return
la tarde	afternoon
cenar	to have supper
acostarse (me acuesto)	to go to bed

⊘ Reflexive verbs

A reflexive verb is one whose subject performs the action of the verb upon himself or herself. In Spanish this idea is conveyed by a reflexive pronoun ('myself', 'yourself', etc.): the pronoun is not normally used in English, e.g. **levantarse**, 'to get up' [*literally* 'to raise oneself']:

(yo) <u>me</u> levanto	(nosotros/as) <u>nos</u> levant<u>amos</u>
(tú) <u>te</u> levant<u>as</u>	(vosotros/as) <u>os</u> levant<u>áis</u>
(él/ella/usted) <u>se</u> levant<u>a</u>	(ellos/as/ustedes) <u>se</u> levant<u>an</u>

In the infinitive (**levantarse**) and the imperative (**levántate**), the reflexive pronoun is added to the end of the verb. Note the accent in the imperative form.

Other reflexive verbs:

acostarse	to go to bed	**ducharse**	to have a shower
peinarse	to comb one's hair	**vestirse**	to get dressed
lavarse	to have a wash		

⊘ Radical-changing verbs

Radical-changing verbs are verbs in which the vowel in the stem ('radical' = stem) changes in the singular forms and in the third person plural. In all other ways they follow the pattern of regular **-ar**, **-er**, and **-ir** verbs. The verbs **volver** ('to return') and **acostarse** ('to go to bed') are radical-changing verbs. In the singular and third person plural forms, **o** changes to **ue**:

volver: v<u>ue</u>lvo, v<u>ue</u>lves, v<u>ue</u>lve, volvemos, volvéis, v<u>ue</u>lven
acostarse: me ac<u>ue</u>sto, te ac<u>ue</u>stas, se ac<u>ue</u>sta, nos acostamos, os acostáis, se ac<u>ue</u>stan

The verb **tener** ('to have') is also a radical-changing verb, as well as being irregular (see p. 63).

In vocabulary lists from now on, the first person singular of such verbs will be shown in brackets after the infinitive, e.g. **volver (vuelvo)**.

ACTIVITY 8

Complete this account of Pepe's day. Here's his timetable:

Pepe gets up at 7 o'clock and works from 9.15 until 1.15. He eats at 2 o'clock and returns to work at 4. He works until 7.45. He goes to bed at 11.30.

Pepe se levanta a las siete …

 Now do activities 9 and 10 on the recording.

What time does the film start?

¿A qué hora empieza la película?

🔊 **ACTIVITY 11** is on the recording.

ACTIVITY 12

What happens at each of these times?

Example: 4.30 p.m. El cine abre a las cuatro y media.

a 7.15 p.m.   b 9 p.m.   c 10 a.m.

DIALOGUE 3

■ ¿Vamos al cine esta tarde?
○ Sí, pero yo quiero visitar el museo también.
■ De acuerdo. ¿A qué hora empieza la película?
○ La película empieza a las siete y cuarto.
■ ¿Cuánto dura?
○ Dos horas más o menos. Termina a las nueve.
■ ¿El museo está abierto los domingos?
○ Sí, está abierto todos los días menos los lunes.
■ ¿A qué hora abre por la mañana?
○ A las diez. Y por la tarde cierra a las ocho.
■ Comemos en un restaurante cerca del museo y por la tarde vamos al museo y luego vamos al cine a las siete.
○ ¡Estupendo! Quedamos en la puerta del museo a las dos.

VOCABULARY	
empezar	to start, begin
la película	film
¿vamos … ?/vamos	shall we go …?/let's go
el cine	cinema
visitar	to visit
durar	to last
más o menos	more or less
terminar	to finish
abierto	open
todos los días	every day
menos	except
abrir	to open
cerrar	to close
¡estupendo!	great! terrific!
quedar	to meet

LANGUAGE BUILDING

✓ More radical-changing verbs

empezar ('to begin'), **cerrar** ('to close'), and **pensar** ('to think') are all **-ar** verbs which are radical-changing: in the singular and the third person plural, the **e** in the stem changes to **ie**:

empiezo, empiezas, empieza, empezamos, empezáis, empiezan

querer ('to want') is an **-er** verb which behaves in the same way:

quiero, quieres, quiere, queremos, queréis, quieren

It is followed by a verb in the infinitive:

Quiero **visitar** el museo. I'd like to visit the museum.

✓ Days of the week

All days of the week in Spanish are masculine and are not capitalized:

los días de la semana: lunes, martes, miércoles, jueves, viernes
weekdays: Monday, Tuesday, Wednesday, Thursday, Friday
el fin de semana: sábado, domingo
the weekend: Saturday, Sunday

To say 'on Monday' etc. or 'at the weekend' in Spanish, you use the definite article, with no preposition:

El lunes tengo clase. On Monday I have a class.
Los sábados no trabajo. On Saturdays I don't work.
Los fines de semana descanso. At the weekend I relax.

ACTIVITY 13

Use the following information to write eight sentences.

Example: La Máscara del Zorro empieza a las cinco y termina a las siete.

1 La Máscara del Zorro: **tarde** 5–7, 7.30–9.30, 10–12
2 Pastelería: **mañana** 9.30–1.30; **tarde** 4.30–8 (**sábados**: 10–2)
3 Museo: **lunes**: cerrado; **martes–sábado** 10–7, domingo 11–5

ACTIVITY 14

Write a short dialogue using Dialogue 3 as a model:

A: ¿el cine/esta tarde?
B: ¿a qué hora/empezar/película?
A: empezar/7/terminar/9.
B: cenar/después

Now do activities 15 and 16 on the recording.

81

6.4 A typical day in Spain
Un día típico en España

ACTIVITY 17

Read the letter from Miguel describing his typical day and find out the following information:

1. what time he gets up.
2. what he does in the middle of the morning.
3. where he has lunch.
4. what time he has dinner.
5. what he does on Sundays.

Hola David,

¿Cómo estás? Me preguntas cómo son los horarios típicos en España. Me levanto a las seis y media y empiezo a trabajar a las ocho. Desayuno muy rápido: café o leche, zumo de naranja, magdalenas, tostadas. A media mañana mucha gente toma un café en un bar cerca de su trabajo. Yo tomo un almuerzo de tortilla de patata u otra cosa.

Normalmente termino el trabajo a la una y vuelvo a casa para comer. Después tomo un café, descanso. Ésta es la costumbre de la sobremesa. Hay programas especiales en la televisión. Vuelvo a trabajar a las cuatro y trabajo hasta las ocho. A media tarde tomo un café con un pastel. Después, en casa, a las nueve y media ceno algo ligero.

Los fines de semana es distinto. Como a las dos y media. Los domingos mucha gente da un paseo con la familia. Hablan y toman café o un aperitivo con los amigos antes de comer. Las comidas de domingo son más especiales y comemos con la familia en casa o en un restaurante, más tarde, a las dos y media o a las tres.

Un abrazo,

Miguel

me preguntas	you ask(ed) me
la magdalena	cupcake
la tostada	toast
la gente	people
el almuerzo	mid-morning snack
la tortilla	omelette
u	or [*used instead of o before a word beginning with 'o'*]
la costumbre	custom
sobremesa	*the period immediately after lunch when people sit around the table chatting* [*literally* over the table]
el programa	television programme
ligero	light
distinto	different
dar un paseo	to take a walk, a stroll
el aperitivo	aperitif
antes de	before
un abrazo	best wishes

ACTIVITY 18

Now describe your own daily routine, using the letter as a model. Use the verbs that appear in the letter and add times and activities to describe your own situation. Use the vocabulary section to help you.

ACTIVITY 19

Find eight words which have something to do with meals or food.

T	O	R	T	I	L	L	A	B	A
Z	O	X	Q	B	Y	G	L	U	P
A	V	S	D	P	P	H	A	F	E
L	E	T	T	P	O	W	N	K	R
M	A	G	D	A	L	E	N	A	I
U	Z	D	Q	S	D	A	N	O	T
E	X	R	R	T	I	A	T	Y	I
R	E	S	C	E	Z	I	M	L	V
Z	U	M	O	L	M	S	L	V	O
O	S	O	B	R	E	M	E	S	A

UNA INVITACIÓN A CENAR
AN INVITATION TO DINNER

Cuando María sale del trabajo, va al Bar España. Jorge la sigue. Se presenta como el hombre del mercado, y le ofrece una bebida. Hablan …

When María leaves work, she goes to the Bar España. Jorge, who has been waiting for her, follows her. In the bar he introduces himself as the man in the market, and offers to buy her a drink. They get talking …

¡salud!	cheers! [*literally* health!]
bastante	quite
largo	long
fijo	fixed
el sueldo	salary
las vacaciones	holidays
de vacaciones	on holiday
exactamente	exactly
de viaje	(travelling) on business
conmigo	with me
así	therefore, that way
continuar	to continue
la conversación	conversation
hasta luego	see you later [*literally* until then]

ACTIVITY 20

Who …

1 offers whom a drink?
2 has an orange juice?
3 works very long hours?
4 doesn't have a very interesting job?
5 has a good salary?
6 invites whom to dinner?
7 suggests which restaurant to go to?
8 suggests they meet in the bar?

ACTIVITY 21

Match these questions to the correct answers from the dialogue.

1 ¿Le conozco?
2 ¿Quiere tomar algo?
3 Trabajas muchas horas, ¿verdad?
4 ¿Es interesante tu trabajo?
5 ¿Quiere cenar conmigo?

a Una cerveza por favor.
b Sí, es un día bastante largo, pero normal.
c Soy el señor del mercado.
d De acuerdo. Pero primero voy a mi casa.
e No es muy interesante pero el sueldo es bueno.

STORY TRANSCRIPT

Jorge	Buenas tardes. Me llamo Jorge Jimeno.
María	¿Le conozco?
Jorge	Soy el señor del mercado ... la cartera ...
María	¡Ah sí! Mucho gusto. Soy María.
Jorge	¿Quieres tomar algo?
María	Bueno, una cerveza, por favor.
Jorge	Para mi un zumo de naranja. Gracias. ¡Salud!
María	¡Salud!
Jorge	¿A qué hora terminas el trabajo?
María	A las ocho.
Jorge	Trabajas muchas horas, ¿verdad?
María	Bueno. Trabajo de nueve a una y media y de cuatro y media a ocho. Sí, es un día bastante largo, pero normal. ¿Y usted? ¿Trabaja muchas horas?
Jorge	Yo no tengo horario fijo pero trabajo muchas horas. ¿Es interesante tu trabajo?
María	Bueno, no mucho. Trabajo en una oficina. No es muy interesante pero el sueldo es bueno. ¿Está usted de vacaciones?
Jorge	No exactamente. Estoy de viaje.
María	¡Oh! Son las nueve menos cuarto. Muchas gracias por la cerveza. Voy a cenar. Es muy tarde.
Jorge	¿Quieres cenar conmigo en un restaurante y así continuamos la conversación?
María	Mmm ... De acuerdo. Pero primero voy a mi casa. Hay un restaurante aquí al lado del bar ... se llama Goya. ¿Quedamos aquí a las nueve y media y vamos al restaurante?
Jorge	De acuerdo ... Hasta luego. Sr. España, otro zumo, por favor.

Test

Now it's time to test your progress in Unit 6.

1 **¿Qué hora es?** Write the following times in full in Spanish, using the phrases **de la mañana**, **de la tarde**, or **de la noche**. (2 points for a correct answer, 1 for one mistake).

1 7.15 a.m.   4 11 p.m.
2 1.30 p.m.   5 4.45 p.m.
3 6.30 p.m.

10

2 **¿Qué horario tienen?** Write down in words the hours these people work, using **desde … hasta**. (2 points for a correct answer, 1 for one mistake).

1 Jaime: 9 a.m.–1 p.m.; 4 p.m.–8 p.m.
2 Carmen: 8.30 a.m.–1.30 p.m.; 4.30 p.m.–7.30 p.m.
3 Jorge: 8 p.m.–6 a.m.
4 Puri: 8 a.m.–5 p.m.
5 Alfonso: 2.45 p.m.–8.30 p.m.

10

3 Write nine sentences about your day, saying what time you usually do things. Use the following verbs:

levantarse / desayunar / salir / llegar / comer / terminar / volver / cenar / acostarse

9

4 Use the correct verb in the correct form to complete these sentences.

1 La tienda _____ a la una del mediodía.
2 La película _____ tres horas.
3 El cine _____ a las once de la noche.
4 La película _____ a las ocho y _____ a las once.
5 El museo _____ a las diez de la mañana.

6

5 **¿Qué quieres hacer?** Complete the dialogue. (2 points for a correct answer, 1 for one mistake).

    A: ¿Quieres ir al cine?
    Tú: (No, you don't want to go to the cinema.)
    A: ¿Qué quieres hacer?
    Tú: (You want to have supper in a restaurant.)
    A: ¿A qué hora quedamos?
    Tú: (You'll meet him at 7.30 at the restaurant.)

                                                               6

6 Replace the infinitive in brackets with the correct form of the verb (all are irregular).

    1 Por la mañana yo (**salir**) de casa a las ocho.
    2 María (**volver**) a casa a mediodía.
    3 Yo (**tener**) dos hermanos.
    4 Mis padres no (**querer**) café.
    5 Yo (**conocer**) a tu amigo, Juan.

                                                                5

7 Make sentences using **querer** + another verb. (2 points for a correct answer, 1 for one mistake).

    1 You want to have dinner.
    2 You want to go out.
    3 You want to visit your parents.
    4 You want to go home.

                                                                8

8 Complete the following sentences by translating the words in brackets. Note that some of them are reflexive verbs: you will need to include the correct reflexive pronoun.

    1 (**I get up**) a las siete.
    2 (**I eat dinner**) a las nueve de la noche.
    3 (**I go to bed**) a las once.
    4 (**I have a shower**) por la mañana.
    5 (**I relax**) después de comer.
    6 (**I go out**) a las ocho.

                                                                6

                            TOTAL SCORE   **60**

If you scored less than 50, look at the Language Building sections again before completing the Summary on page 88.

Summary 6

Now try this final test, summarizing the main points covered in this unit.

How would you:
1 ask the time?
2 say it's a quarter to nine in the morning?
3 say you work in a shop and he works in an office?
4 say you work from nine to five?
5 say they get up at seven in the morning and go to bed at 11?
6 say the film starts at five and finishes at seven?
7 say the shop opens at ten and closes at six?
8 say she wants to have lunch?
9 say you'll meet someone at the restaurant at eight?
10 say that on Monday you work?

REVISION

Practise saying the time to yourself in Spanish. Get into the habit of practising the different structures for saying the time: **son las dos menos cuarto**, etc. Look at timetables and practise saying complete sentences: **abre a las diez**, etc. What is your daily routine? Work through it in Spanish.

Revise your vocabulary for jobs by identifying the jobs done by your friends and family in Spanish. Extend the vocabulary by using your dictionary to look up the Spanish for jobs you don't know. Practise your own details whenever you get the chance: **Me llamo...**, **trabajo en ...**, **me levanto a las ... trabajo de ... a ...**, etc. Do this for other people as well to improve your fluency.

This unit is full of new verbs, some of them irregular. It's important to practise saying them over and over. Pay particular attention to the reflexive verbs and the radical-changing verbs.

7

Eating out
En el restaurante

OBJECTIVES

In this unit you'll learn how to:

☑ talk about different kinds of food and drink

☑ order items from the menu in a restaurant

☑ complain about things in a restaurant

☑ ask for the bill

And cover the following grammar and language:

☑ the disjunctive pronouns **mí**, **ti**, etc.

☑ the verb **poder** ('to be able') followed by the infinitive

☑ more irregular verbs

☑ **se** in passive constructions

LEARNING SPANISH 7

Use a tape recorder to record yourself speaking Spanish and to help you improve your pronunciation. First of all, listen to the stress, intonation, and rhythm of people speaking Spanish on the recording, then try to reproduce it yourself. Don't underestimate the value of simply listening to sentences and copying them as exactly as you can. It's all good practice. Start by doing this with individual words, and then build up to longer sentences.

Now start the recording for Unit 7.

7.1 What's on the menu?
¿Qué hay en el menú?

ACTIVITY 1 is on the recording.

ACTIVITY 2

Sort the items: **primer plato**, **segundo plato**, **postre**, or **bebida**?

fruta	sopa	cocido	agua	flan
cordero	ensalada	vino	pescado	

DIALOGUE 1

○ ¿Qué hay en el menú del día?
▼ De primero hay sopa o ensalada. De segundo hay cocido, pescado o cordero, y de postre hay flan o fruta.
■ Para empezar, quiero la ensalada y el cordero de segundo.
○ De primero quiero sopa y de segundo pescado. ¿Qué pescado es?
▼ Es merluza a la plancha.
○ Bueno. Pues quiero la merluza.
▼ Muy bien. ¿Y para beber?
○ Vino tinto, por favor, y agua.
▼ ¿Qué van a tomar de postre?
○ Pues el flan.
■ Para mí también.

VOCABULARY

el menú (del día)	menu (of the day)
el plato	dish
el postre	dessert
la bebida	drink
la sopa	soup
el cocido	*meat and chickpea stew*
el agua	water
el flan	crème caramel
la ensalada	salad
para empezar	to begin
a la plancha	grilled
para beber	to drink
el vino tinto	red wine

✓ Disjunctive pronouns after a preposition

After prepositions, such as **para** ('for'), **con** ('with'), **sin** ('without'), **de** ('of, from'), an emphatic form of the pronoun, known as the disjunctive pronoun, is used:

para <u>mí</u> for me	**con <u>nosotros/as</u>** with us
para <u>ti</u> for you	**sin <u>vosotros/as</u>** without you
con <u>él</u>/<u>ella</u> with him/her	**sin <u>ellos/as</u>** without them

con + mí becomes **conmigo** and **con + ti** becomes **contigo**. Note that **mí** has an accent to distinguish it from the possessive pronoun **mi** ('my'), but **ti** has no accent.

✓ *De primero/de segundo/de postre*

The preposition **de** [*literally* 'of'] means 'for' in the following expressions when ordering a meal. The ordinal numbers **primero** ('first') and **segundo** ('second') can be used either on their own or with the noun **plato** ('course'). If used with the noun, **primero** drops the final **-o**.

De primer plato quiero la sopa de champiñon. For the first course I'd like the mushroom soup.
De primero hay ensaladilla rusa o ensalada mixta. For the first course there's Russian salad or mixed salad.
De segundo plato quiero pollo al ajillo. For the second course I'd like garlic chicken.
¿Qué va a tomar **de postre**? What are you having for dessert?

✓ *para* + infinitive

para is frequently used for the English equivalent of 'to'. It is followed by the infinitive: **para empezar** ('to begin'), **para beber** ('to drink').

ACTIVITY 3

Complete the sentences using the appropriate word or phrase from the list below.

empezar / beber / de primero / cómo / quiero / qué

1 ____ _____ hay ensalada mixta.
2 Para _____ quiero la sopa.
3 ¿_____ es la merluza? A la plancha.
4 ¿_____ es pollo al ajillo? Es pollo con ajos.
5 ¿El pescado o el cordero? … _____ el pescado.
6 ¿Qué quiere _____? Agua mineral, por favor.

(🎧) Now do activities 4 and 5 on the recording.

7.2 There's a knife missing
Falta un cuchillo

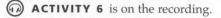 **ACTIVITY 6** is on the recording.

ACTIVITY 7

¿Alfonso o Carmen? Quién …

1 ¿… toma café sólo?
2 ¿… toma un cortado?

3 ¿… no tiene cuchara?
4 ¿… no tiene cuchillo?

DIALOGUE 2

○ ¿Qué hay de postre?
▼ Hay flan, helado, fruta del tiempo, tarta de whisky.
○ Para mí, fruta, una manzana.
■ Para mí, tarta de whisky.
▼ Sí, se toma con nata.
■ Muy bien.
▼ ¿Toman cafés?
■ Un café solo, por favor.
○ Y para mí un cortado.

■ No tengo cuchara. ¡Oiga! ¿Puede traer una cuchara?
▼ Sí, señorita. Ahora la traigo.
○ Y falta un cuchillo para la fruta. ¿Puede traer uno?
▼ Sí, señor, ahora lo traigo.
■ Falta un café. ¿Puede traerlo?
▼ Sí, en seguida lo traigo.

○ Oiga, por favor. ¿Puede traer la cuenta?
▼ Sí, ahora la traigo.

VOCABULARY	
faltar	to lack, to be missing
el cuchillo	knife
la cuchara	spoon
la fruta del tiempo	seasonal fruit
la tarta (de whisky)	tart, cake (with whisky)
se toma	it is eaten [*from* **tomarse**]
la nata	cream
traer (traigo)	to bring
en seguida	immediately
la cuenta	bill

LANGUAGE BUILDING

✓ *poder* + infinitive

poder ('to be able') is a radical-changing verb (see the Grammar Summary page 231) and also page 95 and Unit 8 for more on its uses. It is followed by an infinitive. **¿puede ...?** ('could you ...?') is used to ask someone formally for something.

No **puedo terminar** el pollo. I can't finish the chicken.
¿Puede traer la cuenta? Could you bring the bill?
¿Puede limpiar la mesa? Could you clean the table?

Note that the direct object pronoun is added to the infinitive:

La mesa está sucia. ¿Puede limpiar**la**? The table is dirty. Could you clean it?

✓ More irregular verbs

traer is an irregular **-er** verb which adds **g** in the first person singular and changes the **e** to **i**:

Ahora **traigo** la cuenta. I'll bring the bill now.
Ahora **trae** la copa. He's bringing the wine glass now.

The rest of the verb is regular. The following verbs also add **g** in the first person singular: **hacer**, 'to do' (**hago, haces**, etc.), **tener**, 'to have' (**tengo, tienes**, etc.), **venir**, 'to come' (**vengo, vienes**, etc.), **salir**, 'to leave' (**salgo, sales**, etc.), **poner**, 'to put' (**pongo, pones**, etc.)

✓ *faltar* ('to be missing, lacking')

This verb is used in the following way:

Falta un cuchillo. There's a knife missing. [*literally* A knife is missing.]
Faltan dos vasos. There are two glasses missing.

✓ *se* in passive constructions

se is often used in passive constructions or where there is no specific subject. It is followed by a verb in the third person singular or plural:

Se toma con nata. You eat it [*literally* it is eaten] with cream.
Se puede comer frío. You can eat it/It can be eaten cold.

ACTIVITY 8

Write these sentences in Spanish.

1 What is there for dessert?
2 There isn't a fork.
3 Could you bring some coffee?
4 They'll bring the bill now.
5 I can't finish my dessert.
6 You eat it cold.

 Now do activities 9 and 10 on the recording.

The soup is cold

La sopa está fría

🔊 **ACTIVITY 11** is on the recording.

ACTIVITY 12

What's the problem with each of the following?

1 the table   4 the bill
2 the soup   5 the restaurant
3 the fish

DIALOGUE 3

○ ¡Oiga! La mesa está sucia. ¿Puede limpiarla, por favor?
■ En seguida.

○ Por favor … La sopa está fría. ¿Puede calentarla, por favor?
■ Sí, señora.

○ El pescado está quemado. ¿Puede cambiarlo?
■ Sí, señora.

○ Oiga, señor. La cuenta está equivocada. ¿Puede mirarla?
■ A ver. Sí, sí, tiene razón.
○ Este restaurante es muy malo. Las mesas están sucias, la sopa está fría, el pescado está quemado y yo estoy muy enfadada.
■ Lo siento mucho, señora.

VOCABULARY	
la mesa	table
sucio	dirty
limpiar	to clean
frío	cold
calentar	to heat up
quemado	burnt
cambiar	to change
equivocado	wrong, mistaken
tener razón	to be right
malo	bad
enfadado	angry, annoyed
lo siento (mucho)	I'm (very) sorry

✅ More uses of *estar* and *ser*

estar is used to describe where someone or something is located. It can also be used to describe a temporary state:

La mesa **está** sucia. The table is dirty.
La sopa **está** fría. The soup is cold.

In these examples the temporary state can be remedied (by cleaning, heating, or replacing). Compare this with the following example:

El restaurante **es** muy malo. The restaurant is very bad.

This statement describes a more permanent state, which would take some time to change, so the verb **ser** is used.

✅ More on *¿puede ...?* + the infinitive and direct object pronouns

When **¿puede ...?** + the infinitive is used with a direct object pronoun in the plural, the forms **los** and **las** are used.

dos cuchillos – ¿Puede traer**los**? Could you bring them?
estas cucharas – ¿Puede cambiar**las**? Could you change them?

ACTIVITY 13

Complete this story, using the correct form of **ser** or **estar** and the correct form of the adjective.

El restaurante Cuatro Estaciones _____ muy (**bueno**). _____ enfrente del cine Cervantes. La comida _____ (**bueno**) también. Pero hoy hay un problema. Hay dos camareros (**nuevo**). _____ (**malo**). La sopa _____ (**frío**) y la carne _____ (**quemado**). Los clientes _____ (**enfadado**). La señora Martínez _____ una persona (**muy importante**). Ella _____ (**enfadado**). La comida _____ (**malo**) y su cuenta _____ (**equivocado**).

ACTIVITY 14

Add the correct form of the direct object pronoun to the infinitive.

Example: la sopa – ¿Puede cambiar**la**?

1 la carne – cambiar
2 el vino – cambiar
3 las cucharas – cambiar
4 los platos – cambiar
5 el cordero – cambiar
6 la cuenta – mirar
7 la mesa – limpiar

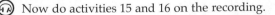 Now do activities 15 and 16 on the recording.

95

Spanish cuisine
La cocina española

ACTIVITY 17

Read the following text about some of Spain's famous dishes and study the new vocabulary. Then identify which dish is described in each of the statements below.

1 You need batter for this dish.
2 It's a cold soup.
3 You can eat this hot or cold.
4 You can make it with different kinds of meat or seafood.
5 A kind of stew with lots of ingredients.
6 You need plenty of potatoes and enough olive oil.
7 There is no cooking involved in this dish.
8 You need plenty of water to boil the vegetables.

España es muy famosa por su cocina y hay platos especiales y regionales. El gazpacho es una sopa fría que se toma en el verano. Es un plato típico de Andalucía en el sur de España. Tiene pimiento, cebolla, tomate, aceite, vinagre y sal. Se cortan todos los ingredientes y se añade agua. Es una comida muy sencilla y muy buena.

La paella es otro plato muy típico de España. La base de la paella se hace con arroz, guisantes, cebolla, pimiento, tomate, aceite y agua. Hay paellas con pollo, con conejo y con mariscos.

La tortilla de patata es un plato tradicional en toda España. En todos los bares hay tapas de tortilla de patata. Se come caliente o fría. El secreto está en las patatas. Se frien las patatas muy bien en aceite de oliva. Es importante usar muchas patatas y bastante aceite.

Otro plato típico es calamares 'a la romana'. Se rebozan los calamares en harina y huevo. Luego se frien en aceite de oliva y se comen calientes. Éste plato es una tapa muy popular en los bares.

El cocido es un plato que tiene trozos de carne, de verdura y de chorizo, y lo más importante, garbanzos o judías blancas. Se hierve mucha agua y se añaden los ingredientes. Se hierve todo. Se sirve caliente.

CULTURE

la cocina	cuisine
el verano	summer
porque	because
el pimiento	pepper [*vegetable*]
la sal	salt
cortar	to cut
añadir	to add
sencillo	simple
el arroz	rice
guisantes	peas
el conejo	rabbit
los mariscos	seafood
caliente	hot, warm
freír	to fry
rebozar	to cover in batter
la harina	flour
el huevo	egg
la mezcla	mixture
los garbanzos	chickpeas
las judías blancas	white beans
hervir	to boil
servir	to serve

ACTIVITY 18

1 ¿Qué tiene el gazpacho?
2 ¿Cómo se hace el gazpacho?
3 ¿Qué se puede hacer con pollo, conejo y mariscos?
4 ¿Qué se puede comer caliente o frío?
5 ¿Qué platos típicos son populares en los bares de España?
6 ¿Qué tiene el cocido?
7 ¿Cómo se hace el cocido?

ACTIVITY 19

How do you make fish and chips? Use the following
vocabulary to help you.

se reboza(n)	se calienta(n)	el pescado	el huevo
se corta(n)	se sirve(n)	las patatas	la salsa (sauce)
se fríe(n)		la harina	

ACTIVITY 20

Choose another simple recipe and write down the instructions
in Spanish. Use your dictionary to find any words you don't
know.

LA CENA
DINNER

Jorge y María están en el restaurante. Pero María está muy nerviosa. ¿Qué le pasa?

nervioso	nervous
tener hambre	to be hungry
de verdad	really
pedir	to ask for
¿qué te pasa?	what's the matter (with you)? [*informal*]
entender (entiendo)	to understand
realmente	really
el / la turista	tourist
decir	to say
no entiendo nada	I don't understand at all
complicado	complicated
quizás	perhaps
hasta mañana	see you tomorrow [*literally* until tomorrow]
explicar	to explain

ACTIVITY 21

¿Verdadero o falso?

1 María no termina el pollo porque está quemado. V/F
2 María quiere helado de postre. V/F
3 María no quiere pedir la cuenta. V/F
4 María quiere más información de Jorge. V/F
5 Jorge no puede decir la verdad. V/F
6 Salen del restaurante juntos. V/F

ACTIVITY 22

The following lines are taken from the dialogue, but they are in the wrong order. Rearrange them so that they make sense.

a No, de verdad, no quiero nada más. ¿Pedimos la cuenta?
b ¿Quieres café?
c ¿Qué te pasa?
d ¿No terminas el pollo? Está muy bueno.
e No importa. ¿Quieres postre?

f No. Lo siento. No tengo mucha hambre. No puedo terminarlo.

g Sí, del bar España.

h No, gracias.

i ¿Quién es usted? Le conozco, ¿verdad?

j Eres muy importante para mí.

ACTIVITY 23

Complete this account of the story by filling the gaps with the appropriate form of the verb from the list below. Use the present tense. Some verbs may be used more than once.

> querer / tener / comer / entender / irse / conocer / estar / poder

Jorge y María (1) _____ en el restaurante. María no (2) _____ porque no (3) _____ hambre. No (4) _____ postre ni café. (5) _____ pedir la cuenta. María no (6) _____ problemas en el trabajo. El problema es Jorge. María (7) _____ a Jorge. Jorge dice que conoce a María pero no (8) _____ decirle nada. María no (9) _____ y (10) _____ del restaurante.

STORY TRANSCRIPT

Jorge	María. No comes. ¿No terminas el pollo? Está muy bueno.
María	No. Lo siento. No tengo mucha hambre. No puedo terminarlo.
Jorge	No importa. ¿Quieres postre? ¿Quieres helado?
María	No, gracias.
Jorge	¿Quieres café?
María	No, de verdad, no quiero nada más. ¿Pedimos la cuenta?
Jorge	Estás muy nerviosa, ¿verdad? ¿Qué te pasa?
María	Nada. No tengo mucha hambre.
Jorge	¿Tienes problemas en el trabajo?
María	No. Trabajo mucho, pero no tengo problemas. El problema es usted.
Jorge	No entiendo. ¿Qué pasa?
María	¿Quién es usted? Le conozco, ¿verdad?
Jorge	Sí, del bar España.
María	No, no. De antes.
Jorge	Mira. Me llamo Jorge Jimeno. Soy representante de ventas y vivo en Granada.
María	Sí, pero ¿quién es usted realmente?
Jorge	Soy turista en la ciudad, nada más.
María	¿Por qué está aquí? ¿Por qué no me dice la verdad? ¿Por qué?
Jorge	María, yo te conozco, sí. Eres muy importante para mí. Pero ahora no puedo decirte más. Lo siento.
María	No entiendo nada. Me voy. ¡Adiós!
Jorge	Por favor, ¡María! La situación es muy complicada. Ahora no puedo decirte quién soy. Mañana quizás.
María	No entiendo nada. ¡Adiós!
Jorge	Bueno. Hasta mañana.

Test

Now it's time to test your progress in Unit 7.

1 Give the Spanish for:

    1 the first course   5 dessert
    2 two first course dishes   6 two dessert dishes
    3 the second course   7 the bill
    4 two second course dishes

      10

2 Complete the questions about food on the menu, then
  supply the answers, using the words in brackets.

    1 ¿___ ___ en el menú? (pollo, pescado, cordero)
    2 ¿___ ___ el pescado? (a la plancha)
    3 ¿___ ___ la sopa? (de verduras)

      3

3 Complete this dialogue using the words below.

estoy	**quiero**	**beber**	**segundo**	**para**
hay	**nada**	**empezar**	**vas**	**bueno**

  A: ¿Qué _____ a tomar de primero?
  B: Para _____ quiero la sopa.
  A: Yo _____ la ensalada
  B: ¿Y de _____?
  A: El cordero, por favor.
  B: _____ mí, el pollo. ¿Y para _____?
  A: Agua mineral.
  A: ¿Qué _____ de postre?
  B: El helado es _____. ¿Y para usted?
  A: No quiero _____. _____ lleno.

      10

4 Using **faltar**, tell the waiter what's missing.

  Example: no plate – Falta un plato.

    1 no knife.   3 no glass.   5 no plates at all.
    2 no spoon.   4 no glasses.   6 no fork.

      6

5 Read the dialogues and complete your part. (Score 2 points for a correct answer, 1 point if you make one mistake.)

1 You: (Call the waitress. Ask her to bring the soup.)
Camarera Sí, sí, lo siento. Ahora la traigo.

2 You: (Tell the waitress that your chicken is cold.)
Camarera: Lo siento.
You: (Ask her to change it.)
Camarera: Sí, en seguida.

3 You: (Ask the waitress to bring the bill.)
Camarera: Ahora la traigo.
You: (Tell her the bill is wrong.)

9

6 Choose between **ser** and **estar** to complete the following sentences.

1 El restaurante (**es/está**) muy bueno.
2 La casa (**es/está**) grande.
3 El vino blanco no (**es/está**) frío.
4 La cuenta (**es/está**) equivocada.

4

7 Complete the following sentences, choosing the appropriate verb from list A and the appropriate direct object pronoun from list B:

A cambiar / calentar / traer / limpiar / mirar
B lo / la / los / las

1 El pollo está quemado. ¿Puede _____, por favor?
2 La sopa está fría. ¿Puede _____ ,por favor?
3 Las copas están sucias. ¿Puede _____, por favor?
4 La mesa está sucia. ¿Puede _____, por favor?
5 Faltan dos cafés. ¿Puede _____, por favor?
6 Falta un plato. ¿Puede _____, por favor?
7 La cuenta está equivocada ¿Puede _____, por favor?
8 Quiero la carne con patatas, no con ensalada. ¿Puede _____, por favor?

16

TOTAL SCORE 58

If you scored less than 48, look at the Language Building sections again before completing the Summary on page 102.

Summary 7

 Now try this final test, summarizing the main points covered in this unit.

How would you:
1 say you want salad for the first course?
2 say you want soup to start with?
3 complain that the fish is burnt and ask the waiter to change it?
4 say there are two knives missing?
5 and ask the waiter to bring them?
6 ask someone you don't know well what they want for dessert?
7 say the restaurant is bad?
8 ask for the bill?

REVISION

If you're eating out, see if you can translate the dishes into Spanish. How would you order in Spanish? Use constructions you have learned in this unit: **para mí, para empezar, para beber, de primero,** etc. Think about the other questions you would use when eating out in Spain: **¿cómo es el cordero? ¿qué tiene la sopa? ¿qué es el cocido?** Can you answer the questions yourself?

Go through the verbs in this unit. Practise the impersonal form when you talk about something: **se toma, se hierve, se sirve,** etc. Look at the irregular and radical-changing verbs, for example **traer, poder,** and practise them in any spare moment you have. Then make up sentences using them.

Finally, practise the difference between **estar** and **ser** by noting different situations as you go through the day. Think about how you would describe things, such as a shop – **es bonito** ('it's nice') and **está abierta** ('it's open') – or a street – **la calle es ancha** ('the street is wide') and **está sucia** ('it's dirty'), and so on.

Review 2

VOCABULARY

1 Give the appropriate adjective of nationality.

    1 una mujer de Francia   4 dos hombres de México
    2 un chico de Alemania   5 un señor de Canadá
    3 dos chicas de Escocia

2 Match the jobs and translate the English sentences, making sure you give the correct form [masc., fem., sing., or pl.].

    1 José is a journalist.   a secretario
    2 María is a teacher.   b contable
    3 Señora Gil is an accountant.   c periodista
    4 Gustavo and Javier are engineers.   d recepcionista
    5 Alicia and Celia are receptionists.   e profesor
    6 Alfonso is a secretary.   f ingeniero

3

Le presento a la familia Suárez. El Sr. Suárez es el _____ de Juan y Josefina y el _____ de la señora Suárez. La señora Suárez es la _____ de Juan y Josefina. Josefina es la _____ de Juan y Juan es el _____ de Josefina. ¿Cuántos _____ tienen los Suárez? Dos, un _____ y una _____.

4 Unscramble the words to identify these rooms in a house.

    A A R T E N D   A N C C O I   R T O O I D M R I O
    N S Ó L A   R O M E C D O

5 Complete this description using the following verbs

    me acuesto me ducho ceno   vuelvo a termino
    llego a   salgo de   desayuno descanso me levanto

    _____ a las siete de la mañana. _____ y _____ cereales a las siete y media. _____ casa a las ocho y _____ mi trabajo a las ocho y media de la mañana. _____ mi trabajo a las seis de la tarde y _____ mi casa. _____ a las nueve de la noche, _____ después de cenar. _____ a las once de la noche.

6 Insert the correct word: **éste, ésta, éstos, éstas**.

    1 _____ es mi marido.
    2 _____ son mis hijos.
    3 _____ es mi madre.
    4 _____ es mi jefe.
    5 _____ son las chicas.

7 Write down the correct form of the verb.

    1 Nosotros (**trabajar**) en una empresa juntos.
    2 Mi hermano (**vivir**) en Barcelona.
    3 Mis padres (**comer**) en un restaurante los viernes.
    4 Yo (**viajar**) de Madrid a Barcelona los sábados.
    5 ¿Tú (**escribir**) a tus padres?
    6 Yo (**querer**) sopa de primero.
    7 ¿Cuántos años (**tener**) tú?

8 Translate into Spanish.

    1 We get up at seven o'clock.
    2 He goes to bed at eleven.
    3 She gets dressed at eight.
    4 Do you [*sing.*] shower at seven?

9 Choose an appropriate verb in the correct form for each of the following sentences.

    1 La mesa está sucia. ¿Puede _____la, por favor?
    2 La carne está fría. ¿Puede _____la, por favor?
    3 Falta el vino. ¿Puede _____lo, por favor?
    4 Faltan los vasos. ¿Puede _____los, por favor?

10 These things are dirty. Ask questions choosing the correct direct object pronoun: **¿puede limpiarlo/la/los/las?**

    1 la mesa   3 los platos
    2 el coche   4 las cucharas

11 **estar** or **ser**? Choose the appropriate verb and write it down in the correct form.

    1 La mesa (**ser**/**estar**) grande.
    2 El café (**ser**/**estar**) bueno.
    3 El hospital (**ser**/**estar**) malo.
    4 La comida (**ser**/**estar**) frío.
    5 El pollo (**ser**/**estar**) pequeño.

12 You'll hear some messages from three people inviting you to go out. For each message write down the correct time and information mentioned.

Time: 1.30 / 5.00 / 7.00 / 7.45 / 8.00 /9.30 / 10.00 / 12.00

Information: have a drink before / have supper before / have supper after

	Message 1	Message 2	Message 3
Time			
Information			

13 Listen to the conversation in the restaurant and decide: **¿verdadero o falso?**

1 The man chooses a salad.   V / F
2 The chicken comes with potatoes and salad.   V / F
3 The woman wants salad with her chicken.   V / F
4 They both want wine.   V / F
5 The spoon is dirty.   V / F
6 The woman's chicken comes with potatoes.   V / F
7 She eats it anyway.   V / F

14 María is asking you about your family. Prepare your side of the conversation first, then listen to her questions on the recording and answer in the pauses.

María: ¿Usted tiene familia?
You: (Say yes, you're married and have two boys and a girl.)
María: ¿Cuántos años tienen?
You: (Say the girl is twelve and the boys are eight and six.)
María: ¿En qué trabaja?
You: (Tell her you're an engineer.)
María: Usted no es español, ¿verdad?
You: (Tell her you're English and ask her where she's from.)
María: Soy española.
You: (Tell her you have an uncle in Spain. He lives in Valencia.)
María: ¡Qué interesante!

15 Practise saying the following in Spanish. You may prefer to write your answers down before checking them against the recording.

In the restaurant order soup for the first course, chicken for the main course. Ask for a beer to drink.
Order an ice cream, say you don't have a spoon, and ask the waiter to bring you one.
Order a black coffee. When the coffee comes say it's a white coffee and ask the waiter to change it.
Ask for the bill.
Complain that the bill is wrong.

Getting around
El transporte público

OBJECTIVES

In this unit you'll learn how to:

- ✓ ask about train and bus times
- ✓ buy a ticket
- ✓ reserve tickets
- ✓ talk about different modes of transport

And cover the following grammar and language:

- ✓ the prepositions **a** and **para** to describe going to and being in or at a place
- ✓ the prepositions **a** and **de** to express distance
- ✓ the prepositions **en** and **a** used with modes of transport
- ✓ verbs followed by the infinitive (**poder**, **querer**, **necesitar**, **desear**)
- ✓ **hay que** + infinitive and **tener que** + infinitive to express obligation
- ✓ possessive pronouns **el mío**, **el tuyo**, **el suyo**, **el nuestro**, **el vuestro**

LEARNING SPANISH 8

Check the television programme listings for Spanish-language films. They are usually shown in the original version and carry subtitles. You'll find that you'll pick up a lot of vocabulary by making use of the subtitles, especially for words and expressions that occur regularly. If you have satellite television, try watching other programmes in Spanish. Don't worry about trying to understand everything, but get used to hearing everyday Spanish spoken at normal speed.

Now start the recording for Unit 8.

8.1 The next train for Valladolid
El próximo tren para Valladolid

ACTIVITY 1 is on the recording.

ACTIVITY 2

1 The train is on time.	V/F
2 Josefina wants a return ticket.	V/F
3 Josefina smokes.	V/F
4 The train leaves from platform 3.	V/F

DIALOGUE 1

○ Por favor, ¿a qué hora sale el próximo tren para Valladolid?
■ Hay un Inter-City dentro de una hora, a las tres. Lleva veinte minutos de retraso.
○ De acuerdo. ¿Puedo comprar un billete de segunda clase?
■ ¿De ida?
○ No, de ida y vuelta. Quiero volver el miércoles.
■ ¿Fumadores o no fumadores?
○ No fumadores, por favor. ¿A qué hora llega a Valladolid?
■ A las seis. Son treinta euros.
○ Tome. ¿De qué vía sale?
■ De la vía dos.

```
VOCABULARY
```

el tren	train
próximo	next
dentro de	within, inside
llevar retraso	to be delayed
comprar	to buy
el billete (de segunda clase)	(second-class) ticket [*for travel*]
(el billete) de ida	single (ticket)
(el billete) de ida y vuelta	return (ticket)
reservar	to reserve
fumadores/no fumadores	smoking/non-smoking
tome	here you are [*formal*] [*literally* take]
la vía	platform
¿de qué vía sale?	which platform does it leave from?

⊘ *a* ('to, in, at') and *para* ('for')

The preposition **a** is used for *going* to a place, or *arriving in* or *at* a place:

Vamos **a** Madrid. We're going to Madrid.
¿**A** qué hora llegamos **a** Valladolid? What time do we arrive in Valladolid?
El tren llega **a** la estación. The train arrives at the station.

However, in the following situations **para** is used:

¿A qué hora sale el tren **para** Valladolid? What time does the Valladolid train [*literally* the train for Valladolid] leave?
Un billete **para** Madrid, por favor. A ticket to/for Madrid, please.

⊘ *llevar ... retraso*

To talk about delays, the construction **llevar** + [time] + **de** is used:

¿Lleva retraso? Is it late?/¿Cuánto retraso lleva? How late is it?
El tren **lleva veinte minutos de retraso**. The train is 20 minutes late.

⊘ Verbs followed by the infinitive

When **poder** ('to be able') and **querer** ('to want') are followed by another verb, that verb is in the infinitive:

¿**Puedo comprar** un billete? Can I buy a ticket?
¿**Quiere reservar** la vuelta? Do you want to reserve the return journey?

necesitar ('to need to') and **desear** ('to wish') are also followed by the infinitive in this construction:

Necesito cambiar el billete. I need to change the ticket.
¿**Desea cambiar** la habitación? Do you wish to change room?

The constructions **hay que** + infinitive and **tener que** + infinitive are covered in this unit on pages 111 and 113.

ACTIVITY 3

Complete the following sentences using **a**, **para** or **de**.

1 ¿____ qué hora llega el tren?
2 Ahora llegamos ____ Madrid.
3 Quiero un billete ____ Barcelona, por favor.
4 El autobús llega dentro ____ media hora.
5 Lo siento; el autobús lleva media hora ____ retraso.

⊙ Now do activities 4 and 5 on the recording.

8.2 Shall we go by car or by bus?
¿Vamos en coche o en autobús?

ACTIVITY 6 is on the recording.

ACTIVITY 7

	Advantages	Disadvantages
Car		
Bus		

DIALOGUE 2

○ ¿Vamos a Madrid en coche o en autobús?
■ El coche es más rápido.
○ Pero no quiero conducir.
■ Yo puedo conducir, si quieres.
○ ¿A cuántos kilómetros está Madrid?
■ A seiscientos. Está muy lejos. ¿Cuánto tardamos en el coche?
○ Siete horas. Hay que comer en la cafetería de la autopista.
■ En el autobús podemos leer, descansar, es más cómodo.
○ Pero el coche es más rápido.
■ Bueno, pero el transporte público es muy bueno en Madrid.
○ No sé. El autobús es muy barato.
■ Pero no podemos llevar mucho equipaje si vamos en el autobús.
○ Es verdad. Podemos dejar las cosas dentro del coche.

VOCABULARY

rápido	fast
costar	to take (time) [*literally* to cost]
¿cuánto tarda?	how long does it take?
hay que ...	it's necessary to ...
la autopista	motorway
leer	to read
cómodo	comfortable
no sé	I don't know [*from* **saber** to know]
llevar	to take, carry
el equipaje	luggage
dejar	to leave (something)

✓ Prepositions *a* and *de* to express distance

The preposition **a** is used in questions or statements about how far away something is, either in distance or time:

> ¿**A** cuántos kilómetros está Madrid? How far away is Madrid?
> Está **a** cien kilómetros. It's 100 kilometres away.
> El museo está **a** diez minutos. The museum is 10 minutes away.

To say how far one place is from another, **de** is used:

> Barcelona está a seiscientos kilómetros **de** Madrid. Barcelona is 600 km from Madrid.

✓ *¿cuánto tardas?*

The verb **tardar** is used to say how long something takes. Unlike English, which uses an impersonal construction ('it takes ...), the form of **tardar** used is determined by the person(s):

> **Tardo / Tardan** media hora. It takes (me / them) half an hour.

✓ *hay que* + infinitive

hay que is an impersonal construction used to express an obligation. It is always followed by an infinitive:

> **Hay que** preparar el coche. We have to prepare the car.
> **Hay que** descansar en la autopista. It's necessary to have a break on the motorway.

✓ Prepositions *en* and *a* with modes of transport

en is used for most modes of transport, with one exception:

> Voy a mi trabajo **en coche/en tren/en motocicleta**. I go to work by car /by train/by motorbike.
> Mi hermano va al instituto **a pie**. My brother goes to school on foot.

ACTIVITY 8

Translate the following sentences into Spanish.

1　How far away is Seville?
2　It takes half an hour by bus.
3　It takes me 15 minutes on foot.
4　It's 300 km to Madrid.

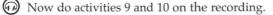 Now do activities 9 and 10 on the recording.

8.3 How do you get to work?
¿Cómo vas a tu trabajo?

ACTIVITY 11 is on the recording.

ACTIVITY 12

¿Carmen o Juan?

1 Tarda más tiempo para ir a su trabajo.	C/J
2 No tiene que cambiar.	C/J
3 Trabaja cerca de su casa.	C/J
4 No puede ir en coche.	C/J
5 A veces tarda diez minutos en llegar a su trabajo.	C/J

DIALOGUE 3

○ Trabajas en Madrid, ¿verdad? ¿Cómo vas a tu trabajo?
■ Voy en autobús y en metro.
○ ¿Cuánto tardas?
■ Tardo cincuenta minutos más o menos. Tengo que cambiar de línea en el metro. ¿Cómo vas tú?
○ Voy a pie o en el autobús, o en el coche de mi vecino. Trabajamos juntos.
■ ¿Y cuánto tardas en llegar?
○ Si voy a pie tardo veinte minutos. En el coche tardo diez o quince minutos. ¿Por qué no vas en coche?
■ Porque no hay sitio para aparcar.
○ Mi trabajo sólo está a dos kilómetros de mi casa.
■ El mío está a quince kilómetros por lo menos.

VOCABULARY	
el metro	underground
tener que	to have to
la línea	line
el vecino/la vecina	neighbour
en llegar	to get there
¿por qué no (vas) ... ?	why don't you (go) ... ?
	[*used as a suggestion*]
el sitio	(parking) space
aparcar	to park
sólo	only
el mío	mine
por lo menos	at least

✓ *tener que* + infinitive

tener que followed by the infinitive is used to express a personal obligation, often in excuses for not being able to do something:

No puedo. **Tengo que ir** a Madrid. I can't. I have to go to Madrid.
Tengo que llevar el coche al garaje. I have to take the car to the garage.

Note the contrast between **tener que**, indicating something that *you personally have to do*, and **hay que**, indicating *an external obligation*:

Tengo que hacer los deberes. I have to do my homework.
Hay que descansar en la autopista. It's necessary to have a break on the motorway.

✓ Possessive pronouns

Possessive pronouns ('mine', 'yours', etc.) always agree in gender and in number with the nouns they refer to:

Mi trabajo está cerca de mi casa. My work is near my house.
El mío está lejos de mi casa. Mine is a long way from my house.

	sing.		*pl.*	
	masc.	*fem.*	*masc.*	*fem.*
mine	**el mío**	**la mía**	**los míos**	**las mías**
yours [*informal*]	**el tuyo**	**la tuya**	**los tuyos**	**las tuyas**
his/hers /yours [*formal*]	**el suyo**	**la suya**	**los suyos**	**las suyas**
ours	**el nuestro**	**la nuestra**	**los nuestros**	**las nuestras**
yours [*informal*]	**el vuestro**	**la vuestra**	**los vuestros**	**las vuestras**
theirs/yours [*formal*]	**el suyo**	**la suya**	**los suyos**	**las suyas**

ACTIVITY 13

Complete the sentences by inserting the correct form of **tener que** + an appropriate verb from the following list:
ir, visitar, comer, hacer.

1 A: ¿Dónde están tus hermanos?
   B: _____ _____ _____ los deberes.
2 A: ¿Por qué te vas?
   B: _____ _____ _____ a mi abuela.
3 A: ¿Podemos ir a un restaurante?
   B: No. _____ _____ _____ en casa.
4 A: ¿_____ _____ ___?
   B: Sí tenemos que ir ahora.

🔊 Now do activities 14 and 15 on the recording.

8.4 Bikes and underground in tandem
La bici en el metro

ACTIVITY 16

The text below describes an experiment to allow cyclists to travel with their bicycles on the Madrid Metro. Read through the passage and answer the following questions, using the context to guess the meanings of the words that are not given in the vocabulary.

1 The experiment is limited to certain days and times; what are they?
2 Can cyclists go on any carriage in the train?
3 Do cyclists have to pay more for a ticket?
4 Can they travel on all lines?
5 In what circumstances might the authorities withdraw the service temporarily?
6 What is the maximum number of bicycles per carriage?
7 What will happen if the experiment is a success?
8 What should you do if you require more information?

Los ciclistas urbanos de Madrid ahora pueden montar en el Metro con sus bicicletas. El Ayuntamiento de Madrid hace un experimento que permite transportar la bicicleta en el suburbano los sábados, domingos y días de fiesta entre las diez de la mañana y las cuatro de la tarde. El precio del billete es igual que un billete normal. Y no hay restricciones de líneas y trayectos.

Los ciclistas no pueden montar las bicicletas dentro de las instalaciones del Metro. Las normas sólo permiten dos bicicletas por vagón y los ciclistas están obligados a utilizar el primer vagón del tren. Si hay mucho público dentro de las instalaciones, la compañía reserva el derecho de anular este servicio. Si funciona el experimento, puede continuar. Buenas noticias para los ciclistas urbanos. El Metro atiende las consultas sobre este servicio en el teléfono 91/552 59 09.

el/la ciclista	cyclist
montar	to ride [*on a bike, train, bus, etc.*]
el Ayuntamiento	town council
hacer un experimento	to carry out an experiment
el suburbano	underground
igual que	the same as
el trayecto	route
las instalaciones	facilities
las normas	regulations
el vagón	carriage [*of a train*]
obligado	obliged
utilizar	to use
reservar el derecho	to reserve the right
anular	to cancel
buenas noticias	good news
atender (las consultas)	to be available (to answer enquiries)
sobre	about, on

ACTIVITY 17

Choose **hay que** + infinitive or the correct form of **poder** to complete the following sentences.

1 _____ viajar con bicicleta antes de las diez de la mañana.
2 _____ viajar en el primer vagón del tren.
3 _____ salir de la estación si hay mucho público.
4 No _____ viajar más que dos bicicletas por vagón.
5 El experimento _____ continuar si funciona.
6 _____ llamar por teléfono si quieres más información.
7 _____ viajar entre las diez y las cuatro.

ACTIVITY 18

Translate the sentences in brackets using the appropriate possessive pronoun – **el mío**, etc.

Example: Mi casa es grande. (Yours [sing.] is small.)
La tuya es pequeña.

1 Mis padres viven en México. (Theirs live in Guatemala.)
2 Mi coche es viejo. (His is new.)
3 Su trabajo es interesante. (Mine is interesting as well.)
4 Nuestra universidad es buena. (Yours [*pl.*] is bad.)
5 Vuestros hijos son mayores. (Ours are small.)

8.5 Un forastero en la ciudad

 TENGO MUCHA PRISA
I'M REALLY IN A HURRY

María explica al Sr. España que va a visitar a su madre porque quiere hablar con ella.

preocupado (por algo)	worried (about something)
tener prisa	to be in a hurry
siempre	always
enfermo	ill, sick
ya	now
mayor	old (person)
difícil	difficult
¿tardas ...?	does it take you ...?
urgentemente	urgently
irse	to go, leave
el viaje	journey
un secreto	a secret
no diga nada	don't say anything

ACTIVITY 19

These questions are taken from the story. Listen again and write down the replies.

1 Tu madre vive sola, ¿verdad? _____.
2 ¿Vas en tren? _____.
3 ¿Tardas mucho en llegar? _____.
4 ¿Vas por mucho tiempo? _____.
5 ¿Tienes un problema, María? _____.

ACTIVITY 20

¿Quién ...

1 está preocupado/a?
2 tiene prisa?
3 no está bien?
4 vive solo/a?
5 vive cerca de Toledo?
6 va en tren?
7 viene al bar?
8 sale del bar?

ACTIVITY 21

¿Verdadero o falso?

1 María looks worried.	V / F
2 It takes a long time to get to the village.	V / F
3 There is a bus service to the village.	V / F
4 Her boss has given her time off.	V / F
5 She doesn't want Sr. Jimeno to know about her journey.	V / F

STORY TRANSCRIPT

Sr. España	¡Hola María! ¿Qué te pasa? ¿Estás preocupada por algo?
María	Sí, tengo que visitar a mi madre y no tengo mucho tiempo. Tengo mucha prisa.
Sr. España	¿Tu madre no está bien?
María	Bueno … está siempre un poco enferma. Y ya es muy mayor. Pero tengo que hablar con ella. Es muy importante.
Sr. España	Tu madre vive sola, ¿verdad?
María	Sí, vive sola en un pueblo cerca de Toledo.
Sr. España	No está muy lejos de aquí.
María	No está muy lejos … a ciento cincuenta kilómetros más o menos, pero es difícil llegar.
Sr. España	¿Vas en tren?
María	Voy en tren hasta Toledo; luego hay un autobús a un pueblo que está cerca. Tengo que ir en un taxi desde ese pueblo. No hay servicio de autobús.
Sr. España	¿Tardas mucho en llegar?
María	Sí, bastante.
Sr. España	¿Vas por mucho tiempo?
María	Voy desde el viernes hasta el lunes. Tengo que pedir dos días de vacaciones a mi jefe y tengo mucho trabajo.
Sr. España	¿Tienes un problema, María?
María	Sí, señor. Tengo un problema. Tengo que hablar urgentemente con mi madre.
Sr. España	¡Ah! Mira quién viene. El señor Jimeno.
María	Bueno … me voy. No puedo hablar con él ahora. Tengo que irme. Adiós, Señor España. Hasta el lunes. Ah, mi viaje es un secreto. No diga nada.

Now it's time to test your progress in Unit 8.

1 Give the Spanish for these questions.

  1 What time is the next train to Madrid?
  2 Can I buy a return ticket?
  3 What time does it arrive?
  4 Is it delayed?
  5 Which platform does it leave from?

  10

2 Complete the following by inserting the appropriate word in each of the gaps.

  vía / equipaje / ida / cómodo / vuelta / próximo / dentro / retraso / rápido / comprar

  El _____ tren para Madrid sale de la _____ dos _____ de diez minutos. Lleva cinco minutos de _____. ¿Usted quiere _____ un billete de ____ y _____? Es un viaje muy _____ y el tren es muy _____ . ¿Tiene mucho _____?

  10

3 Look at the grid below and write five sentences giving the distance between each city. (Score 2 points for a correct answer, 1 point if you make one mistake.)

Madrid – Barcelona	621 KM
Zaragoza – Barcelona	300 KM
Madrid – Sevilla	542 KM
Zaragoza – Bilbao	290 KMS
Barcelona – Valencia	270 KM

  1 Madrid _____ Barcelona.
  2 Zaragoza _____ Barcelona.
  3 Madrid _____ Sevilla.
  4 Zaragoza _____ Bilbao.
  5 Barcelona _____ Valencia.

  10

4 **¿Cómo vas a tu trabajo?** Reply in Spanish.

1 You go by motorbike. Sometimes you walk.
2 You go by train and then by bus.
3 You go by car but sometimes you go on foot.
4 You go by underground and bus.
5 You go on foot to the bus stop and then by bus.

10

5 Make excuses to decline your friend's suggestions using **tener que**. (Score 2 points for a correct answer, 1 point if you make one mistake.)

A: ¿Quieres ir al cine esta tarde?
You: (You can't because you have to work at home.)
A: ¿Quieres ir mañana?
You: (You can't. You have to visit your mother.)
A: ¿Vamos a la piscina?
You: (You can't. You have to take the car to the garage.)
A: ¿Quieres venir a mi casa el sábado?
You: (You are sorry, but you have to clean the house.)
A: Voy a la playa dentro de una semana. ¿Por qué no vienes conmigo?
You: (You can't. You have to go to work.)

10

6 Replace the underlined possessive adjective and noun with the correct possessive pronoun in the following sentences.

1 <u>Mis hijos</u> son mayores.
2 <u>Nuestro coche</u> es nuevo.
3 <u>Los libros de mi marido</u> son muy interesantes.
4 <u>Mis clases</u> son buenas. ¿Cómo son <u>tus clases</u>?
5 ¿Estos platos son <u>de vosotros</u>?
6 <u>La casa de Alfonso</u> es muy bonita.
7 <u>Tus hermanos</u> son pequeños.
8 <u>Nuestro apartamento</u> en la playa es muy bonito.
9 <u>Tus abuelos</u> son buenos.
10 <u>Tu coche</u> es nuevo.

10

TOTAL SCORE **60**

If you scored less than 50, look at the Language Building sections again before completing the Summary on page 120.

Summary 8

 Now try this final test, summarizing the main points covered in this unit.

How would you:
1 ask what time the next train for Madrid leaves?
2 ask if you can buy a return ticket?
3 say the train is 20 minutes late?
4 ask which platform the train leaves from?
5 ask what time we arrive in Barcelona?
6 say the bus is leaving in five minutes?
7 say you have to work?
8 ask how far Madrid is from Barcelona?
9 say it takes you half an hour to get to work by bus?

REVISION

Learn the different modes of transport and practise saying them with the appropriate preposition. Remember that **en** is used except when you go on foot: **a pie**. Also practise talking about distances: first asking how far something is: **¿a cuántos kilómetros está …?**, and then replying using distances that you know, for example, how far your town is from another: **está a cincuenta kilómetros de …** or how far the bus stop is: **está a diez minutos de aquí**, and so on.

Every day, run through the things you have to do and practise saying what they are in Spanish using **tengo que**; for example **tengo que trabajar**, **tengo que comprar comida**, **tengo que llamar a mis padres**, and so on.

Practise saying what you can do when you have free time, using **poder** followed by the infinitive: **puedo leer el periódico hoy, puedo cenar en un restaurante**.

Finally, practise using the possessive pronouns from this unit: **el mío, la mía, los míos, las mías**, etc. Refer to your friends' or family's possessions as well so that you practise other possessive pronouns apart from 'mine'.

People
Gente

OBJECTIVES

In this unit you'll learn how to:

- ✓ describe people physically
- ✓ describe people's personalities
- ✓ describe clothes and gifts

And cover the following grammar and language:

- ✓ the verb **ser** with adjectives of physical description
- ✓ the verb **ser** with adjectives of personality
- ✓ comparatives
- ✓ demonstrative pronouns and adjectives

LEARNING SPANISH 9

Although speaking and understanding spoken Spanish is important, don't underestimate the value of writing in Spanish. The activities in this book provide plenty of written practice, but you may also find it helpful to write your own sentences, even keep a simple diary, using the Spanish you already know.

Writing is a useful consolidation exercise, since you can take your time to consider what you want to say. Start off simply, concentrating on verb endings and choosing appropriate vocabulary. Think about gender and number agreement. Use your dictionary to look up any words you don't know. As you learn more vocabulary and grammar your writing will become more fluent.

Now start the recording for Unit 9.

9.1 Your children are very beautiful
Sus hijos son muy guapos

ACTIVITY 1 is on the recording.

ACTIVITY 2

	tall	short	slim	plump	dark	fair
Carmen						
José						
María José						
Pablo						
Patricia						

DIALOGUE 1

○ Sus hijos son muy guapos. Patricia es como usted.
■ Ésa es María José. Patricia lleva un jersey.
○ Ah sí. Perdón.
■ Sí, y Pablo es como su padre.
○ Es muy alto. Y son muy morenos los tres, Patricia, Pablo y María José.
■ Sí, es verdad. Todos somos morenos. ¿Y sus hijos?
○ José, el pequeño, es moreno, bajo y un poco gordo.
■ Sí, y Carmen es alta, delgada y rubia. ¡Muy diferentes!
○ Carmen es como mi mujer. Es rubia y alta también. Son muy parecidas.

VOCABULARY

guapo	beautiful, pretty
como	like, similar to
llevar	to wear
alto	tall
moreno	dark [*complexion, hair*]
bajo	short [*stature*]
gordo	fat, plump
delgado	thin, slim
rubio	blond(e)
diferente	different
parecido	similar
el pelo	hair

⊘ *ser* and *estar* in physical descriptions

The verb **ser** is used to describe permanent physical characteristics:

José es **moreno**; Patricia **es alta**. José is dark. Patricia is tall.
Pepe **es de estatura mediana**. Pepe is (of) average height.

estar is only used if a characteristic is temporary, for example, if a child has grown a lot since you last saw her, you might say: **estás muy alta**. If you were telling someone that you were tanned, you would say **estoy moreno/a**.

⊘ Adjective agreement

Remember that the adjectives agree in number and gender with the person or people being described. Note the use of **ser** and **estar** in the examples:

Juan y Pablo son morenos. Juan and Pablo are dark.
Carmen es rubia. Carmen is blonde.
Somos altos. We are tall.
Estoy delgada. I'm slim [*at the moment*].
Estás muy gorda. You've put on weight [*you're plump at the moment*].
Gustavo tiene los ojos **azules**. Gustavo has blue eyes.

ACTIVITY 3

Complete the sentences below, by supplying the appropriate opposite. Make sure you make the adjective agree.

Example: María es **morena**, pero su hermano es **rubio**.

1 Raúl es alto, pero su hermana es _____.
2 Regina es delgada, pero su padre es _____.
3 Mis padres son rubios, pero los tuyos son _____.
4 Sois muy bajos. Nosotras somos muy _____.
5 El hermano de Alfonso es moreno, pero su hermana es _____.
6 Soy un poco gordo. Mis padres son _____.

Now choose the correct form of the verb **ser**.

7 Beatriz y su hermana _____ muy morenas.
8 Javier _____ alto.
9 Mi padre y yo _____ altos.
10 Yo _____ delgado, pero mi hermana _____ gorda.

⊕ Now do activities 4 and 5 on the recording.

9.2 What sort of person is he?
¿Cómo es su personalidad?

ACTIVITY 6 is on the recording.

ACTIVITY 7

1 Sr. Blasco works with Juan.	V/F
2 Juan is very hardworking.	V/F
3 The job involves working alone.	V/F
4 Juan is a popular member of staff.	V/F
5 Sra. Muñoz needs a calm person for this job.	V/F

DIALOGUE 2

○ ¿Usted cree que Juan tiene la personalidad adecuada para este trabajo?

■ Bueno. Creo que sí. Trabajo con él. Es muy trabajador y muy honrado.

○ ¿Trabaja bien con sus compañeros?

■ Sí, sí, es muy simpático.

○ Pero necesitamos una persona tranquila.

■ Juan es muy tranquilo y tiene un temperamento fuerte.

○ Muy bien. Es perfecto.

■ Sí, es una persona inteligente, abierta, y sincera.

○ ¿Puede ser un buen jefe?

■ Sí, estoy seguro.

○ Bueno. Muchas gracias.

VOCABULARY

la personalidad	personality
creer (que)	to believe (that)
adecuado	suitable
trabajador	hard-working
honrado	honest
el compañero/la compañera	colleague
simpático	friendly
tranquilo	calm
el temperamento	temperament
fuerte	strong
inteligente	intelligent
abierto	open, frank
sincero	sincere
seguro	sure

✓ Expressing an opinion using *creer que*

The verb **creer** followed by **que** is used to ask for or express an opinion:

¿Usted **cree que** tiene la personalidad adecuada? Do you think he has the right personality?
Creo que Celia es perezosa. I think Celia is lazy.
Creo que sí. **Creo que** no. I think so. I don't think so.

✓ Agreement of adjectives ending in -e or a consonant

With the exception of nationalities (see page 49), most adjectives ending in **-e** or a consonant have the same form in the singular. In the plural, an **-s** is added to those ending in **-e**, and **-es** to those ending in a consonant.

María es **inteligente** y sus hermanas son **inteligentes**. María is intelligent and her sisters are intelligent.
Manuel es **hábil** y sus hermanos son **hábiles**. Manuel is skilful and his brothers are skilful.

There are also some adjectives which vary slightly from the regular -**o** pattern, e.g. **trabajador** ('hardworking'):

Juan es **trabajador** y María es **trabajadora**. Juan y Pablo son **trabajadores**. María y Josefina son **trabajadoras**.

Note that in Spanish the noun **persona** is feminine, and any adjectives used with it must be feminine:

Juan es **simpático**. Es **una persona abierta**.
Juan is friendly. He is an open person.

ACTIVITY 8

Choose three adjectives from the list below to describe the person in each sentence. Remember to make the adjectives agree. You may use the same adjective more than once.

Example: Él estudia mucho. Es **inteligente, serio, trabajador**.

nervioso / tranquilo / inteligente / generoso / serio / sincero / antipático / perezoso / honrado / feliz / trabajador / simpático / abierto

1 Raúl tiene muchos amigos.
2 Alicia tiene un trabajo muy difícil.
3 Él y su mujer son felices.
4 Él tiene problemas en su trabajo.

🔊 Now do activities 9 and 10 on the recording.

I need to buy ...

Tengo que comprar ...

ACTIVITY 11 is on the recording.

ACTIVITY 12

There are 6 mistakes. Correct them.

Hoy es el cumpleaños de la madre de (1) Beatriz y tiene que comprarle un regalo. Beatriz recomienda (2) un vestido pero Antonio prefiere una pulsera. Beatriz necesita (3) una blusa y Antonio tiene que comprar (4) una camisa. (5) Antonio tiene una buena idea. Él va a la sección de ropa de caballeros y Beatriz busca (6) una pulsera.

DIALOGUE 3

○ Tengo que comprar un pantalón.
■ ¡Y yo un vestido para la fiesta de cumpleaños de tu madre!
○ ¡Ah sí! ¿Qué puedo comprar para mi madre?
■ Mira. Esta blusa blanca. Es preciosa.
○ Sí, es bonita. Pero ésta es más bonita. Mira.
■ Sí, también. ¡Ah, ésta! Es la más bonita de todas.
○ Sí. Es muy bonita. Pero creo que una pulsera es mejor.
■ Mira. Tengo una idea. Tengo que comprar un vestido. ¿Por qué no vas a la sección de ropa de caballeros, compras el pantalón y después un regalo para tu madre?
○ De acuerdo. Quedamos en la cafetería a las seis.

VOCABULARY

el pantalón/los pantalones	pair of trousers
el cumpleaños	birthday
el vestido	dress
la pulsera	bracelet
la blusa	blouse
la camisa	shirt
buscar	to look for
el regalo	gift
la fiesta	party
precioso	beautiful
éste	this one
mejor	better
la sección	department
la ropa (de caballeros)	(men's) clothing

✓ Demonstrative pronouns

There are three forms of the demonstrative pronoun: **éste** ('this one'), **ése** ('that one'), and **aquél** ('that one'). Their endings vary depending on gender and number:

sing.		*pl.*	
masc.	*fem.*	*masc.*	*fem.*
éste	ésta	éstos	éstas
ése	ésa	ésos	ésas
aquél	aquélla	aquéllos	aquéllas

The demonstrative pronoun is the same as the demonstrative adjective, except that the pronouns take an accent:

Quiero **este jersey**. Me gusta **éste**. I want this sweater. I like this one.
Quiero **esa camisa**. Me gusta **ésa**. I want that shirt. I like that one (just over there).
Quiero **aquellos pendientes**. Me gustan **aquéllos**. I want those earrings. I like those ones (right over there, far away).

✓ Comparatives and superlatives

To form the *comparative*, **más** ('more') or **menos** ('less') is added before the adjective. To make an explicit comparison, **que** is used:

La casa es **más grande** que la mía. The house is bigger than mine.
Esta película es **menos interesante que** la otra. This film is less interesting than the other one.
Estas pulseras son **más caras que** las otras. These bracelets are more expensive than the others.

A number of adjectives have irregular comparative forms:

bueno – mejor	good – better	**grande – mayor**	big – bigger
malo – peor	bad – worse	**pequeño – menor**	small – smaller

For the *superlative*, the appropriate definite article is added to the comparative form. **de** ('of') is used for 'in':

Estos anillos son **los más caros de** la tienda. These rings are the most expensive in the shop.

ACTIVITY 13

Using the correct form of the comparative, describe a house in 4 sentences:
It's [bigger / smaller / better / worse] than this house.

Describe the house again, this time using the superlative:
It's the [biggest / smallest / best / worst] house in the street.

 Now do activities 14 and 15 on the recording.

In the department store
En los grandes almacenes

ACTIVITY 16

Study Juan's shopping list and decide which department he has to go to for each item. You may not have seen these items in Spanish before, but you can probably guess most of them.

1	disco compacto	7	anillo
2	perfume	8	vídeo
3	raqueta de tenis	9	carrete de fotos
4	blusa	10	sobres
5	chaqueta	11	disquete
6	collar	12	sandalias

Write sentences to consolidate your answers, for example:

Compra un disco compacto en la sección de sonido.

DIRECTORIO

Planta

6ª   CAFETERÍA, Oportunidades

5ª   ELECTRÓNICA. T.V. Vídeo, Sonido, Telefonía, Informática

4ª   DEPORTES, Camping

3ª   Moda Jóven EL Y ELLA

2ª   Moda Sport, Zapatería

1ª   LIBROS, DISCOS, Películas de vídeo, REGALOS

Bª   COMPLEMENTOS MODA:
Cinturones, Bolsos, Medias, Pañuelos, Sombreros

Sº 2   FOTOGRAFÍA, RELOJERÍA, JOYERÍA, BISUTERÍA, PAPELERÍA, PERFUMERÍA, COSMÉTICA, MARROQUINERÍA, TURISMO

Sº 3   APARCAMIENTO

Sº 4   APARCAMIENTO

ACTIVITY 17

Read the article about Spanish department stores and answer the following questions.

1 Look at the following words from the article. They are similar to English words. What do they mean?

el centro / la reunión / moderno / la variedad / el artículo / el objeto / en general / la diferencia / el aire acondicionado

2 ¿Los españoles van a los grandes almacenes sólo a comprar?

3 ¿Pueden comer en los grandes almacenes?

4 En el directorio, ¿qué plantas visita si quiere comprar las cosas mencionadas en el texto?

5 ¿Cuál es la gran diferencia entre los grandes almacenes y las tiendas normales?

6 ¿Qué tienen los grandes almacenes en el verano?

Los grandes almacenes no sólo son un centro de compras sino también un centro de reunión para los españoles. Allí se encuentran los amigos para mirar chaquetas, faldas, trajes, vestidos y zapatos, y también para merendar en su moderna cafetería o comer en el restaurante.

Los grandes almacenes ofrecen gran variedad de artículos, objetos para hacer camping, vídeos, ordenadores, teléfonos, discos, libros y muchas cosas más.

Los horarios de los grandes almacenes son diferentes de los horarios de las tiendas en general. La gran diferencia es que no cierran a mediodía. Además tienen aire acondicionado en el verano y podemos estar cómodos a la hora de la siesta.

sino	but
la chaqueta	jacket
la falda	skirt
el traje	suit
el zapato	shoe
merendar	to have an afternoon snack
el ordenador	computer

9.5 Un forastero en la ciudad

MARÍA Y SU MADRE
MARÍA AND HER MOTHER

María está en casa de su madre en el pueblo. Pregunta por la familia y por los amigos de la familia. También habla del Sr. Jimeno.

preguntar por	to ask about
regular	OK
el vecino/la vecina	neighbour
el primo/la prima	cousin
preocupado	worried
extraño	strange
¡qué susto!	what a shock!

ACTIVITY 18

The people mentioned in the dialogue are listed below. Underneath are words used to describe each person.

1 Sort the words into physical descriptions and descriptions of personality.

2 Write down who is being described by each phrase. Don't forget to make the adjectives agree.

	1 delgado
	2 extraño
	3 fuerte
	4 generoso
la vecina	5 gordo
la tía Leticia	6 guapo
Julia	7 inteligente
Tomás	8 mayor
la madre de Julia y Tomás	9 misterioso
Jorge	10 moreno
	11 perezoso
	12 preocupado
	13 simpático
	14 trabajador

ACTIVITY 19

Who …

1 helps María's mother?
2 goes out every night?
3 has a shock?
4 has no husband?
5 knows a man in Madrid?
6 talks with the neigbour?
7 lives in the house on the corner?
8 studies a lot?

STORY TRANSCRIPT

María	Mamá, ¿cómo estás?
Madre	Regular. Una vecina me ayuda mucho. Trae la leche y las compras.
María	¿La vecina?
Madre	Sí, Rosa. ¿No la conoces?
María	No. ¿Es la vecina nueva? No está casada ¿verdad?
Madre	No. Hablamos mucho juntas. Es muy simpática y generosa.
María	¿Dónde vive?
Madre	En aquella casa en la esquina.
María	¡Ah sí! ¿Y cómo está la tía Leticia?
Madre	Muy bien. Está bastante gorda ahora, y más vieja. Pero es fuerte.
María	¿Y los primos, Tomás y Julia? ¿Cómo están?
Madre	Julia está muy bien. Es muy inteligente y trabajadora. Estudia mucho y ayuda a su madre.
María	Pero Tomás no, ¿verdad?
Madre	No, Tomás es perezoso. Sale todas las noches con los amigos, bebe, no quiere trabajar. No sé. Su madre está muy preocupada.
María	Tengo que ir a su casa y hablar con él. Me quiere mucho.
Madre	Sí, es una buena idea.
María	Bueno, mamá. Quiero hablarte de una cosa. Conozco a un hombre que es de Granada y ahora está en Madrid. Creo que le conoces tú.
Madre	¿Cómo se llama?
María	No sé su nombre completo, pero se llama Jorge.
Madre	¡Jorge! ¿Y cómo es?
María	Bueno es bastante mayor, de tus años, más o menos, alto, bastante guapo, moreno, delgado.
Madre	¿Y dice que me conoce?
María	Sí. Es un poco extraño … es muy misterioso. Y tiene fotos …
Madre	Pues, no sé … no sé. No le conozco. Es imposible. ¡Ay!
María	Mamá, ¿qué te pasa? ¿Estás bien? ¿Quieres agua?
Madre	Sí, hija, gracias. Estoy bien. ¡Qué susto!

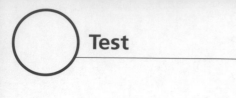

Now it's time to test your progress in Unit 9.

1 Give the Spanish for these sentences. (Score 3 points for a correct answer, and deduct 1 point for each mistake.)

1 He is tall, slim, and very good-looking.
2 She is short with long blonde hair.
3 The brothers are dark, strong, and short.
4 The sisters are slim and blonde.
5 The man is older; he's dark and tall.

15

2 Complete the sentences using an appropriate adjective from the list below, making sure you make the adjective agree.

simpático / inteligente / nervioso / trabajador / sincero

1 Él trabaja mucho. Es muy _____ .
2 Son buenos amigos. Son _____ .
3 Ella estudia en la universidad. Es muy _____ .
4 Él dice la verdad. Es muy _____ .
5 Hoy Juan hace los exámenes. Está muy _____ .

5

3 Your friend tells you what she thinks about another friend. You think the opposite. Complete the responses with the appropriate adjective.

Example: A: Jorge es perezoso. B: No. Es trabajador.

1 A: Gloria es tranquila. B: No. Es _____
2 A: Carlos es malo. B: No. _____
3 A: Javier no es inteligente. B: Sí. _____
4 A: Luis no tiene la personalidad adecuada. B: Sí. _____
5 A: Manuel es antipático. B: No. _____

5

4 Complete the following items of clothing.

1 c _ _ _ _ _ _ _   5 v _ _ _ _ _ _
2 c _ _ _ _ _   6 f _ _ _ _
3 p _ _ _ _ _ _ _   7 z _ _ _ _ _ _
4 b _ _ _ _   8 j _ _ _ _ _

8

5 Write a sentence in Spanish saying who each gift is for.

Example: ring – grandfather: **El anillo es para mi abuelo**.

1 bracelet – mother   2 necklace – sister
3 ring – grandmother   4 book – brother
5 blouse – friend   6 compact disc – father
7 video – male friend   8 sweater – aunt

16

6 You want some things from a shop. Choose the appropriate demonstrative pronouns.

Example: You don't want this book. You want that one.
No quiero este libro. Quiero **ése**.

1 You don't want that skirt. You want that one a bit further away.
2 You don't want this bracelet. You want this one.
3 You don't want this dress. You want this one.
4 You don't want that sweater over there. You want that one on the other side of the shop.
5 You don't want that ring over there. You want that one.
6 You don't want these earrings. You want these.

6

7 Make comparative sentences following the example.

Example: Este anillo es bonito. **Ése es más bonito**.

1 Esta casa es grande.   4 Esta película es mala.
2 Este coche es nuevo.   5 Este programa es interesante.
3 Este libro es bueno.

5

TOTAL SCORE 60

If you scored less than 50, look at the Language Building sections again before completing the Summary on page 134.

Summary 9

 Now try this final test, summarizing the main points covered in this unit.

How would you:
1 say he is very tall?
2 say they're very dark
3 say you think Juan is sincere?
4 say you have to buy a gift for your father?
5 say you want this bracelet?
6 (looking at rings) say you don't want this one, you want that one?
7 say your house is bigger than theirs?
8 say your house is the biggest in the street?
9 say that this film is better than the other?

REVISION

Write a list of people you know – friends, work colleagues, other aquaintances – and write down words to describe their physical appearance and their personality.

Use every opportunity to compare things: prices in a supermarket – **más barato**, **más caro** – buildings in a street – **grande, más grande, (el/la) más bonito**, and so on.

When you're at home, practise demonstrative adjectives and pronouns by saying what items are next to you, a little further away, and further away still. Build your vocabulary at the same time by learning the names for everyday household objects, together with their gender.

10

Free time
El tiempo libre

OBJECTIVES

In this unit you'll learn how to:

✓ talk about your likes and dislikes

✓ talk about your hobbies and interests

✓ say what you do in your free time

✓ say what you did last weekend

✓ talk about parties and other celebrations

And cover the following grammar and language:

✓ the past tense of regular verbs

✓ the past tense of **hacer** and **ir**

✓ the construction **gustar** + noun for describing likes and dislikes

✓ the construction **gustar** + infinitive for describing what you like doing

✓ the preposition **a** to express frequency

LEARNING SPANISH 10

Try to get hold of any Spanish language material such as newspapers and magazines. If you live in a big city this shouldn't be too difficult. The Internet can also be a useful resource. Begin by reading some of the shorter articles and see how much you can understand without resorting to the dictionary. Try to work out the meaning of the words you don't know. Don't worry about the meaning of every word, but concentrate on the main point of the story and only look up key words for comprehension. You will soon find that your reading speed and vocabulary acquisition increase considerably.

 Now start the recording for Unit 10.

10.1 What do you do in your free time?
¿Qué haces en tu tiempo libre?

ACTIVITY 1 is on the recording.

ACTIVITY 2

Who might say the following: Pepe, Margarita, or Margarita's husband?

1 Mi mujer siempre quiere ir al teatro. Yo prefiero descansar.
2 Quiero ir al concierto, pero tengo mucho trabajo.
3 ¿No quieres ir al teatro conmigo? No quiero ir sola.
4 ¡Niños! ¿Queréis ir al cine? Vamos todos.
5 Podemos ver películas en la televisión.

DIALOGUE 1

○ ¿Le gusta la música clásica?
■ Sí, me gusta mucho.
○ Hay un concierto de Mozart esta noche. ¿Quiere ir?
■ No puedo. Tengo que preparar unos documentos para la conferencia. Es una lástima. Me gusta mucho la música.
○ A mí me gusta mucho el teatro. Pero a mi marido no le gusta. Trabaja mucho y quiere descansar en casa.
■ ¿Le gusta el cine?
○ No, no me gusta mucho. Pero veo muchas películas en la televisión.
■ A mí me gustan las películas buenas. Pero a mis hijos les gustan las películas de dibujos animados. Vamos al cine a ver películas para niños.

VOCABULARY	
gustar	to please, to be pleasing
la música clásica	classical music
el concierto	concert
esta noche	tonight
preparar	to prepare
el documento	document
la conferencia	conference
es una lástima	it's a pity
varios	several
el teatro	theatre
los dibujos animados	cartoon film

✓ Expressing likes and dislikes

To say that you like something, you use the verb **gustar** with an indirect object pronoun:

Me gusta el cine. I like the cinema. [*literally* The cinema pleases me.]

The thing that is liked – **el cine** – is the subject of the sentence and determines the ending of the verb **gustar**, in this case the third person singular. The pronoun refers to the person(s) doing the liking:

¿**Te gusta** el teatro? Do you like the theatre?
Le gusta la tele. He/she likes television.
Les gusta el coche nuevo. They like their new car.

When you're referring to more than one thing, the verb is plural (**gustan**):

Me gustan las películas buenas. I like good films.

To say that you don't like something, you use the simple negative form:

No me gusta el cine. I don't like the cinema.
No me gustan las películas. I don't like films.

To emphasize or qualify the negative, you can use **nada** [*literally* 'nothing'] or **mucho**:

No me gusta nada/mucho. I don't like it at all/much.

a + noun/ disjunctive pronoun is used to identify or emphasize the person expressing the like or dislike. The pronoun is still included:

A mi marido no le gusta la música clásica. My husband doesn't like classical music. [*literally* To my husband classical music is not pleasing.]
A mí me gusta el cine, pero **a mis hijos les gusta** la televisión. I like the cinema, but my children like television.

The verb **encantar** ('to love') is used in the same way as **gustar: me encanta** el cine ('I love cinema').

ACTIVITY 3

Complete the dialogue with the correct form of **gustar**.

Juan: ¿_____ _____ el cine?
Ana: ¡Ah sí! ____ encanta el cine. A mis padres también _____ _____ el cine.
Juan: Tengo una hermana. ____ _____ el cine también.
Ana: A mis hermanos no ____ _____ el cine.
Juan: ¿A ellos ____ _____ las discotecas?
Ana: Sí mucho. A mí también.

Now do activities 4 and 5 on the recording.

10.2 What did you do last night?
¿Qué hiciste anoche?

🎧 **ACTIVITY 6** is on the recording.

ACTIVITY 7

Rewrite correcting the mistakes.

Bernardo went dancing until midnight and didn't get to bed until about half past one in the morning. His sister woke him up at seven to go shopping. Bernardo helped her with her shopping and then went to a bar to meet some friends. After playing football he went to a friend's house to study. Elena feels sorry for Bernardo. She understands that he is tired because he went out dancing and played football. She'll call him tomorrow.

DIALOGUE 2

○ ¿Por qué no quieres salir? ¿Estás enfermo?

■ No estoy enfermo. Estoy cansado.

○ ¿Por qué? ¿Qué hiciste anoche?

■ Fui a bailar. Bailé hasta la una de la mañana.

○ ¡Qué tarde!

■ A las ocho de la mañana mi madre llamó a la puerta.

○ ¿Te levantaste?

■ Claro. Me levanté y fuimos al centro de compras. La ayudé con las compras y después fui a jugar al fútbol con mis amigos. Después del partido, fuimos a un bar a tomar algo y un amigo me llevó a casa. Luego me llamaste tú.

○ Bueno. Te gusta salir por la noche, ¿verdad? Te gusta bailar. Te gusta jugar al fútbol. Vamos a tomar algo ahora.

VOCABULARY	
anoche	last night
enfermo	ill
cansado	tired
bailar	to dance
claro	that's right, of course
ayudar	to help
jugar	to play
el fútbol	football
el partido	match
llevar	to take, to give someone a lift

✓ The simple past of regular verbs

The simple past is used to describe a specific event in the past: **bailé anoche** ('I danced last night'). To form the past tense of regular **-ar**, **-er**, and **-ir** verbs, the following endings are added to the stem:

bail**é**	com**í**	sal**í**
bail**aste**	com**iste**	sal**iste**
bail**ó**	com**ió**	sal**ió**
bail**amos**	com**imos**	sal**imos**
bail**asteis**	com**isteis**	sal**isteis**
bail**aron**	com**ieron**	sal**ieron**

-er and **-ir** verbs are conjugated in exactly the same way. Note that the first person plural in **-ar** and **-ir** verbs is the same in the present and simple past tense:

Cenamos en aquel restaurante. We have dinner/had dinner in that restaurant.
Salimos a la una. We leave/left at one.

✓ The past tense of *hacer* and *ir*

hacer and **ir** are irregular in the past tense:

hacer: hice, hiciste, hizo, hicimos, hicisteis, hicieron
ir: fui, fuiste, fue, fuimos, fuisteis, fueron

Note that the past tense of **ir** is exactly the same as **ser** (see page 141).

¿Qué **hiciste** (tú) anoche? What did you [*informal*] do last night?
¿Adónde **fuiste** (tú) ayer? Where did you [*informal*] go yesterday?
Fui al cine. I went to the cinema.

To say you went dancing/skiing, etc., you use the past of the verb **ir** followed by the preposition **a** + infinitive:

Fuimos a bailar. We went dancing.

ACTIVITY 8

Put the verb in brackets in the simple past.

1 Anoche Juan y Ana (**cenar**) en aquel restaurante.
2 Ayer yo (**salir**) con mis amigos.
3 Nosotros (**bailar**) hasta la una.
4 Juan, ¿dónde (**ir**) anoche?
5 Mi madre (**comprar**) un anillo para su hermana.
6 Carmen, ¿qué (**hacer**) anoche?

Now do activities 9 and 10 on the recording.

Yesterday was my birthday
Ayer fue mi cumpleaños

🎧 **ACTIVITY 11** is on the recording.

ACTIVITY 12

¿Bernardo o Elena? ¿Quién …

1 hace deporte?
2 prefiere estar en casa?
3 viajó a América?

4 celebró su cumpleaños ayer?
5 escucha música?
6 celebra su compleaños en julio?

DIALOGUE 3

○ Ayer fue mi cumpleaños.
■ ¿Ah sí? ¡Felicidades! ¿Qué hiciste?
○ Por la noche salí con unos amigos. ¿Cuándo es tu cumpleaños?
■ En el verano, en julio. El mes que viene. El año pasado viajé a América el día de mi cumpleaños.
○ ¿Adónde fuiste?
■ Fui a Puerto Rico. Nadé, comí muy bien, bailé.
○ Yo bailo. Hago clases de baile tres veces a la semana. El mes pasado gané un premio en un concurso de baile.
■ A mí me gustan los deportes. En el invierno juego al fútbol.
○ Yo prefiero estar en casa. Me gusta ver la tele, escuchar música.

VOCABULARY

¡felicidades!	congratulations!
¿cuándo?	when?
el verano	summer
el mes que viene	next month
el año pasado	last year
¿adónde?	where (to)?
nadar	to swim
los deportes	sports
el invierno	winter
las clases de baile	dance classes
tres veces a la semana	three times a week
el mes pasado	last month
ganar	to win [*a prize or competition*]
el premio	prize
el concurso	competition

✓ The past tense of *ser*

The past tense of **ser** is exactly the same as the past tense of **ir**:

fui, fuiste, fue, fuimos, fuisteis, fueron

Ayer **fue** mi cumpleaños. Yesterday was my birthday.
La semana pasada Juan **fue** a América. Last week Juan went to America.

✓ *gustar* and *encantar* + infinitive

You've already seen how to talk about *things* you like: **me gusta el cine**.
To describe *activities* you like doing, you use **gustar** or **encantar** followed by the infinitive:

Me **gusta** escuchar música. I like listening to music.
¿Te **gusta** viajar? Do you like travelling?
Nos **encanta** bailar. We love dancing.

Note that **encantar** is not generally used in the question form.

✓ Saying how often you do something

To say you do an activity a number of times a week, month, or year, use the following expressions:

Bailo **tres veces a la semana**. I dance three times a week.
Viajo **dos** veces al **año**. I travel twice a year.

To say you do something every day, week, or month, use either of the following expressions:

Voy a la piscina **cada semana**. I go to the pool every week.
Voy a la piscina **todas las semanas**. I go to the pool every week.

ACTIVITY 13

Translate these sentences using the past tense of **ser** or **ir**.

1 We went to the cinema yesterday.
2 The film was good.
3 Yesterday was my father's birthday.
4 They went to Peru for their holidays.
5 Did you [*plural*] go to the party?
6 Was it you who rang?

Now do activities 14 and 15 on the recording.

10.4 Spanish national holidays

Las fiestas nacionales de España

ACTIVITY 16

Below is a list of dates and Spanish national holidays. Several are the same in Spain and the UK, for example **25 diciembre – Día de Navidad**. Can you work out which fiestas have an English equivalent and match them with the appropriate date? Then translate the remaining fiestas into English and try to work out the dates for each of them.

1	1 enero	a	Año Nuevo
2	6 enero	b	Noche Vieja
3	marzo/abril	c	Todos los Santos
4	12 octubre	d	Semana Santa: Pascua
5	1 noviembre	e	Fiesta Nacional: la Virgen del Pilar
6	6 diciembre	f	Los Reyes Magos
7	24 diciembre	g	Noche Buena
8	25 diciembre	h	Día del Trabajo
9	31 diciembre	i	Día de Navidad
10	1 mayo	j	Día de la Constitución

ACTIVITY 17

The following phrases describe the fiestas a–j. Match each description with the correct fiesta.

1 Hay procesiones religiosas por las calles. La gente sale a las calles para ver las procesiones.
2 La gente celebra esta fiesta el veinticuatro por la noche. Las familias celebran la fiesta en casa y hacen una cena especial.
3 Trabajamos mucho. Esta fiesta es para nosotros.
4 Esta fiesta se celebra por todo el mundo a las doce de la noche. La gente come doce uvas, una por cada campanada del reloj. En el centro de Madrid, la gente acude a la Puerta del Sol para escuchar las doce campanadas.
5 El día después de la cena de número 2.
6 Para celebrar la ley democrática española.
7 En esta fiesta tres señores importantes traen regalos a los niños.
8 Durante este día todo el mundo duerme después de la fiesta de la noche anterior.
9 Esta fiesta es para recordar a las personas muertas de la familia. La gente visita los cementerios.

10 Esta fiesta religiosa se celebra en honor de la Virgen María.

la procesión	procession
celebrar	to celebrate
las uvas	grapes
la campanada	bell toll [*from a clock tower*]
el reloj	clock
acudir	to gather
la ley	law
anterior	previous
recordar	to remember
muerto	dead
el cementerio	cemetery

ACTIVITY 18

Using some of the sentences from Activity 17, describe what you did on some of the fiestas.

Example: ¿Qué hiciste en la Noche Vieja? Comimos uvas y escuchamos las doce campanadas.

1 ¿Qué hiciste en Semana Santa?
2 ¿Qué hicisteis en la Noche Buena?
3 ¿Qué hiciste el día del Año Nuevo?
4 ¿Qué hiciste el día de Todos los Santos?
5 ¿Qué hicisteis el día de los Reyes Mayos?

ACTIVITY 19

In this word search find eight of the fiestas from the list above.

C	Y	Q	R	A	Q	B	A	S	Y	B	U
O	U	S	T	N	P	R	X	X	Z	G	S
N	L	V	R	O	N	O	K	L	Q	P	T
S	E	M	A	N	A	S	A	N	T	A	T
T	A	F	B	U	O	U	X	A	Q	S	S
I	Z	I	A	E	Q	U	W	V	R	C	M
T	F	J	J	V	E	Z	V	I	S	U	U
U	G	H	O	O	X	I	R	D	T	A	P
C	M	R	E	Y	E	S	M	A	G	O	S
I	N	W	G	E	T	H	D	D	O	P	C
O	N	O	C	H	E	B	U	E	N	A	D
N	O	C	H	E	V	I	E	J	A	W	V

10.5 Un forastero en la ciudad

 ¿QUIÉN ES JORGE?
WHO IS JORGE?

La madre de María está preocupada por su hija. Le pregunta sobre su trabajo, su casa y sus amigos. Le enseña unas fotos y una postal.

preocuparse (por)	to worry (about)
demasiado	too much, too many
enseñar	to show
explicar	to explain
recibir	to receive
decir	to say
prometer	to promise

ACTIVITY 20

Listen to the story again: **¿verdadero o falso?**

1	A María le gusta su trabajo.	V/F
2	No tiene mucho trabajo.	V/F
3	Vive sola y no tiene amigos.	V/F
4	Sale mucho al cine y al teatro y le gusta bailar.	V/F
5	La madre se preocupa por María.	V/F
6	La foto es del año pasado.	V/F
7	Es una foto de María y su madre.	V/F
8	Jorge mandó una postal a María a casa de su madre.	V/F
9	La madre de María le explica todo.	V/F

ACTIVITY 21

Imagine you are a friend of María in Madrid and her mother is telling you she is worried about María. Respond to each statement using the information given in the conversation. Use extra phrases where necessary to reassure her.

Example: María trabaja mucho. **Sí, trabaja mucho pero le gusta trabajar.**

1 Vive sola.
2 No tiene amigos.
3 No come bien, está muy delgada.
4 Está cansada.
5 Hace demasiadas cosas.

STORY TRANSCRIPT

Madre	¿Qué tal tu trabajo?
María	Bien. Me gusta bastante.
Madre	Trabajas mucho, ¿verdad?
María	Sí, hay mucho trabajo pero me gusta trabajar.
Madre	¿Y, que haces en tu tiempo libre? Estás sola en el piso. ¿Tienes amigos?
María	Sí, Mamá. No te preocupes. Prefiero vivir sola pero tengo muchos amigos y salgo mucho al teatro y al cine. También me gusta bailar. Estoy bien.
Madre	No comes bien. Estás muy delgada, hija.
María	Mamá, no te preocupes. Estoy muy bien. Vivo muy bien.
Madre	Pero, estás cansada, ¿verdad? Haces demasiadas cosas. Me preocupo por ti.
María	Pues no te preocupes. Hago muchas cosas pero no demasiadas.
Madre	Es que ya no eres mi hija pequeña. Eres una mujer. Es difícil para mí.
María	Ya lo sé.
Madre	Tengo que enseñarte una cosa. Mira lo que tengo aquí. Unas fotos tuyas. En ésta, tienes tres años.
María	¡Ah, sí! ¡Qué bonita! ¡Pero, mamá! ¿Quién es el señor que está en la foto a tu lado?
Madre	¿Le conoces, verdad? Es el señor de Granada. Se llama Jorge. Mira. Te mandó esta postal de cumpleaños el año pasado.
María	A ver. "De Jorge, desde Granada. Tengo que explicarte muchas cosas." Mamá, no la recibí.
Madre	Porque Jorge mandó la postal a esta casa, no a Madrid y no te la mandé. No sé por qué. Es que Jorge es … es …
María	Es mi padre, ¿verdad? ¡Jorge es mi padre!
Madre	Sí, hija, sí. Lo siento. No puedo explicarte más ahora. Y no puedes decirle nada a Jorge. Por favor. ¿Me lo prometes? Necesito tiempo.
María	Te lo prometo.

Test

Now it's time to test your progress in Unit 10.

1 Choose something you like and something you don't like from each of the three lists and write a sentence about them using **gustar**.

el cine	la fruta	los periódicos
el teatro	la verdura	los libros
la televisión	la carne	los dibujos animados
la música (pop/clásica)	el chocolate	
las películas de Hollywood		

6

2 Now write down two activities you like doing and two activities you don't like doing from the following:

1 dance   2 read   3 work   4 listen to music

8

3 Insert the appropriate indirect and direct pronouns and the correct form of **gustar**.

Example: Mi madre. **A ella le gusta** el cine.

1 Mi padre. _____ los restaurantes italianos.
2 Mi hermano y yo. _____ la música rock.
3 Mis amigos. _____ el fútbol.
4 Tú y tu hermana. _____ las discotecas.
5 Yo. _____ el teatro.
6 Tú. _____ la ciudad.
7 Las hermanas. _____ su trabajo.

14

4 Complete your side of this conversation.

A: ¿Quieres ir a un concierto de música clásica?
B: (You're very sorry. You don't like classical music at all.)
A: No importa. ¿Te gusta la música popular?
B: (You don't like it much. You don't like music. You prefer the cinema. Ask if she likes the cinema.)
A: Sí, a mí también me gusta. ¿Te gusta bailar?
B: (No you don't.)
A: A mí me gusta mucho salir.

B: (You like going to the cinema once a month, but you prefer to be at home reading a book or watching the television.)

| 10

5 Read the following commentary on what Raúl did yesterday. Put the verbs into the correct form of the simple past tense.

Ayer, sábado, (**levantarse**) pronto, a las ocho. Mi amiga Elisa y yo (**ir**) al centro de la ciudad a comprar ropa y regalos para mis hermanos. Yo (**comprar**) dos camisas y Elisa (**comprar**) una falda muy bonita. (**Comer**) en un restaurante y después (**ir**) a buscar a las amigas de Elisa. Ellas (**ir**) al cine. Yo (**visitar**) a un amigo que está en el hospital. Después de la visita (**ir**) a mi casa. (**Salir**) a las ocho de la tarde y (**encontrarse**) a un amigo, Enrique, en un bar cerca de mi casa. Enrique y yo (**tomar**) una cerveza.

| 12

6 Ask these questions in Spanish.

1 Ask a colleague formally what he did yesterday.
2 Ask the same colleague where he went the day before yesterday.
3 Ask your friend what she did last week.
4 Ask your friend where she went last month.
5 Ask two colleagues formally where they went yesterday.

| 10

7 Complete these sentences, using the appropriate time expression.

1 Juego al fútbol _____ . (twice a week)
2 Hago clases de baile _____ . (three times a week)
3 Visito a mis padres _____ . (once a month)
4 Viajo a Valladolid _____ . (three times a year)
5 Tomo café _____ . (twice a day)
6 Voy a la piscina _____ . (every week)

| 12

TOTAL SCORE | 70

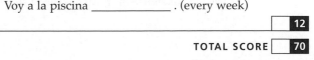

If you scored less than 60, look at the Language Building sections again before completing the Summary on page 148.

Summary 10

Now try this final test, summarizing the main points covered in this unit.

How would you:
1 say you like classical music?
2 ask someone you don't know well if he likes the cinema?
3 ask your friend if she likes dancing?
4 say you don't like it at all?
5 ask your brother what he did last night?
6 ask your sister where she went last week?
7 say yesterday was your birthday?
8 say your birthday is next month?
9 say your parents visited you last week?
10 say you swim three times a week?

REVISION

First make a list of *things* you like, for example, which cars, books, films, or newspapers do you like, and which do you not like at all? Practise saying them in Spanish. You may need to use your dictionary to look up any words you don't know. Build up your list of likes and dislikes and practise using the constructions **me gusta** and **me gustan**.

Now think about *activities* you like, for example skiing (**esquiar**), skating (**patinar**), or walking (**caminar**), and practise using **gustar** + infinitive. Again, use your dictionary to find new verbs.

Note down the things you do regularly – every day, every week, every month, every year – and make sentences, for example: **voy al cine dos veces al mes/una vez a la semana**. Then think about the last time you did a particular thing practise the past tense of **ir: fui al cine la semana pasada**.

Review 3

1 En la estación. Complete the gaps with the appropriate word from the list below.

retraso / billete / reserva / tren / ida / ida y vuelta / vía / lleva

El 1 _____ sale a las diez de la 2 _____ número tres, pero 3 _____ veinte minutos de 4 _____. Aquí tengo dos 5 _____, uno de 6 _____ para ti, porque no vuelves, y otro de 7 _____ __ _____ para mí. Yo vuelvo el miércoles. Tengo 8 _____.

2 Roberto is tall, dark, and thin. He has long straight hair. His sister is the opposite. They both have blue eyes. Describe them in Spanish.

1 Roberto es _____, _____, y _____. Tiene el pelo _____ y _____.
2 La hermana de Roberto es _____, _____, y _____. Tiene el pelo _____ y _____.
3 Tienen ___ _____ _____.

3 Describe each of these people using the correct form of the adjectives given.

1 sincero: Roberto
2 honrado: Juana
3 inteligente: los hermanos
4 tranquilo: mi padre
5 nervioso: mi madre
6 serio: las hermanas
7 simpático: Javier
8 antipático: Carmen
9 feliz: los niños
10 generoso: mi abuelo

GRAMMAR AND USAGE

4 Choose the correct preposition: **para** or **a**?

   1 Un billete _____ Madrid, por favor.
   2 ¿A qué hora llegamos _____ Madrid?
   3 Tomamos un tren _____ Valladolid.
   4 Este tren va _____ Madrid.

5 Translate these sentences into Spanish, using the verbs below.

   querer / viajar / cambiar / poder / necesitar / tomar / desear / tener que / comprar

   1 I want to buy a return ticket.
   2 Can you have a coffee in the waiting room?
   3 They need to buy a ticket.
   4 We wish to change our room.
   5 I have to travel to Seville.

6 Ask your friend the following questions.

   1 How long does it take to get to work?
   2 How long do you take to go to work on the bus?
   3 How far away is your work (in kilometres)?

7 Complete the sentences with the correct form of the demonstrative pronouns **éste**, **ése**, or **aquél**.

   1 El anillo: _____ (this one) es más caro que _____ (that one nearby) y mucho más caro que _____ (the one over there).
   2 Las pulseras: _____ (the ones over there) son mejores que _____ (these), pero _____ (those nearby) son las mejores.
   3 La camisa: _____ (the one nearby) es bonita, pero _____ (the one over there) es más bonita. No me gusta _____ (this one).
   4 Los zapatos: Me gustan _____ (these) pero son muy caros. _____ (those nearby) son buenos pero prefiero _____ (those over there).

8 Write the Spanish for the following:

   1 These shoes are better than those.
   2 My job is worse than yours.
   3 His car is bigger than my car.
   4 His car is better than my car.
   5 The film isn't as interesting as the book.

9 Write the following in Spanish using the appropriate form of **gustar**.

    1 I like the cinema.
    2 I like playing football.
    3 They like fast cars.
    4 We like cartoons.
    5 Do you [*informal*] like listening to music?
    6 I don't like the theatre at all.

10 Javier talks about his terrible day. Put the verbs in brackets into the simple past tense.

Ayer 1_____(**ser**) un día terrible. 2_____(**levantarse**) tarde. 3_____(**desayunar**) rápidamente y 4_____(**salir**) de casa. El autobús 5_____(**llegar**) tarde y yo 6_____(**llegar**) muy tarde a mi trabajo. A mi jefe no le 7_____ (**gustar**), es muy antipático. 8_____ (**terminar**) mi trabajo y 9_____ (**ir**) a mi casa. Cuando 10_____ (**entrar**) tú me 11_____ (**llamar**).

 LISTENING

11 Listen to these conversations and decide which of the people below is being described. Listen as many times as you like for each description.

    1 This person is rather plump and quite short.
    2 This person is tall and dark, with long straight hair, and always wears white trousers.
    3 This person is tall and a bit fat, and wears big sweaters all the time.
    4 This person has blue eyes and blonde hair, and is quite tall.
    5 This person is short, dark, and thin.
    6 This person is neither short nor tall and has blonde hair.

Now listen again and fill in the extra information for each person.

12 Josefina is talking to María and Gustavo about what to do tonight. They all want to go out, but can't decide where.

Listen once and indicate who likes what by ticking the appropriate column.

	música clásica	música rock	baile	cine	bar	restaurante
Josefina	☐	☐	☐	☐	☐	☐
María	☐	☐	☐	☐	☐	☐
Gustavo	☐	☐	☐	☐	☐	☐

Now listen again. Say which two things they all like doing but can't do. Give the reason they can't do them.

 SPEAKING

13 You're buying a train ticket. Prepare your side of the conversation and then check it against the recording.

A: ¿Qué desea?
You: (Say you'd like a ticket to Barcelona.)
A: ¿De ida o de ida y vuelta?
You: (You want a return.)
A: ¿Para cuándo?
You: (You want to go tomorrow and come back on the seventeenth.)
A: Hay un tren a las nueve de la mañana.
You: (Ask how long it takes.)
A: Cuatro horas y media. ¿De primera o segunda clase?
You: (You want second class.)

14 Tell a friend about what you did yesterday. Prepare your answers and then check the recording to see if you got them right.

Example: You got up at eight. **Me levanté a las ocho.**

You went to town with your friend.
You bought some shoes.
You ate at a restaurant.
You went home.
You studied.
Your friends called you.
You all went to a bar.
You all went to the cinema.
You went home by bus at eleven.

Talking about the past
Hablamos del pasado

OBJECTIVES

In this unit you'll learn how to:
- ✓ describe holidays, visits, and events
- ✓ say what you did in the past
- ✓ talk about what you used to do
- ✓ describe important events in your life

And cover the following grammar and language:
- ✓ the past tense of more regular verbs
- ✓ the past tense of irregular verbs: **estar**, **tener**
- ✓ the imperfect tense

LEARNING SPANISH 11

You should now be expanding your stock of common expressions to include everyday things that do not appear in this book. Make a mental note of subjects you discuss at work, at home, and with your friends. Be alert to phrases that come up again and again in conversation, and think to yourself: 'how do you say that in Spanish?' If you're lucky enough to know someone who speaks Spanish, or, better still, a Spaniard or Latin American, ask them to help you with the Spanish versions of what you want to say. Otherwise, make use of a good dictionary, which will not only give translations of single words, but provide examples of context and common expressions.

🎧 Now start the recording for Unit 11.

11.1 Where did you go on holiday?
¿Adónde fuiste de vacaciones?

ACTIVITY 1 is on the recording.

ACTIVITY 2

1 ¿Por qué está morena Beatriz?
2 ¿Estuvieron en hoteles Beatriz y Antonio?
3 ¿Cuándo estuvo Beatriz en Londres?
4 ¿Con quién fue Antonio a Londres?
5 ¿Cómo se llama el castillo que visitó Antonio?

DIALOGUE 1

○ ¡Qué morena estás!
■ Sí. Ayer volví de vacaciones.
○ Yo fui a Londres con mis padres. ¿Adónde fuiste de vacaciones tú?
■ Fui a la playa, a un apartamento con dos amigas.
○ Yo estuve en un hotel con mis padres. Vimos el Parlamento y el Big Ben. Fuimos en un barco por todo el Támesis.
■ Yo estuve en Londres hace dos años. Fue muy interesante pero llovió constantemente. Prefiero descansar, nadar en la playa y no hacer nada.
○ ¿Te bañaste todos los días?
■ Sí, me bañé porque hizo muy buen tiempo y mucho sol.
○ Nosotros visitamos el castillo de Windsor.
■ Pues yo un día fui a un monasterio.

VOCABULARY	
ir de vacaciones	to go on holiday
¡qué morena estás!	how tanned you are!
la cosa	thing
el barco	boat
el Támesis	Thames
hace dos años	two years ago
llover	to rain
constantemente	constantly
bañarse	to bathe
hacer buen tiempo	to be fine (weather)
hacer sol	to be sunny
el castillo	castle
pasear	to walk, stroll
el monasterio	monastery

⊘ The simple past of *estar* and *tener*

In the simple past tense, **estar** changes its stem:

est<u>uve</u>	est<u>uvimos</u>
est<u>uviste</u>	est<u>uvisteis</u>
est<u>uvo</u>	est<u>uvieron</u>

tener and verbs related to it also change in this way: **tener (tuve)**, **obtener (obtuve)**, 'to obtain', **detener (detuve)**, 'to detain', **sostener (sostuve)**, 'to sustain'.

⊘ The simple past of *volver* and *ver*

Although **volver** and **ver** are irregular in the present, they are regular in the simple past and their stems do not change:

Ayer **volví** de mis vacaciones. Yesterday I came back from my holidays.
Vimos el Parlamento. We saw Parliament.

⊘ Describing the weather

The verb **hacer** ('to do', 'to make') is used in many expressions describing the weather:

Hace buen/mal tiempo. The weather is good/bad.
Hace un buen día. It's a fine day.
Hace sol/calor/frío. It's sunny/hot/cold.

⊘ Expressing time in the past using *hace*

To say how long ago something happened, use **hace** [*literally* 'it makes'] + the period of time:

Fui a Londres **hace dos años**. I went to London two years ago.
Le vi **hace cinco minutos**. I saw her five minutes ago.
Comí **hace poco**. I ate a short while ago.
Fui a Australia **hace mucho**. I went to Australia a long time ago.

ACTIVITY 3

Write these sentences in Spanish.

1 I was in a good hotel.
2 I went to the beach on holiday.
3 They came back yesterday.
4 We came back three days ago.
5 It rained a lot.
6 The weather was bad.
7 They saw the Thames.
8 I saw Juan an hour ago.

⊕ Now do activities 4 and 5 on the recording.

Me gusta la playa

(🎧) **ACTIVITY 6** is on the recording.

ACTIVITY 7

¿Antonio o Beatriz? ¿(A) quién …

1 fue a la playa y a quién le gusta el sol?
2 no le gusta el sol?
3 fue a las montañas?
4 le gustan los campamentos?
5 le gustan las vacaciones organizadas?

DIALOGUE 2

○ ¿No te gusta la playa? ¿No te gusta bañarte en el mar?
■ Sí, me gusta un poco, pero prefiero ver monumentos.
○ A mí también me interesa. Cuando era pequeña, mi padre me llevaba por muchas ciudades de Europa.
■ A mí me gustan las montañas. Cuando era pequeño mis padres me llevaban a campamentos. Visitábamos pueblos pequeños.
○ Una vez yo fui a un campamento en las montañas, pero no me gustó. No me gusta el camping.
■ Sí, pero si vas de camping, puedes hacer lo que quieres.
○ De acuerdo. Pero yo prefiero las vacaciones organizadas por una agencia. No tienes que preocuparte de nada. Te diviertes más.
■ Yo creo que no. Yo odio las vacaciones 'turísticas'.

VOCABULARY	
el mar	sea
interesar	to interest
acordarse	to remember
la montaña	mountain
el campamento	holiday camp [*for young people*]
ir de camping	to go camping
la agencia	agency
divertirse	to enjoy oneself
odiar	to hate

✓ The imperfect tense of -ar verbs and ser

The imperfect tense is used to describe events or states in the past which continued for some time or which occurred repeatedly. It is often translated in English by 'used to' or 'was -ing'. The following endings are added to the stem:

llevar	llevaba	llevábamos
	llevabas	llevabais
	llevaba	llevaban

Note that in the singular the first and third person are the same, and in the plural the first person is stressed on the first syllable after the stem.

Mi padre me **llevaba** a visitar las ciudades de Europa. My father used to take me to European cities.
Visitábamos pueblos pequeños. We used to visit small villages.

ser is irregular:

era	éramos
eras	erais
era	eran

It is used to describe a state persisting over a long period:

Cuando **era** pequeña ... When I was young ...

ACTIVITY 8

Write the imperfect form of the verb in brackets for this account of Carmen's memories.

Cuando yo (1 **ser**) pequeña mi madre (2 **trabajar**) para una empresa muy importante. Mi padre y yo (3 **comprar**) toda la comida para la semana en el supermercado. Cada año nosotros (4 **visitar**) a mis abuelos. Durante aquellos años nosotros (5 **estar**) en Barcelona.

 Now do activities 9 and 10 on the recording.

When I was young

Cuando era joven

ACTIVITY 11 is on the recording.

ACTIVITY 12

1	Margarita lived in a big house.	V/F
2	Her family was quite rich.	V/F
3	Pepe lived in a big flat.	V/F
4	Margarita didn't see much of her father.	V/F
5	Pepe used to go to the coast in summer.	V/F

DIALOGUE 3

○ Tengo recuerdos muy buenos de mi juventud. Cuando era joven vivíamos en una casa muy grande en las afueras de la Ciudad de México. Éramos bastante ricos.

■ Nosotros vivíamos en un piso pequeño en Madrid. Éramos cinco hermanos. Mi padre perdió su trabajo. Éramos muy pobres.

○ ¿Ah sí? Mi vida era muy diferente. Mi padre viajaba mucho. Nosotros íbamos a la costa durante el verano.

■ Pues yo pasaba el verano en el centro de Madrid. No teníamos dinero, pero mis padres estaban siempre con nosotros. Nunca podíamos ir de vacaciones.

○ ¡Qué triste!

■ No, no, éramos una familia muy feliz.

○ Yo era feliz también, pero echaba de menos a mi padre.

VOCABULARY

el recuerdo	memory
la juventud	youth, childhood
las afueras	outskirts [of a city]
enorme	huge
rico	rich
perder	to lose
pobre	poor
la vida	life
pasar	to spend [time]
nunca	never
triste	sad
echar de menos	to miss

✅ The imperfect tense of *-er* and *-ir* verbs

The imperfect tense of **-er** and **-ir** verbs is formed as follows:

tener		vivir	
tenía	teníamos	vivía	vivíamos
tenías	teníais	vivías	vivíais
tenía	tenían	vivía	vivían

ir is irregular: **ir: iba, ibas, iba, íbamos, ibais, iban**

✅ Use of the imperfect and simple past

The imperfect is used to describe things that either went on for a long time, or to describe things that happened regularly in the past:

Vivíamos en un piso muy pequeño. We lived in a very small flat.
Íbamos a la costa durante el verano. We used to go to the coast in the summer.

In contrast the simple past is used to describe one specific action that occurred once in the past:

Fuimos a la costa el año pasado. We went to the coast last year.
Mi padre **perdió** su trabajo. My father lost his job.

✅ Describing numbers of people

The verb **ser** is used to describe how many there are in a group:

Éramos cinco hermanos. There were five brothers and sisters.
Somos tres. There are three of us.

ACTIVITY 13

Rewrite the following acount in Spanish, using the imperfect or the simple past for each verb as appropriate.

When I was young I used to live in the city, but every summer I used to go to my grandparents' house with my two brothers. My grandparents had a big old car and I remember that once, my grandfather took us to the mountains. My father worked a lot and he didn't have long holidays, but every weekend he came to see us and gave us presents.

ACTIVITY 14

Now write a few sentences about your childhood, including one or two things that only happened once. Use your dictionary for words you haven't yet seen.

 Now do activities 15 and 16 on the recording.

(11.4) Spanish fiestas
España en fiestas

ACTIVITY 17

Read the passage below about Spanish fiestas and answer these questions.

1 Name five things that you get in a Spanish fiesta.
2 Name one thing you have to do in a Spanish fiesta.
3 Name one thing you can't do.
4 Which is probably the most internationally known fiesta, and why?
5 What is las Fallas?

España es un país de fiestas: fiestas regionales, fiestas de las ciudades, fiestas de los pueblos, fiestas del campo; fiestas grandes y fiestas pequeñas. Todas tienen las mismas características: los toros, la música, el baile, el vino, los fuegos artificiales, los juegos infantiles, el ruido y el no dormir. Si vives en un pueblo pequeño durante las fiestas, olvídate de dormir. Durante varias noches, hay música en la plaza hasta las cuatro de la mañana. La gente está por la calle durante toda la noche.

Desde marzo hasta octubre, en toda España, celebran fiestas. La más famosa, inmortalizada por el escritor americano Ernest Hemingway, es San Fermín, que se celebra en julio en Pamplona, una ciudad pequeña que está en el noreste de España. Lo más importante de estas fiestas son los encierros: los toros corren por las calles de la ciudad. Los jóvenes, vestidos de blanco con pañuelos rojos, corren delante de toros enormes. Por la tarde hay una corrida en la plaza con los toreros profesionales.

Muchos otros pueblos de España tienen su versión, en pequeño, de San Fermín. Los toros corren por las calles; los jóvenes corren delante. Pero los toros de los pueblos son más pequeños, se llaman vaquillas.

Cada comunidad tiene su fiesta especial. En Valencia, en marzo se celebran las Fallas. Son unas fiestas espectaculares en las que queman enormes estatuas de cartón y fuegos artificiales impresionantes.

En Sevilla, la Fería de Abril celebra la primavera con música y baile flamenco.

el toro	bull
los fuegos artificiales	fireworks
los juegos infantiles	children's games
el ruido	noise
el no dormir	lack of sleep, not sleeping
olvidar	to forget
inmortalizado	immortalized
el escritor/la escritora	writer
el encierro	*the practice of running with bulls in the street*
correr	to run
los jóvenes	young people
el pañuelo	handkerchief
coger	to catch
la corrida	bullfight
la plaza de toros	bullring
el torero	bullfighter
en pequeño	in miniature, in a smaller version
la vaquilla	calf
la herida	injury
la comunidad	community
quemar	to burn
las estatuas de cartón	cardboard statues
la primavera	spring

ACTIVITY 18

Write five sentences in the simple past about what you did at the fiesta.

1 You went to the fiesta in a village.
2 You danced until four in the morning.
3 You saw the fireworks.
4 You ran in front of the bulls.
5 You didn't sleep all night.

Now try to write five more sentences using information from the passage.

11.5 Un forastero en la ciudad

MARÍA Y JORGE HABLAN POR TELÉFONO
MARÍA AND JORGE TALK ON THE PHONE

María quiere hablar más con Jorge. Le invita a cenar.

saber	to know
comportarse	to behave
amable	kind, friendly
quizás	perhaps
entonces	then
por casualidad	by coincidence

ACTIVITY 19

¿Verdadero o falso?

1 María invita a Jorge a cenar en un restaurante.
2 Le invita porque la otra cena fue muy buena.
3 María dice que fue a visitar a unos amigos.
4 Le invita porque quiere hablar.
5 Jorge no puede aceptar la invitación.
6 Jorge no quiere decir cómo se llama la persona a quien visita.
7 Jorge y María fueron a Las Fuentes por casualidad.
8 Pueden cenar juntos el sábado.

ACTIVITY 20

Answer the questions using the appropriate information from this episode of the story. Your answer doesn't have to be exactly the same as in the recording.

Jorge: ¿Adónde fuiste?
María: _____
María: ¿Quiere venir a mi casa a cenar?
Jorge: _____
María: ¿El pueblo está lejos?
Jorge: _____
María: ¿Cómo se llama el pueblo?
Jorge: _____
Jorge: ¿Podemos cenar el viernes por la noche?
María: _____

ACTIVITY 21

Complete this part of the story by filling in the gaps. All the words which are missing consist of one or two letters only.

Fui 1_____ ver 2_____ unos amigos. Mire usted, 3_____ llamo para invitar 4 _____ 5 _____ cenar 6_____ 7_____ casa. Es que, 8_____ otra noche, 9_____ comporté muy mal. ¿Quiere venir? Quiero hablar con usted 10_____ algunas cosas.

STORY TRANSCRIPT

Jorge	¿Dígame?
María	Señor Jorge, hola, soy yo, María.
Jorge	¡Ah! ¡Hola! ¿Qué tal estás? ¿Cómo sabes mi número de teléfono?
María	Por el señor España.
Jorge	¡Ah sí! ¿Qué tal el viaje? ¿Adónde fuiste?
María	Oh, fui a ver a unos amigos. Mire usted, le llamo para invitarle a cenar en mi casa. Es que, la otra noche, me comporté muy mal. ¿Quiere venir? Quiero hablar con usted de algunas cosas.
Jorge	Oh, no te preocupes, no fue nada. Eres muy amable y gracias por la invitación, pero lo siento, no puedo ir.
María	Ah … bueno, no importa. Quizás otro día.
Jorge	Tengo que ir a un pueblo a visitar a una vieja amiga.
María	Ah. ¿Está lejos?
Jorge	No, está bastante cerca de Toledo, a unos ciento cincuenta kilómetros de aquí.
María	¿Cómo se llama el pueblo?
Jorge	Se llama Las Fuentes – es muy pequeño.
María	¡Las Fuentes! ¿El pueblo se llama Las Fuentes?
Jorge	Sí, sí, Las Fuentes. … María – ¿estás bien?
María	Sí, sí, no pasa nada. Conozco el pueblo, muy bien. ¡Y usted va allí!
Jorge	¡Qué casualidad! Es muy pequeño.
María	Dice que va a visitar a una amiga. ¿Cómo se llama? Quizás la conozca.
Jorge	Oh, es una amiga que conocí hace muchos años. Vuelvo el viernes. ¿Podemos cenar el viernes por la noche?
María	Sí, sí. Podemos cenar en mi casa.
Jorge	Estupendo. Podemos hablar entonces.
María	De acuerdo. Hasta el viernes.
Jorge	Adiós.

Test

Now it's time to test your progress in Unit 11.

1 Complete this postcard using the correct form of the verb in the simple past.

¡Hola Pepe! ¿Qué tal estás? Ayer (yo) (1 **volver**) de mis vacaciones. ¿Dónde (2 **ir**) (tú?) Mis padres y yo (3 **ir**) a Barcelona. (Nosotros) (4 **hacer**) muchas cosas en Barcelona. (Nosotros) (5 **estar**) en un hotel. (Nosotros) (6 **ver**) el Tibidabo. (Yo) (7 **bañarse**) en el mar. (Nosotros) (8 **visitar**) un monasterio. ¡Adiós! Ana.

8

2 Write the correct form of these reflexive verbs.

1 Mi hermano (**bañarse**) en el mar ayer.
2 Mis padres (**levantarse**) tarde ayer.
3 Me gusta (**divertirse**) en el baile.
4 No (**acordarse**) de como termina la película.
5 Ellos (**aburrirse**) los domingos.

5

3 Give the Spanish for these sentences using the simple past of **ser**, **estar**, or **ir**, as appropriate.

1 Yesterday I went to the village.
2 They were in Madrid.
3 It was a big car.
4 We went to a castle.
5 It was a good film.

5

4 How would you describe the weather in Spanish?

1 It's raining.   4 It's hot.
2 It's sunny.   5 The weather is good.
3 It's cold.

10

5 Supply the Spanish for each response below.

   1 A: ¿Cuándo fuiste a Sevilla?
      (You went two years ago.)
   2 A: ¿Dónde está Pablo?
      (You saw him five minutes ago.)
   3 A: ¿Quieres un café?
      (You had a coffee a short while ago.)
   4 A: ¿Cuándo fuiste a Madrid?
      (You went to Madrid a long time ago.)
   5 A: ¿Tu coche es nuevo?
      (You bought it two years ago.)

10

6 Translate these sentences into English.

   1 Vivieron en la costa durante muchos años.
   2 Yo trabajaba antes en una empresa de muebles.
   3 Fuimos a ver el partido de fútbol el domingo.
   4 Íbamos a ver el fútbol los domingos.
   5 Mi padre conducía muy mal.
   6 Estuvo en la discoteca.
   7 Siempre estabas en el cine.
   8 Ayer compré un regalo para mi amiga.

16

7 Here is an advertisement for the Barcelona region. Read the
   information, then write a short letter to a friend telling him
   what you did there. Use the simple past tense.

Querido Juan,
Fui a Barcelona …

> **Visitar Barcelona**
> • Pasear por las Ramblas
> • Visitar el Tibidabo
> • Comprar en los grandes almacenes
> • Comer en buenos restaurantes
> • Bañarse en el Mediterráneo
> • Bailar en las discotecas
> • Ver la arquitectura de Gaudí

7

TOTAL SCORE **51**

If you scored less than 41, look at the Language Building
sections again before completing the Summary on page 166.

Summary 11

 Now try this final test, summarizing the main points covered in this unit.

How would you:
1 ask someone where he went for his holidays?
2 say you went to England?
3 say you and your parents were in a hotel?
4 say it's good weather?
5 say it's cold?
6 say you went to Australia three years ago?
7 say you saw Juan a short while ago?
8 say you lived in a big house when you were young?
9 say you used to visit your grandparents?
10 say you don't like the beach?

REVISION

Think of the things you used to do or things you did lots of times when you were younger. Practise using the imperfect tense to say or write down these things in Spanish. For example, if you used to go to the cinema every Sunday, practise saying **iba al cine los domingos**. Then find an example of something you did once only on a specific occasion and say it using the simple past, for example: **Vi una película muy buena.**

Making plans
Haciendo planes

OBJECTIVES

In this unit you will learn how to:

✓ talk about your future plans and activities

✓ invite someone to do something

✓ accept and refuse invitations

✓ apologize for not being able to accept an invitation

And cover the following grammar and language:

✓ the future tense

✓ the verb **ir** + **a** + infinitive for describing plans

✓ the conditional tense used for invitations

✓ the verb **querer** + infinitive for invitations

LEARNING SPANISH 12

Practise improvising ways of getting your meaning across when speaking spontaneously, even if you don't know the exact words or phrases in Spanish. If you know a Spanish speaker, he or she will probably help you when you get into difficulties. If not, think of things you might want to say whenever you have spare time – while you're travelling, for example. A basic example is the use of tenses. If you don't know the past tense but want to talk about yesterday, use the verb in the present tense and use the word 'yesterday'. With practice, you'll find that you will improve your ability to approximate and to describe things, even if you are aware that you do not have the exact vocabulary or specific phrases. Use facial expressions, hand movements, anything to get your meaning across. The important thing is to build up confidence so you're not afraid of getting involved in a conversation.

Now start the recording for Unit 12.

Would you like to come?

¿Te gustaría venir?

ACTIVITY 1 is on the recording.

ACTIVITY 2

Complete the sentences.

Example: **No voy a hacer nada** porque estoy cansado.

1 _____ porque tengo que trabajar en mi casa.
2 _____ porque es una casa bonita.
3 _____ porque va a hacer buen tiempo.
4 _____ porque mi hijo va a jugar al fútbol.
5 _____ porque su mujer tiene que estudiar.

DIALOGUE 1

○ ¿Qué vas a hacer este fin de semana?

■ No voy a hacer nada. ¡Estoy tan cansado! Voy a dormir y a descansar.

○ ¡Qué suerte! Yo voy al campo con la familia. Vamos a preparar la casa para el verano. Es mucho trabajo.

■ Pero vale la pena, ¿verdad? Es una casa muy bonita.

○ ¿Te gustaría venir, con la familia? Podemos hacer una barbacoa en el jardín.

■ A mí me gustaría ir pero no podemos. Mi hijo va a jugar al fútbol el sábado.

○ ¡Qué lástima! Pero ¿por qué no venís el domingo?

■ No sé. Mi mujer tiene un examen el lunes. Va a estudiar todo el domingo.

○ ¿Quieres venir tú solo con los niños? Tu mujer puede estudiar tranquilamente.

■ Sí, es una buena idea. Voy a preguntarle a mi mujer si está de acuerdo.

VOCABULARY	
¡qué suerte!	you lucky thing! [*literally* what luck!]
vale la pena	it's worth it
¿te gustaría venir?	would you like to come?
la barbacoa	barbecue
el examen	exam
tranquilamente	quietly

✅ Talking about the future with *ir* + *a* + infinitive

ir + **a** followed by the infinitive is used to talk about plans for the future. It is very similar to the English construction 'going to (do)':

¿Qué vas **a hacer** este fin de semana? What are you going to do this weekend?
Voy a visitar a mis padres. I'm going to visit my parents.
Vamos a preparar la casa. We're going to prepare the house.
No voy **a hacer** nada. I'm not going to do anything.

✅ Giving invitations and expressing wishes

The verb **gustar** is used in the conditional to give invitations and to express what you would like to do:

¿Te gustaría venir? Would you like to come?
Me gustaría ir al campo. I'd like to go to the countryside.

There is more on the conditional on page 183.

✅ Using *¡qué!* in exclamations

The structure **¡qué!** (meaning 'what (a)' or 'how') + an appropriate noun/adjective is often used for exclamations:

¡Qué suerte! What luck!   **¡Qué inteligente es!** He's so intelligent.
¡Qué lástima! What a pity!   **¡Qué moreno estás!** You're so tanned.

ACTIVITY 3

Change the subjects of these sentences as indicated.

Example: Voy a estudiar esta noche. (**nosotros**)
Nosotros vamos a estudiar esta noche.

1 No voy a salir con mis amigos mañana. (**ellos**)
2 No vamos a salir el sábado. (**vosotros**)
3 Vamos a estar en casa todo el fin de semana. (**tú**)
4 ¿Vas a venir a mi fiesta de cumpleaños? (**ella**)
5 Van a comprar un coche nuevo. (**yo**)
6 No va a visitar a sus padres. (**tú**)
7 ¿Vais a ir al teatro? (**él**)

Now do activities 4 and 5 on the recording.

12.2 We'll go in the morning
Iremos por la mañana

ACTIVITY 6 is on the recording.

ACTIVITY 7

¿Quién(es) …

1 … irá(n) por la mañana?
2 … hará(n) una barbacoa?
3 … jugará(n)?
4 … no podrá(n) ir?
5 … prepará(n) la comida?
6 … llamará(n) a Alfonso?

DIALOGUE 2

○ Alfonso nos invita a su casa de campo el fin de semana.
■ Este fin de semana yo no puedo ir. Voy a estudiar.
○ Ya lo sé pero podemos ir los niños y yo.
■ Es una buena idea. ¿A qué hora iréis?
○ Iremos pronto por la mañana. Es una casa preciosa, en el campo. Haremos una barbacoa en el jardín. Los niños jugarán. ¿No puedes venir? ¡Qué lástima!
■ Sí, pero estudiaré mejor sola sin los niños.
○ Además, tienen una piscina. Nos bañaremos y tomaremos algo en el patio.
■ ¡Qué envidia!
○ Quizás podremos ir todos otro día.
■ Pues no sé. Creo que iré con vosotros. Llevaré mis libros y estudiaré en el jardín mientras tú y Alfonso preparáis la comida. ¿Qué te parece?
○ ¡Estupendo! Llamaré a Alfonso ahora mismo.

VOCABULARY

pronto	early
precioso	beautiful, wonderful
sin	without
el patio	patio
¡qué envidia!	I'm so envious, jealous! [*literally* what envy!]
mientras	while
¿qué te parece?	what do you think?
¡estupendo!	great!
ahora mismo	right now

✅ The future tense

In Spanish there are two ways of talking about the future: **ir + a +** infinitive and the future tense. Both are roughly equivalent to the English 'will' and 'going to', and there is not the same difference between them as in English. In many ways they are interchangeable.

For regular **-ar**, **-ir**, and **-er** verbs, the future is formed by adding the following endings to the infinitive:

trabajar	trabajar**é**	trabajar**emos**
	trabajar**ás**	trabajar**éis**
	trabajar**á**	trabajar**án**

Trabajaré mañana. I'll work/I'm going to work tomorrow.
Iremos el fin de semana. We'll go/We're going at the weekend.
Llevaré mis libros. I'll take/I'm going to take my books.

The following verbs change stems in the future, but the endings are regular: **venir (vendr-)**, **tener (tendr-)**, **hacer (har-)**, **poder (podr-)**, **salir (saldr-)**.

✅ More about the future

In Spanish there is not the same perceived difference as there is in English between saying **voy a estudiar esta noche** ('I'm going to study tonight') and **estudiaré esta noche** ('I'll study tonight'). Spanish uses either form – **ir + a +** infinitive or the future tense – from the point of view of the speaker, sometimes depending on the proximity of the event:

Son las once. Voy a ir a la cama. It's 11 o'clock. I'm going to bed.
Iré a la cama más tarde. I'll go to bed later.
Vamos a salir esta noche. We're going to go out/We'll go out tonight.
Me quedaré en casa. I'm going to stay in/I'll stay in tonight.

ACTIVITY 8

Translate the following into Spanish.
We'll go early next Saturday morning. We'll arrive at the house at ten o'clock. The children will play in the garden and swim in the pool while I prepare lunch. We'll be able to go for a walk in the afternoon and we'll visit the village. You'll come in the evening and we'll all have supper together. We'll have to go to bed early because we're going to leave early in the morning for Madrid. We'll arrive in Madrid at about midday and I'll call my mother. In the evening we'll relax and watch television.

 Now do activities 9 and 10 on the recording.

12.3 We're going to the cinema
Vamos al cine

ACTIVITY 11 is on the recording.

ACTIVITY 12

Translate the phrases which are true into Spanish.

1 Elisa won't be able go to the cinema tonight.
2 She's busy.
3 She'll stay at home tonight.
4 She can go on Sunday.
5 The boys can't go on Sunday.
6 They'll do something else tonight.
7 Elisa will call at 5.30.
8 They'll go and see a Spanish comedy film.
9 They'll decide later.

DIALOGUE 3

○ Hola, Elisa, Federico y yo vamos al cine esta noche.
¿Quieres venir?
■ Me gustaría pero no puedo. Lo siento.
○ ¿Qué te pasa? ¿Estás enferma?
■ No, estoy ocupada. Voy a una boda mañana y tengo que
preparar las cosas. Me quedaré en casa esta noche.
○ ¿Y el domingo? ¿Te gustaría venir el domingo? Esta noche
haremos otra cosa.
■ De acuerdo. ¿Dónde quedamos y a qué hora?
○ Yo estaré en casa el domingo a partir de las cinco de la
tarde. ¿Me puedes llamar?
■ De acuerdo. Te llamaré a las cinco y media. ¿Está bien?
○ ¿Y qué película vamos a ver?
■ No sé. Hay una española cómica muy buena.
○ Vale, ya decidiremos el domingo.

VOCABULARY	
ocupado	busy
la boda	wedding
quedarse	to stay
otra cosa	something else
la (película) cómica	comedy (film)
vale	OK
decidir	to decide

172

✓ Making excuses

Estoy enfermo/a.	I'm not well/I'm ill.
Estoy cansado/a.	I'm tired.
Estoy ocupado/a.	I'm busy.
Estoy resfriado/a.	I have a cold.
Mi madre está enferma.	My mother is ill.
Voy a una boda mañana.	I'm going to a wedding tomorrow.
Tengo que preparar las cosas.	I have to prepare things.

ACTIVITY 13

Make excuses for these invitations using the constructions
estar or **tener que**.

1 ¿Quieres venir al cine? (You're tired.)
2 ¿Te gustaría salir con nosotros esta noche? (You aren't well.)
3 ¿Por qué no vamos a bailar? (You're busy.)
4 ¿Quieres salir mañana? Podemos ir a tomar algo.
  (You have to visit your mother.)
5 ¿Quieres venir a comprar con nosotros?
  (You have to prepare lunch.)
6 ¿Te gustaría salir mañana? Es mi cumpleaños.
  (Tomorrow you're going to Barcelona.)

ACTIVITY 14

In the sentences below, you will see one form of the future.
Complete your response using the other form: for example if
you see **voy a comer** you respond using **comeré**.

1 Voy a comer en el restaurante Goya. ¿Y tú?
  Yo_____ (restaurante Bella Vista).
2 Visitaré a mis tíos en Argentina.
  Yo _____ (México).
3 Vamos a trabajar todo el fin de semana.
  Nosotros _____ (toda la semana).
4 ¿Saldrán a las siete?
  No. Ellos _____ (a las ocho).
5 Vamos a llegar a las diez, ¿verdad?
  No, vosotros _____ (a las once).

🎧 Now do activities 15 and 16 on the recording.

12.4 Entertainments and listings
La cartelera

Spaniards are great cinema-goers. Read the following passage, then answer the questions which follow.

El cine es muy popular en España. En las ciudades hay muchos cines que ponen todo tipo de películas, nuevas y antiguas, desde las cinco de la tarde hasta la medianoche. Casi todas las películas (normalmente americanas) son dobladas por los directores y actores más famosos de España. Algunas películas se presentan en versión original con subtítulos.

Las películas están recomendadas para distintas edades, por ejemplo: 'Todos los públicos', '13 años', '18 años'.

El teatro es menos popular que el cine pero en muchas ciudades hay por lo menos un teatro que pone obras populares o clásicas. Y también hay espectáculos, a veces con cena incluida, con canciones, baile y karaoke.

poner (una película)	to show (a film)
todo tipo	all sorts
casi	almost
doblado	dubbed
presentarse	to be shown, presented
versión original	original version
el subtítulo	subtitle
la edad	age
la obra	play, work
el espectáculo	show
la canción	song

ACTIVITY 17
¿Verdadero o falso?

1 El cine es más popular que el teatro.
2 Hay más películas americanas que españolas.
3 Muchas películas se presentan en versión original.
4 Un niño de diez años puede ver una película recomendada para 'Todos los públicos'.
5 Hay dos o tres teatros en todas las ciudades.
6 Puedes cenar y ver un espectáculo.

ACTIVITY 18

Study **la cartelera** and answer the questions.

1 ¿Cuántas salas hay en el cine Aragón?
2 ¿En qué película actúa Nicolas Cage?
3 ¿Por qué calle entras al cine Fleta?
4 ¿Tienes que tener dieciocho años o más para ver 'El chico ideal'?
5 Quieres reservar una entrada para el teatro. ¿A qué número llamas?
6 ¿Cómo se llama el restaurante que tiene karaoke?

CARTELERA

TEATROS

TEATRO DE LA ESTACION. – Teniente Coronel Pueyo (junto Aljafería) presenta **Más o menos Shakespeare,** de Rafael Campos. Hoy, 22,30 h.; sábado, 22,30 h.; domingo, 20,00 h. ¡Local climatizado! Reservas: 976 445 011.

CINES

ARAGON. 3 SALAS. – Cádiz, 13 (Centro Comercial Independencia). 976 213 160. Dolby SR.
ARAGON. – Hampones. 5-7,30-10,30. 18 años.
ARAGON. – El Coyote. 5-7-9-11. Todos públicos.
ARAGON. – Mejor... imposible. 24 semanas. ¡Ultimos días! 5-7,30-10,30. Todos públicos.
CERVANTES. – DDS. 5-7-9-11. **City of Angels.** Nicolas Cage, Meg Ryan. Apta.
CINE COLISEO. – Digital SDDS. Paseo Independencia, 19. **Asesinos de reemplazo.** 5-7-9-11. 18 años.

CINE DON QUIJOTE. – DDS. 5-8-11. **Armageddon.** Bruce Willis. Apta.
CINE FLETA. – Entrada por avenida César Augusto. **El chico ideal.** 5-7-9-11. Todos públicos.

RESTAURANTES ESPECTACULO

CLUB NAUTICO. – Magníficas cenas, copas, música y karaoke. Teléfonos 976 293 400 y 976 446 666.
GARDEN. – Restaurante espectáculo. Viernes y sábados, cenas con espectáculo y baile con orquesta, con menús desde 22 euros. Jueves, domingos y festivos, comidas con menú del día. San Juan Bosco, 3. Teléfono 976 551 625.

¿QUÉ TAL EL VIAJE?
HOW WAS THE TRIP?

Jorge vuelve de su viaje. María sabe quién es 'la amiga' de Jorge. Jorge se lo explica todo.

enterarse	to find out
sospechar	to suspect
explicar	to explain
pasar	to happen
pelear(se)	to quarrel, to fight
contigo	with you
entender	to understand
querer	to love
dejar	to give up, leave

ACTIVITY 19

Choose the correct answer for each question:

1 María tiene
   a la tarjeta y la foto.
   b la tarjeta.
   c la foto.
2 María se enteró del secreto
   a cuando vio a Jorge la primera vez.
   b cuando fue a visitar a su madre.
   c durante la cena.
3 Jorge y la madre de María
   a no tenían problemas pero no tenían dinero.
   b tenían dinero pero tenían problemas.
   c tenían problemas y no tenían dinero.
4 Jorge
   a no encontró trabajo y no llamó a su mujer.
   b encontró trabajo y llamó a su mujer.
   c encontró trabajo pero no llamó a su mujer.
5
   a Jorge dejó a su mujer.
   b La mujer dejó a Jorge
   c Se dejaron los dos.

6 Jorge volvió porque quería ver
   a a su mujer y a María.
   b a su mujer.
   c a María.

ACTIVITY 20

Here are the answers to some questions from the dialogue. What are the questions? Check your answers against the transcript.

María	¿_____?
Jorge	Muy bien, gracias. Mi amiga está muy bien.
María	¿_____?
Jorge	Sí, soy yo. Soy tu padre.
Jorge	¿_____?
María	Cuando fui a visitar a mi madre.
María	¿_____?
Jorge	Encontré un trabajo bueno en Granada.
María	¿_____?
Jorge	Porque tengo que verla y tenía que verte a ti también.

STORY TRANSCRIPT

María ¿Qué tal el viaje?
Jorge Muy bien, gracias. Mi amiga está muy bien.
María Mira ... tengo unas fotos. Y esta tarjeta. Yo sé quién es tu amiga. Es mi madre, ¿verdad? Y este señor de la foto eres tú, ¿verdad?
Jorge Sí, soy yo. Soy tu padre. ¿Cuándo te enteraste?
María Cuando fui a visitar a mi madre. Ya lo sospechaba. ¿Me vas a explicar lo que pasó? Le prometí no decir nada pero tenemos que hablar.
Jorge Sí, pero es difícil. Tuvimos muchos problemas durante mucho tiempo. No teníamos dinero. Siempre nos peleábamos. Fui a buscar trabajo en Granada.
María ¿Pero por qué no fuimos contigo?
Jorge ¿No lo entiendes? Tuve que irme.
María Pero, ¿no querías a mi madre?
Jorge Sí, mucho, y ella me quería a mí. Pero no podíamos vivir juntos.
María Entonces, ¿por qué no volviste?
Jorge Encontré un trabajo bueno en Granada y llamé a tu madre. No quería venir a Granada conmigo.
María Y tú no querías volver.
Jorge No, porque no podía dejar mi trabajo. Me quedé allí. Cada año pensaba volver, pero no podía. Al final decidí no volver.
María Y olvidaste a mi madre.
Jorge ¡No, no! Nunca la olvidé. Pero, no podíamos vivir juntos.
María Y ahora. ¿Por qué vuelves?
Jorge Porque tengo que verla y tenía que verte a ti también. ¡Eres mi hija!

Test

Now it's time to test your progress in Unit 12.

1 ¿Qué van a hacer? Write out the sentences in full.

    1 Roberto / ir / cine
    2 Elisa / ir / boda
    3 Nosotros / ir / bailar
    4 Ellos / visitar / unos amigos
    5 Tú / estudiar
    6 Vosotros / preparar / cena
    7 Yo / comprar / coche nuevo
    8 Mis hermanos / jugar / fútbol
    9 Tú y yo / ver / película
   10 Yo / terminar / libro

`20`

2 Write down three ways of inviting someone to the cinema.

    1 ¿____ _____ venir al cine?
    2 ¿ ____ venir al cine?
    3 ¿ ____ al cine?

`6`

3 Write the correct form of the future tense in this letter.

> Querida Sara
> Mañana (1 **ir**) a mi nuevo trabajo. (2 **Empezar**) a
> las nueve. (3 **Estar**) nervioso porque no conozco a mis
> nuevos compañeros. (4 **Salir**) de casa a las ocho porque
> quiero llegar pronto. Mi amiga (5 **venir**) conmigo porque
> trabaja cerca de mi nueva oficina. El primer día (6 **hacer**)
> una visita a varios departamentos. Mis nuevos
> compañeros (7 **comer**) conmigo el primer día. Mis
> compañeros y yo (8 **tener**) mucho trabajo porque es una
> compañía nueva. Mi jefe (9 **tener**) que ayudarme los
> primeros días. Ahora (10 **preparar**) mis cosas.
> Saludos.
> M.

`10`

4 Someone asks you if you want to go out. Make five different excuses.

1 ____ ocupado/a.
2 ____ ____ trabajar.
3 ____ ____ examen.
4 ____ cansado/a.
5 ____ ____ visitar a un amigo.

| 5 |

5 Give the Spanish for the following expressions.

1 You lucky thing!
2 It's worth it.
3 What a pity!
4 What do you think about that?
5 Great!
6 Next week.
7 I'm sorry.
8 It doesn't matter.
9 OK, agreed.
10 What's the matter?

| 10 |

6 In this word search, there are ten verbs in the future tense. Find each verb, and write it down adding the accent in the appropriate place where necessary.

E	S	T	A	R	E	P	N	Y	D
S	X	Q	O	H	X	C	P	U	E
T	J	U	G	A	R	E	M	O	S
A	Y	F	Z	R	W	N	A	E	C
R	W	I	R	A	B	A	M	D	A
A	J	G	H	N	V	R	T	U	N
N	I	P	O	D	R	E	L	J	S
C	K	H	L	L	A	M	A	R	A
S	L	R	F	G	K	O	A	E	R
B	C	I	R	E	I	S	D	I	A

| 10 |

TOTAL SCORE | 61 |

If you scored less than 51, look at the Language Building sections again before completing the Summary on page 180.

Summary 12

Now try this final test, summarizing the main points covered in this unit.

How would you:
1 say you're going to study tonight?
2 say they're going to see a film tomorrow?
3 ask your friend if she would like to go out?
4 say you're sorry but you can't?
5 say you're tired?
6 say you'll go tomorrow?
7 say that he'll come next week?
8 say that you'll stay at home?
9 say it's worth it?
10 ask your friend what she thinks about something?

REVISION

Go over the exclamations in this unit and remember them when you use the English equivalent, for example ¡qué lástima!, ¡qué suerte!, ¡qué envidia!, etc.

Finally, practise inviting people to different outings and events, and also practise turning down invitations. Perhaps you're not feeling well, or you're tired, or you have to do a lot of work, or you have to study your Spanish, for example!

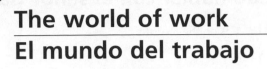

13

The world of work
El mundo del trabajo

OBJECTIVES

In this unit you'll learn how to:

✓ make professional telephone calls

✓ give instructions

✓ make an appointment

✓ introduce yourself and your company

And cover the following grammar and language:

✓ the formal imperative in polite instructions – **pase por aquí, oiga, tenga usted, perdone**

✓ the use of **poder** in formal exchanges

✓ **quisiera** ('I'd like')

✓ the present continuous tense: **estoy trabajando** ('I am working')

✓ the relative pronoun **que** (which, that, who)

✓ **sin** ('without') + infinitive

LEARNING SPANISH 13

Previous units have stressed the importance of a wide vocabulary as the key to effective language learning. There is a great deal of vocabulary in this book, but you'll also find it useful to develop your own personalized vocabulary lists. Perhaps areas of your job or study require specialized vocabulary which it would be useful to learn. This will enable you to talk about these subjects confidently in Spanish. If you have a hobby, do a sport, or are interested in a particular subject, look up some of the relevant vocabulary and start to build it into your speaking and writing practice.

Now start the recording for Unit 13.

13.1 Can I speak to Sr. García?

¿Puedo hablar con el señor García?

ACTIVITY 1 is on the recording.

ACTIVITY 2

1 Why can't Bernardo: a talk to Sr. García?
                            b phone later?
                            c attend the interview?
2 How can the receptionist help?

DIALOGUE 1

○ ¿Dígame?
■ ¿Puedo hablar con el señor García, por favor?
○ Sí. ¿De parte de quién?
■ Bernardo Díaz.
○ Un momentito. Ahora se pone … Oiga, señor Díaz.
   Perdone. El señor García está ocupado en estos momentos.
   Está en una reunión. ¿Podría llamarle usted más tarde?
■ No; estaré fuera. ¿Puedo dejarle un recado?
○ Sí, espere un momento … dígame.
■ Dígale que no podré asistir a la entrevista. Tengo que viajar.
   Quisiera cambiarla.
○ ¿Podría pasar por la oficina el miércoles próximo a las tres
   de la tarde?
■ Perfecto.
○ De nada. Hasta el miércoles.

VOCABULARY

¿de parte de quién?	who's calling?
un momentito	one moment, please
ahora se pone	he's just coming
en estos momentos	at the moment
la reunión	meeting
fuera	away
un recado	a message
esperar	to wait
asistir	to attend
la entrevista	interview
quisiera …	I'd like to …
pasar por la oficina	to come to the office
de nada	that's fine, it's a pleasure

✓ Formal imperatives 2

Formal imperatives – certain expressions used in everyday formal situations such as offices, receptions, or shops, where politeness and formality are expected – are given in Spanish in the subjunctive:

Dígame. Hello. [*literally* speak to me; *used on the telephone*]
Tenga usted. Here you are. [*literally* have]
Pase por aquí. Please come through. [*escorting someone into a room*]
Perdone. I'm sorry.

See 3.1 for more examples and the Grammar Summary, page 235, for more details.

✓ The use of *poder* in formal exchanges

The verb **poder** is often used in the conditional to make an enquiry or a request in a formal situation, for example:

¿**Podría** llamar usted más tarde? Could you call later?
¿**Podría** pasar por la oficina a las tres? Could you come to the office at three?

✓ *quisiera* ... ('I'd like ...')

quisiera is used to say 'I'd like' in formal situations:

Quisiera cambiar la hora. I'd like to change the time.
Quisiéramos hablar con el Sr. García. We'd like to talk to Sr. García.

quisiera is in fact the past subjunctive form of **querer** ('to want'). As with the formal imperatives above, this form does come up a lot in everyday conversation and is worth practising.

ACTIVITY 3

Using Dialogue 1 create a similar dialogue for the following exchange:

Call and ask the receptionist if you can speak to Sra. Blasco. The receptionist asks who is calling and then tells you that Sra. Blasco is in a meeting. Tell her you're calling about the interview on Monday. Say you can't attend the interview and would like to change the time. The receptionist says she can change the date. The receptionist asks if you can come on Wednesday afternoon. That's perfect for you. She asks if you can go to the office at 2 p.m. You agree.

 Now do activities 4 and 5 on the recording.

An interview

Una entrevista

🔊 **ACTIVITY 6** is on the recording.

ACTIVITY 7

What does Sr. García **not** ask Bernardo Díaz in the interview?

1 his reasons for wanting the job
2 his current activities and responsibilities
3 his reasons for leaving his current job
4 when he can start
5 proof of experience
6 necessary qualities for the new job

DIALOGUE 2

○ ¿Por qué está usted interesado en este puesto?
■ Estoy haciendo un trabajo parecido en mi empresa actual,
   pero la empresa es pequeña. Creo que hay más
   posibilidades en una empresa más grande como ésta.
○ Explíqueme qué funciones tiene en su trabajo actual.
■ Soy el encargado de servicio al cliente. Trabajo con un
   equipo de quince personas. El trabajo que estoy haciendo
   es parecido al trabajo que ustedes ofrecen. Yo creo que
   tengo la experiencia adecuada.
○ ¿Cuáles son las cualidades que se necesitan para este
   puesto?
■ Creo que tengo motivación y experiencia. Estoy bien
   cualificado y tengo iniciativa.

VOCABULARY

interesado (en)	interested (in)
el puesto	position, post
actual	current
la posibilidad	possibility
el encargado/la encargada	person responsible
el servicio al cliente	client service
el equipo	team
ofrecer	to offer
la cualidad	quality
la motivación	motivation
cualificado	qualified
la iniciativa	initiative

✓ Present continuous tense

The present continuous describes an action taking place at the moment of speaking. It is formed with the present tense of the verb **estar** + a verb in the gerund. The gerund is made up of the stem of the verb + the endings **-ando** for **-ar** verbs, and **-iendo** for **-er** and **-ir** verbs.

Estoy cen<u>ando</u>/com<u>iendo</u>/viv<u>iendo</u>. I'm having supper/eating/living.
Estoy estudiando en la universidad. I'm studying at the university.

The following verbs do not normally appear in the present continuous: **ser, estar, ir, venir, volver.**

✓ The relative pronoun *que*

This is used in much the same way as the English 'which' or 'that'; unlike English, it must always be included.

El trabajo **que** estoy haciendo es parecido al trabajo **que** ustedes ofrecen. The job (that) I am doing is similar to the job (that) you are offering.

When it refers to a person, **que** is sometimes replaced by **quien**.

El equipo tiene un jugador **que / quien** es muy bueno. The team has a player who is very good.

ACTIVITY 8

Read the following text and write the numbered verbs in the simple present or present continuous form. Which of the verbs are describing a continuing action? Write these in the present continuous. Note that one of the verbs is in the future.

¡Hola! me llamo Pepe. (1 **Vivir**) en Madrid pero no tengo casa. Estos días (2 **vivir**) en la casa de unos amigos mientras están de vacaciones. No (3 **tener**) trabajo. Cada día (4 **ir**) a la oficina de empleo, (5 **comprar**) periódicos y (6 **leer**) los anuncios pero no hay nada. (7 **buscar**) trabajo. Si no (8 **encontrar**) nada (9 **volver**) a mi pueblo. Al mismo tiempo (10 **estudiar**) por las noches. (11 **Querer**) hacer unos exámenes importantes.

 Now do activities 9 and 10 on the recording.

13.3 I'm head of personnel
Soy jefe de personal

ACTIVITY 11 is on the recording.

ACTIVITY 12

1 List three things that information technology allows us to do which we couldn't do in the past.
2 What three questions does Jorge ask at the end?

DIALOGUE 3

○ Me llamo Jorge García. Soy jefe de personal del departamento de informática. Hoy voy a hablar de la influencia que tiene la informática en nuestras vidas. En la actualidad podemos comunicarnos con más rapidez y con más información que nunca. Dentro de unos años la capacidad de nuestros sistemas de informática crecerá mucho. Cuando yo empecé con esta compañía hace veinticinco años, mandábamos la información por correo. Hoy podemos ver la última información sin esperar y mandar mensajes a nuestros compañeros en un segundo. Podemos asistir a reuniones sin salir de la oficina. Estoy llevando a cabo un estudio sobre los efectos de la informática en nuestra vida profesional y hoy quisiera enseñarles los resultados. La cuestion es … ¿Cómo podemos manejar esta explosión de información? ¿La necesitamos? ¿La queremos?

VOCABULARY	
el departamento	department
la informática	information technology
hablar (de)	to talk (about)
la influencia	influence
con más rapidez que nunca	more rapidly than ever
crecer	to grow
llevar a cabo	to carry out
el efecto	effect
enseñar	to show, teach
el resultado	result
la cuestión	question
manejar	to manage, cope with
la explosión	explosion

✓ *sin* + infinitive

The preposition **sin** followed by the infinitive is used for the English construction 'without -ing':

Vemos la información **sin esperar**. We see the information without waiting.
He trabajado dieciocho horas **sin parar**. I worked 18 hours without stopping.

✓ Ways of expressing what you do

To say what you do, use **ser** with the name of your job:

Soy profesor. I'm a teacher.

Other ways of describing what you do are:

Trabajo por mi cuenta. I'm freelance/self-employed [*literally* I work for myself].
Estoy en paro desempleado/a. I'm unemployed.
Tengo mi propio negocio. I have my own business.
Trabajo media jornada. I work part-time.

ACTIVITY 13

Write about yourself in the same way Jorge presents himself. Introduce yourself, give your position, and say what you do and are going to do in the future.

ACTIVITY 14

1 Select the appropriate form of **de, de la, del, de los, de las** in the following sentences.

  1 Voy a hablar _____ efecto de la informática en nuestras vidas.
  2 El profesor habló _____ estudiantes _____ su clase.
  3 Hablaremos _____ vacaciones.
  4 Vamos a hablar _____ contaminación atmosférica.

2 Now complete these sentences using **sin** + an appropriate verb in the infinitive.

  1 I visited my family without seeing my sister.
  2 I worked all day without eating.
  3 I did my exams without studying.
  4 I'm in the office all day and never go out.

(🎧) Now do activities 15 and 16 on the recording.

13.4 Job advertisements

Anuncios de trabajo

ACTIVITY 17

Study the job advertisements from a Spanish newspaper and then answer the questions below.

1 Which post is in a hotel?
2 Which post is in the construction industry?
3 Which post is for a company which has been in the market for more than 10 years?
4 Which post has duties that involve covering all of Spain?
5 What three jobs require experience and knowledge of English?
6 Which job requires a knowledge of information technology?
7 Which jobs require a team leader?
8 Which job insists on a knowledge of written English?

❶

Somos la filial española de una de las empresas líderes europeas en la producción de baterías. Para nuestra expansión en la Península Ibérica, buscamos:
JEFE DE VENTAS PARA ESPAÑA
Se requiere una formación de técnico electrónico o ingeniero, y experiencia en dirección de un equipo de ventas.

❷

Importante Grupo Empresarial necesita
DIRECTOR HOTEL
para Hotel de Cuatro Estrellas en Extremadura
Se requiere: amplia experiencia; capacidad en dirección de equipos; inglés hablado y escrito.

❸

Empresa Multinacional de Ingeniería, Construcción y Mantenimiento
necesita
INGENIERO MECÁNICO SENIOR
Se requiere 10 años de experiencia; dominio del idioma inglés.

❹

> Organización Independiente de Control de Calidad
> en Construcción
> para su área de instalaciones
> necesita
> **INGENIERO TÉCNICO INDUSTRIAL**
> Se requiere
> • experiencia mínima de dos años en control de
>   calidad de instalaciones de edificación
> • conocimientos de inglés

❺

> Compañía líder en el sector de la información y
> gestión de Comercio Exterior con más de 10 años en
> el mercado, requiere
> **PROGRAMADORES**
> requisitos: licenciado (informática, física,
> matemáticas, o ingeniería)

ACTIVITY 18

1 On the left is a list of new words taken from the job
   advertisements. On the right are their English equivalents.
   First find the Spanish words in the advertisements, then
   match each one to the appropriate English translation.

filial	graduate
estrellas	fluency
amplia	leader
dominio	requirements
edificación	subsidiary
líder	stars
licenciado	wide
se requiere/requisitos	building

2 Now rewrite the advertisements in English for the
   companies who wish to recruit English speakers. It may be
   a bit of a challenge!

13.5 Un forastero en la ciudad

 VOY A QUEDARME AQUÍ
I'M GOING TO STAY HERE

Jorge explica más detalles de su negocio y de sus planes. Está buscando empleados.

el motivo	reason, motive
ponerse en contacto	to make contact
ir bien	to go well
la sucursal	branch [*of a company*]
la fábrica	factory
las conservas	canned food products
dirigir	to direct, to manage
con más frecuencia	more frequently
alguien	someone
pronto	soon

ACTIVITY 19

1 Give two reasons why Jorge will stay in Madrid.
2 What most surprises María?
3 Who owns the company in Granada and what position does Jorge hold?
4 Who will take over the work in Granada?
5 What qualities is Jorge looking for in the person he wishes to employ?
6 What does María want to do before anything else?

ACTIVITY 20

Five of the questions below come from the conversation. Which are they? Indicate who asks each question and give the relevant answer.

1 ¿Vas a volver a Granada?
2 ¿Vas a llevar a mi madre?
3 ¿Qué haces en Granada?
4 ¿Qué vas a hacer aquí?
5 ¿Quién va a dirigir la empresa de Granada?
6 ¿Quieres trabajar en mi empresa?
7 ¿Cuándo puedes empezar?
8 ¿Quieres llamar a tu madre?

Now look at the other questions and decide who might have asked them, María or Jorge. Supply a relevant answer from the story.

ACTIVITY 21

Below are some of the things Jorge tells María. Rewrite the text below as if you were María on the telephone to her mother, telling her the news.

Jorge   Voy a quedarme aquí. Quiero estar cerca de mi familia. En Granada, tengo mi propia empresa. Tengo bastante dinero. Estoy buscando un sitio para abrir una sucursal. Tengo un jefe muy bueno allí. Yo me quedo aquí. Necesito un jefe de personal para la compañía aquí en Madrid. Tú eres la persona adecuada.

María   Mamá, Jorge va a quedarse aquí. Quiere estar cerca de su familia ...

STORY TRANSCRIPT

María   ¿Qué vas a hacer? ¿Vas a volver a Granada? ¿Vas a llevar a mi madre?

Jorge   Voy a quedarme aquí. Quiero estar cerca de mi familia.

María   ¿Y tu trabajo?

Jorge   Estoy en Madrid por dos motivos. El primero es ponerme en contacto con vosotras. Pero hay otro motivo.

María   ¿Qué es?

Jorge   En Granada, tengo mi propia empresa. Va muy bien. Tengo bastante dinero. Estoy buscando un sitio para abrir una sucursal. Tengo el dinero. Y la empresa necesita crecer.

María   ¿Qué tipo de empresa es?

Jorge   Es una fábrica de conservas.

María   ¿Y la de Granada? ¿Quién va a dirigir la empresa de Granada?

Jorge   Tengo un jefe muy bueno allí. Yo me quedo aquí.

María   ¡Qué buena idea! Estoy muy contenta, después de tanto tiempo. Estoy contenta por mi madre. Podrás visitarla con más frecuencia.

Jorge   Además ... otra cosa. Necesito un jefe de personal para la compañía aquí en Madrid. Alguien que conoce Madrid. Alguien con experiencia.

María   Yo puedo ayudarte a buscar a alguien.

Jorge   Estoy buscando una persona bien cualificada, con iniciativa y motivación.

María   Bueno.

Jorge   No tengo que buscarla más. Tú eres la persona adecuada. ¿Quieres trabajar en mi empresa?

María   ¡Yo! Pues sí, me gustaría mucho.

Jorge   Estupendo. ¿Cuándo puedes empezar?

María   Pronto. Pero primero quiero llamar a mi madre.

Test

Now it's time to test your progress in Unit 13.

1 Put this jumbled telephone conversation in the correct order.

¿De parte de quién?
Gracias.
¿Dígame?
Un momento, por favor, ahora se pone.
¿Puedo hablar con la señora Gil por favor?
De nada.
Daniel Jiménez.

| 7 |

2 Make the following requests on the telephone in Spanish.

1 Ask if you can speak to Sr. García.
2 Ask someone if they can call back later.
3 Ask if you can leave a message.
4 Say you would like to change the time of an interview.
5 Ask someone if they can come to the office tomorrow.

| 10 |

3 Using formal imperatives, what do you say when:

1 you answer the telephone?
2 you want to attract someone's attention?
3 you want someone to look at something?
4 you give something to someone?
5 you are escorting someone into another office?
6 you want to apologize?

| 6 |

4 Complete each sentence with the appropriate word or phrase from the list below.

una entrevista	el encargado/la encargada	un recado
puesto	una empresa	
las cualidades	una reunión	

1 Soy _____ de la sección de control de calidad.
2 Trabajo para _____ de electrodomésticos.
3 ¿Por qué está usted interesado en este _____?

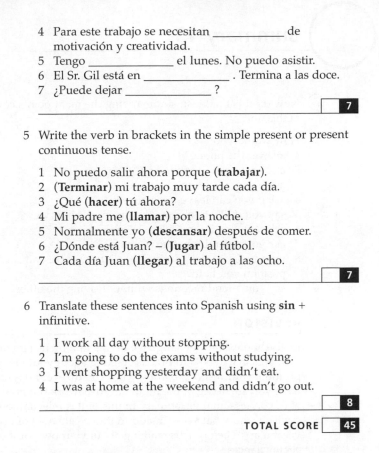

    4 Para este trabajo se necesitan _____ de
motivación y creatividad.

    5 Tengo _____ el lunes. No puedo asistir.

    6 El Sr. Gil está en _____ . Termina a las doce.

    7 ¿Puede dejar _____ ?

                  7

5 Write the verb in brackets in the simple present or present
continuous tense.

    1 No puedo salir ahora porque (**trabajar**).

    2 (**Terminar**) mi trabajo muy tarde cada día.

    3 ¿Qué (**hacer**) tú ahora?

    4 Mi padre me (**llamar**) por la noche.

    5 Normalmente yo (**descansar**) después de comer.

    6 ¿Dónde está Juan? – (**Jugar**) al fútbol.

    7 Cada día Juan (**llegar**) al trabajo a las ocho.

                  7

6 Translate these sentences into Spanish using **sin** +
infinitive.

    1 I work all day without stopping.

    2 I'm going to do the exams without studying.

    3 I went shopping yesterday and didn't eat.

    4 I was at home at the weekend and didn't go out.

                  8

TOTAL SCORE   **45**

If you scored less than 35, look at the Language Building
sections again before completing the Summary on page 194.

Summary 13

 Now try this final test, summarizing the main points covered
in this unit.

How would you:
1 answer the phone?
2 ask if you can speak to Sr. García?
3 ask if you can phone him later?
4 ask if you can leave a message?
5 say you'd like to change the day of the interview?
6 ask someone if they'd like to come this way?
7 ask your friend what he is doing?
8 introduce yourself; say you work for Nexus, and say what
   position you hold?
9 say you attend meetings without leaving the office?

REVISION

Revise and extend the language of this unit by using your
own personal details to practise talking about your job, your
position, your responsibilities, what you do every day, and
what you are doing at the moment. Also, work out how much
of the professional vocabulary in this unit is relevant to your
own job, and what you can add to it to create a set of useful
vocabulary. Then practise talking about your own professional
circumstances.

14

Health and fitness
La salud

OBJECTIVES

In this unit you'll learn how to:

- ✓ describe different kinds of sport and other activities
- ✓ describe illnesses and injuries
- ✓ give instructions

And cover the following grammar and language:

- ✓ the perfect tense
- ✓ the verbs **tener** and **doler** to describe how you feel
- ✓ irregular past participles
- ✓ reflexive verbs in the perfect tense
- ✓ the informal imperative
- ✓ the verb **deber** to express obligation

LEARNING SPANISH 14

Now you've completed the course, the most important thing is to consolidate what you have learned by practising as much as you can. You'll find several useful suggestions throughout the Learning Spanish sections at the beginning of each unit. There are two key elements in learning a language; one is your knowledge (vocabulary, tense, and verb forms) and the other is your ability to communicate fluently. There is no substitute for trying out your Spanish whenever you can. As you grow more comfortable with the language, the more you'll enjoy speaking Spanish and the more fluent you'll become.

Now start the recording for Unit 14.

I've got a temperature

Tengo fiebre

ACTIVITY 1 is on the recording.

ACTIVITY 2

Tick Carmen's symptoms. She says when 2 of them started.
Write this down, beginning **Empezó …**

la fiebre ☐	dolor de garganta		☐
la tos ☐	dolor de pecho		☐
la gripe ☐	inflamación de la garganta	☐

DIALOGUE 1

- ■ Tengo fiebre y me duele la garganta.
- ○ ¿Cuántos días ha estado así?
- ■ Desde el lunes con la fiebre, y la garganta desde el miércoles.
- ○ A ver … abra la boca, por favor … Sí, sí, está inflamada. ¿Tiene tos? ¿Le duele el pecho?
- ■ No, pero me siento muy mal.
- ○ Tiene gripe. Tiene que quedarse en la cama y tomar unas pastillas cada cuatro horas.
- ■ De acuerdo. ¿Puedo tomar algo para la garganta?
- ○ Sí, le voy a recetar un jarabe para el dolor de garganta. Pero lo importante es quedarse en la cama unos días.

VOCABULARY	
la fiebre	temperature, fever
doler (duele)	to hurt
la garganta	throat
la boca	mouth
inflamado	swollen, inflamed
la tos	cough
el pecho	chest
sentirse	to feel
la gripe	flu
la cama	bed
la pastilla	pill, tablet
recetar	to prescribe
el jarabe	syrup [*e.g., cough syrup*]
el dolor	pain

✓ The perfect tense

The perfect tense is used to describe events in the recent past, in much the same way as the English perfect tense ('I have finished', etc.). It is formed using the present of **haber** ('to have') + the past participle of the verb. The past participle is made up of the stem of the verb + the endings **-ado** for **-ar** verbs, and **-ido** for **-er** and **-ir** verbs. It does not vary in gender or number:

He trabajado mucho esta semana. I've worked a lot this week.
El taxi ha llegado ya. The taxi has just arrived.
Has estado en la cama. You've been in bed.
Ha vivido allí siempre. He/she has always lived there.

See the Grammar Summary page 235 for irregular past participles.

✓ Using *tener* and *doler* to describe how you feel

The verb **tener** is often used with a noun to describe how you feel. The definite article (**el, la, los, las**) is not normally used:

Tengo fiebre/tos. I've got a temperature/a cough.
Tengo dolor de cabeza/espalda. I've got a headache/backache.
Tengo frío. I'm cold.

The verb **doler** is used with an indirect object pronoun in the following way to describe symptoms:

Me duele la garganta. My throat hurts.
Te duelen los ojos. Your eyes hurt.

Note that **doler** behaves like **gustar** (see Unit 10). The ending is governed by the thing that hurts rather than the person(s) affected.

ACTIVITY 3

Put the verb in each sentence into the perfect tense.

1 Ayer trabajé mucho.
   Hoy _____.
2 El año pasado mi padre viajó a América.
   Este año _____ a América y Japón.
3 ¿Dónde cenaste ayer?
   ¿_____ esta noche?
4 ¿Dónde estuviste anoche?
   ¿_____ esta semana?

Now do activities 4 and 5 on the recording.

14.2 I've twisted my ankle
Me he torcido el tobillo

ACTIVITY 6 is on the recording.

ACTIVITY 7

1 Both Juan and the other player hurt themselves.   V/F
2 Juan has been in hospital.   V/F
3 The other player is in hospital.   V/F
4 Juan has twisted his knee.   V/F
5 Carmen tells Juan to lie on the bed to ease his ankle. V/F

DIALOGUE 2

○ ¿Qué te ha pasado?
■ Me he torcido el tobillo jugando al fútbol. Un choque con
  otro jugador. Él está en el hospital. Se ha roto la pierna.
  Tengo que ponerme esta pomada.
○ ¿De verdad? El fútbol puede ser muy peligroso.
■ También puedes hacerte daño con otros deportes.
○ Sí, tienes razón. ¡Pero el fútbol es peligroso para las
  piernas! Mi padre jugó durante muchos años y tuvo varias
  lesiones en las rodillas.
■ Pues me ha dicho el médico que no puedo jugar más en
  toda la temporada. ¡Ah! Me duele mucho el tobillo.
○ Levanta la pierna y ponla encima de esta silla.

VOCABULARY	
torcer	to twist
la pomada	ointment
el choque	collision, crash
el jugador/la jugadora	player
romper	to break
la pierna	leg
peligroso	dangerous
hacerse daño	to hurt oneself
la lesión	injury
la rodilla	knee
el médico	doctor
la temporada	(sports) season
encima de	on top of
la silla	chair

✓ Irregular past participles

The following verbs have irregular past participles:

hacer	**hecho** ('done')	romper	**roto** ('broken')
ver	**visto** ('seen')	decir	**dicho** ('said')
poner	**puesto** ('put')	escribir	**escrito** ('written')

✓ Describing injuries using reflexive verbs

To describe an injury, the relevant reflexive verb is used in the perfect tense.
The pronoun comes before **haber**:

> ¿Qué <u>te</u> ha pasado? What has happened to you?
> <u>Me</u> he roto la pierna. I've broken my leg.
> <u>Se</u> ha hecho daño. He has hurt himself.

To say you've hurt a specific part of your body, use the preposition **en**:

> Me he hecho daño **en** la espalda/**en** las piernas. I've hurt my back/legs.
> [*literally* I've hurt myself in the back/legs.]

✓ Informal imperative

For regular verbs the singular informal imperative has the same form as the third person singular. The plural is formed by adding **d** to -**ar** and -**er** verbs. For -**ir** verbs the **e** of the singular is replaced by **id**:

[sing.]	*[pl.]*	
Levanta los brazos.	**Levantad los brazos.**	Raise your arms.
Come.	**Comed.**	Eat (your dinner).
Abre la puerta.	**Abrid las puertas.**	Open the door(s).

The most common irregular verbs used in the imperative form are: **ven**, **venid** ('come'); **haz**, **haced** ('do'); **pon**, **poned** ('put').

ACTIVITY 8

What a day! Write a postcard to your best friend from your holiday apartment:

You've had a terrible day. You have twisted your ankle playing football on the beach, you have got sunburnt, your head aches, and you have a sore throat. The doctor has told you to stay in the apartment for the rest of the holiday and not to play football any more on the beach. You want to go home.

 Now do activities 9 and 10 on the recording.

14.3 You have to lose weight
Tienes que adelgazar

ACTIVITY 11 is on the recording.

ACTIVITY 12

Which of these apply to Antonio and which don't?

1 tiene energía
2 quiere descansar
3 trabaja demasiado
4 hace deporte
5 come mal
6 fuma
7 adelgaza

DIALOGUE 3

○ No sé qué me pasa. No tengo energía. Sólo quiero descansar.

■ Tu problema es que trabajas demasiado, no haces deporte, comes mal.

○ Sí, tienes razón. Pero he dejado de fumar y me encuentro mejor.

■ Muy bien, pero debes comer menos carne y más verduras.

○ Y beber más zumos y menos vino y cerveza.

■ Exactamente. Y debes hacer ejercicio. Tienes que adelgazar.

○ Sí, tengo que perder peso. Pero juego al tenis.

■ Juegas al tenis una vez a la semana con tu hermano. Eso no es deporte. Tienes que entrenar, dos o tres veces a la semana. Ven conmigo al club.

○ No sé si tengo tiempo.

■ No quiero excusas. Tienes que hacer ejercicio.

○ Bueno. ¿Quieres salir a tomar una pizza?

VOCABULARY	
adelgazar	to slim
la energía	energy
demasiado	too much
mal	badly
fumar	to smoke
dejar de fumar	to give up smoking
encontrarse	to feel
deber	to have to
hacer ejercicio/deporte	to take exercise/to do a sport
perder peso	to lose weight
entrenar	to train

✓ *demasiado*

The adjective **demasiado** agrees in gender and number with the noun it describes. It generally comes in front of the noun:

Como **demasiada carne**. I eat too much meat.
Bebe **demasiado alcohol**. He drinks too much alcohol.
Hay **demasiados coches**. There are too many cars.
Están construyendo **demasiadas casas** en esta zona. They're building too many houses in this area.

Used as an adverb, **demasiado** means 'too much' or 'too hard' and its form doesn't change: **trabajas demasiado** ('you work too hard').

✓ *deber*

To express an obligation or to offer advice, the verb **deber**, followed by the infinitive, is used:

Debes comer menos carne. You should eat less meat.
No **debes fumar**. You shouldn't smoke.
Debe adelgazar. He should lose weight.

✓ *dejar de* + infinitive

dejar de followed by the infinitive is used to say you have stopped or given up doing something:

He **dejado de fumar**. I've given up smoking.
Voy a **dejar de jugar** al tenis. I'm going to give up playing tennis.

ACTIVITY 13

Form sentences by matching up the verbs 1–5 with the correct phrase from a–e.

1 Trabajas   a demasiada cerveza
2 Como   b más fruta
3 Bebe   c demasiado
4 Debes comer   d demasiadas patatas
5 Debe   e adelgazar

ACTIVITY 14

Make sentences to describe three things that you do, but which you shouldn't; three things you don't do which you should; and three things you have given up doing over the last few years. Use your dictionary if necessary, and invent if you have to!

 Now do activities 15 and 16 on the recording.

(14.4) Holiday sports
Deportes de vacaciones

ACTIVITY 17

Below is some information on six of the most popular holiday and beach sports in Spain.

1 Find the Spanish equivalent for each sport in this list.

frisbee   kite flying   hiking
pedal boat   beach volleyball   beach tennis

2 What do you think the following words mean in English?
  Try to work them out from the context, and then use your dictionary to check.

a beneficios   e el brazo   i la mano
b volar   f las lesiones   j el estrés
c los reflejos   g el codo   k la torcedura
d fortalecer   h la muñeca   l la ampolla

3 Which of the following sport(s) …
  1 strengthens your arms?
  2 could get you lost and give you blisters?
  3 improves your reflexes?
  4 is great for your heart but watch out for sunburn?
  5 could hurt your fingers?
  6 is a great antidote to stress?

PALAS

El deporte playero más divertido y fácil de practicar. Parecido al tenis pero más sencillo. Unas palas de madera y una pelota. Beneficios: mejora la forma física general, la capacidad de reflejos, la coordinación, y la potencia de los brazos. Peligros: lesiones de codo.

PATINETE DE PLAYA

Una de las actividades veraniegas más practicadas. Beneficios: fortalece las piernas y aumenta la capacidad cardiovascular. Peligros: las quemaduras del sol; hay que llevar crema.

LAS COMETAS

Esta divertida manera de jugar con las posibilidades del viento te permite fortalecer los músculos de las manos y de los pies. Beneficios: coordinación y equilibrio. Excelente antídoto contra el estrés. Ejercita los músculos de las manos y de los brazos. Peligros: lesiones en manos y codos.

DISCO VOLADOR

El disco volador se ha convertido en una imagen habitual en todas las playas del país. Un sencillo disco de plástico volando por las playas. Beneficios: actividad relajante, mejora los reflejos, fortalece piernas y brazos. Peligros: se pueden producir lesiones en los codos y las muñecas.

VOLEIPLAYA

Uno de los deportes que más se practica en las costas. Uno de los juegos que forman parte del programa de las Olimpiadas de verano. Beneficios: mejora la forma física general, los reflejos y la flexibilidad. Fortalece los músculos de las piernas y la capacidad cardiovascular. Peligros: lesiones de dedos de las manos y muñecas.

EXCURSIONISMO

Pasear por el campo, hacer excursiones es algo que todos hemos practicado alguna vez. Es la actividad deportiva más popular en España. Beneficios: mejora la capacidad cardiovascular y la forma física en general. Es bueno para el estrés y fortalece las piernas. Peligros: torceduras de tobillos y ampollas en los pies; la posibilidad de perderse.

mejorar	to improve
el deporte playero	beach sport
la madera	wood
la pelota	ball
la potencia	strength
el equilibrio	balance
los dedos de las manos	fingers
veraniego	summer [*adjective*]
quemaduras del sol	sunburn
algo que …	something that …
la actividad deportiva	sporting activity

LA FAMILIA
THE FAMILY

María invita a Jorge a cenar con ella y su madre. Por fin la familia está reunida.

el champán	champagne
la ayuda	help
el sitio	room, space
ganar	to earn
el edificio	building

ACTIVITY 18

1 ¿Por qué están contentos?
2 ¿Dónde están?
3 ¿Por qué vivirá la madre en el piso de María?
4 ¿Cuántos dormitorios tiene María en el piso?
5 Podrán cambiarse a otro piso si no hay sitio. ¿Cómo?
6 Jorge encontró dos cosas ayer. ¿Cuáles son?
7 ¿Cuándo abrirá la empresa?
8 ¿Por qué estaba triste Jorge?

ACTIVITY 19

Supply the appropriate response from the dialogue, without looking at the transcript.

María Mamá, te vas a quedar aquí conmigo. ¿De acuerdo?
Madre Sí, hija. Quiero _____. ¿Pero tienes sitio?
María Sí, tengo _____.
       ¿Dónde vivirás?
Jorge He encontrado _____.
María ¿Cuándo vamos a empezar?
Jorge _____.

ACTIVITY 20

These phrases are in the order they appear in the story. Rearrange them into chronological order from the past to the future.

1 Aquí estamos los tres.
2 Vamos a abrir el champán.
3 He decidido que no debes vivir sola.
4 Te vas a quedar aquí conmigo.
5 Ganaré más dinero en mi nuevo puesto.
6 Encontré un edificio.
7 Podremos empezar dentro de seis meses.
8 Tendré que hablar con mi jefe pronto.
9 Os dejé hace muchos años.

ACTIVITY 21

Listen to the story again and, without reading the transcript, write sentences about what happened in this episode using the following time expressions:

ayer / dentro de seis meses / pronto / hace muchos años / ahora / hoy

Example: Ayer Jorge encontró un edificio muy bueno para la empresa.

STORY TRANSCRIPT

María	Bueno. Aquí estamos los tres. No sé qué decir. Estoy muy contenta.
Jorge	Yo también. Vamos a abrir el champán.
María	Mamá, he decidido que no debes vivir sola en el pueblo. Estás enferma y necesitas ayuda. Te vas a quedar aquí conmigo. ¿De acuerdo?
Madre	Sí, hija. Quiero estar con mi familia. ¿Pero tienes sitio aquí?
María	Sí, mamá. Tengo dos dormitorios. Si queremos un piso más grande podemos cambiarnos. Ganaré más dinero en mi nuevo puesto. Papá, ¿has encontrado un sitio para la empresa?
Jorge	Sí, ayer encontré un edificio muy bueno para la empresa.
María	¿Dónde vivirás?
Jorge	He encontrado un apartamento muy cerca de aquí. Lo encontré ayer.
María	¡Qué bien! ¿Cuándo vamos a empezar?
Jorge	Yo creo que podremos empezar dentro de seis meses. ¿Qué te parece?
María	Me parece muy bien. Tendré que hablar con mi jefe pronto.
Jorge	Tengo que deciros una cosa. Os dejé hace muchos años. Estuve muy triste durante muchos años. Os echaba de menos pero no podía volver. Pero ahora estoy aquí y voy a quedarme.
María	Hoy ha sido un día muy especial.

Now it's time to test your progress in Unit 14.

1 Describe how you feel using **me duele(n)** or **tengo**.

   1 You have a headache.
   2 You have a temperature.
   3 Your eyes hurt.
   4 You have a pain in your chest.
   5 Your throat hurts.
   6 You have a cough.
   7 Your arms ache.
   8 You have a pain in your back.

16

2 Now say that you feel:

   1 well   4 ill
   2 bad   5 terrible
   3 very well

5

3 Say you have to take the following remedies, beginning
each sentence with **tengo que tomar/ponerme**.

   1 some ointment   3 some aspirin
   2 some pills   4 cough syrup

4

4 Perfect or simple past? Insert the correct form of the verb.

   1 (**Trabajar**) mucho la semana pasada pero no (**trabajar**)
     mucho esta semana.
   2 (**Viajar**) mucho en mi vida. El año pasado (**viajar**) a
     Australia.
   3 (**Vivir**) siempre en esta casa.
   4 ¡Mira! El tren (**llegar**). ¿Cuándo (**llegar**)?
   5 ¡Oh no! Creo que (**perder**) las llaves de la casa.

8

5   ¿Qué te ha pasado? Translate these sentences using the perfect of the appropriate reflexive verb.

    1   I've twisted my ankle.   4   He's hurt his head.
    2   I've hurt my knee.   5   She's burnt herself.
    3   He's broken his leg.

| 10 |

6   Insert the correct form of the informal imperative.

    1   ¡Hola! ¿Qué tal? (**pasar**)
    2   (**Abrir**) la puerta, por favor.
    3   (**Hacer**) los deberes ahora mismo.
    4   Vamos a comer; (**poner**) la mesa.

Now insert the correct form of the formal imperative.

    1   (**Pasar**) por aquí.
    2   (**Levantar**) los pies.
    3   (**Venir**) aquí.
    4   (**Seguir**) esta calle.

| 8 |

7   ¿**Demasiado/a/os/as?** Complete the sentences with the appropriate form of the word.

    1   Trabajo _____.
    2   Bebe _____ alcohol.
    3   Veo la televisión _____.
    4   Siempre está en el sofá. Descansa _____.
    5   Fumas _____ cigarillos.
    6   No come verdura. Come _____ carne.
    7   Estás muy gordo. Comes _____.
    8   Comes _____ patatas.

| 8 |

8   Now give appropriate advice for each sentence in Activity 7, using the correct form of **deber**. For 1 and 8 use the informal form; for 2–7, use the formal.

| 8 |

TOTAL SCORE  | 67 |

If you scored less than 57, look at the Language Building sections again before completing the Summary on page 208.

Summary 14

 Now try this final test, summarizing the main points covered in this unit.

How would you:
1 ask someone you don't know well what the matter is?
2 say you have a temperature?
3 say you have a headache?
4 say you feel terrible?
5 say you have been ill?
6 say you have worked a lot this week?
7 say you've hurt your foot?
8 tell a friend to open the door?
9 tell your friend she shouldn't smoke?
10 tell her you've given up smoking?

REVISION

Now that you've completed this course, go back over all the units and read through the revision notes for each one. In this way you will remind yourself of things you may have forgotten. Practise structures and vocabulary you are less confident about. Develop the subject matter of the earlier units in the light of what you now know.

Constantly practise verb forms and recycle vocabulary every day. Develop your vocabulary by actively adding to your word store. Use a dictionary and make sure you learn the words by using them appropriately. Get hold of articles, newspapers, and books in Spanish and build your vocabulary in this way too. Most important, try to gain the opportunity to speak to Spanish people. The sooner you use your Spanish in real situations the faster it will develop.

Review 4

1 Write the Spanish for the following reflexive verbs.

    1 to get tired   6 to worry
    2 to bathe   7 to enjoy oneself
    3 to get bored   8 to stay
    4 to get burnt   9 to feel
    5 to remember   10 to hurt oneself

2 Complete the story using the following items of vocabulary, giving the correct forms as necessary.

camping / barco / costa / barbacoa / jardín / estupenda

Estuve en un 1_____ durante el verano. Estuvimos en la 2_____. Un día fui de excursión en un 3_____ . Otro día me quedé en el camping y preparé carne para una 4_____ en el 5_____ de un amigo. ¡Fue una comida 6_____!

3 Match the complaints on the left with the appropriate remedy on the right.

    1 la espalda quemada   a pastillas
    2 dolor de cabeza   b una pomada
    3 una tos   c un jarabe

4 What is the Spanish for the following phrases?

    1 You're right. [*informal sing.*]
    2 To miss someone.
    3 It's worth it.
    4 To begin with.

GRAMMAR AND USAGE

5 Give the Spanish for the following.

1 I returned.
2 He was in Alicante.
3 What did they do?
4 We went to the beach.
5 They bought a house in the city.

6 Write three sentences describing good weather and three sentences describing bad weather.

7 Answer the following questions about yourself using **hace** + time period. **¿Cuánto hace que ...**

1 viste la televisión?
2 fuiste de vacaciones?
3 te cambiaste de casa?
4 comiste?
5 te duchaste?

8 Choose the imperfect or simple past to complete these sentences.

1 (**Jugar**) al futbol cada domingo. (Yo)
2 (**Comprar**) la camisa ayer. (Yo)
3 Cuando yo (**ser**) pequeño mi padre (**viajar**) mucho.
4 Nosotros (**vivir**) en esta casa hace muchos años.
5 (**Tener**) fiebre la semana pasada. (Yo)

9 Put the verbs in brackets into the imperative.

1 (**Pasar**) por aquí. (usted)
2 (**Abrir**) la puerta. (tú)
3 (**Poner**) la mesa. (vosotros)
4 (**Levantar**) el pie. (tú)
5 (**Decir**). (usted) [*on the telephone*]

10 Say what these people are doing, using the present continuous.

1 Yo (**estudiar**).
2 Ellos (**comer**).
3 Nosotros (**viajar**) a Madrid.
4 Vosotros (**terminar**) el trabajo.
5 Tú (**vivir**) con un amigo.

11 **¿Qué te ha pasado?** Say what happened using the perfect.

1 (**Torcer**) el tobillo.
2 (**Hacer daño**) en el pie.
3 (**Romper**) el brazo.
4 (**Quemar**) la espalda.

12 Listen to the conversation. What are Antonio and Beatriz doing?

  1 Esta tarde
  2 A las siete
  3 Esta noche
  4 El mes que viene

13 Listen to these phone conversations and answer the questions. Who …

  1 is coming to the phone?
  2 will ring later?
  3 is on holiday?
  4 can't come to the phone?
  5 is in a meeting?
  6 leaves a message; what is it?

SPEAKING

14 Complete your side of the conversation and then check against the recording.

  A: ¡Qué moreno estás!
  You: (Say you've been on holiday.)
  A: ¿Adónde fuiste?
  You: (You went to Alicante.)
  A: ¿Estuviste en un camping?
  You: (You were in your parents' apartment.)
  A: ¿Con quién fuiste?
  You: (You went with some friends.)
  A: ¿Te gusta bañarte?
  You: (Yes, you do, but you also like to visit towns and villages.)
  A: ¿Qué tiempo hizo?
  You: (It was sunny every day except Saturday, when it rained all day.)
  A: ¿Qué hiciste por las noches?
  You: (You danced and enjoyed yourself.)

15 Now answer these questions about yourself using the future or **voy** + **a** + infinitive.

1 ¿Qué harás esta noche?
2 ¿A qué hora te acostarás esta noche?
3 ¿Qué vas a hacer este fin de semana?
4 ¿Tienes planes para el año que viene?
5 ¿Qué vas a hacer la semana que viene?

16 Complete your side of the telephone conversation and then check your answers on the recording.

A: ¿Dígame?
You: (You want to speak to Sr. Solano.)
A: No está. Está de viaje.
You: (Ask when he will be back.)
A: El jueves.
You: (Ask if you can leave a message.)
A: Sí. Un momento. Dígame.
You: (The message is that you called and that you cannot attend a meeting on Friday. Can you change it?)
A: Yo la puedo cambiar. ¿Qué día le va bien?
You: (Suggest next Tuesday.)
A: ¿A qué hora?
You: (Suggest 10 o'clock.)
A: Muy bien.
You: (Say see you on Tuesday.)

Answers

Unit 1

2 1 c; 2 a; 3 b

3 1 usted; 2 tú; 3 usted; 4 tú; 5 usted

7 1 F: they take place in the morning; 2 F; 3 T; 4 F: he asks her what her name is

8 1 c; 2 a; 3 b

12 *María*: zumo de naranja; *Juan*: café con leche, bocadillo de queso

13 1 Un bocadillo de jamón y un bocadillo de queso. 2 Un zumo de manzana y un café.

14 1 d; 2 a; 3 e; 4 f; 5 b; 6 c

17 *Drinks*: café solo, Coca cola, café con leche, limonada, té solo, zumo de tomate, té con limón, té con leche; *Food*: ensalada, pizza, espaguetis, tarta de chocolate, bocadillo de jamón, hamburguesa
María: Quiero la tarta de chocolate y un café solo. *Juan*: Para mí una Coca cola y una ensalada. *Miguel*: Un café con leche/un té con leche y espaguetis, por favor.

18 3, 2, 6, 1, 4, 5

19 1 M; 2 E; 3 S; 4 E; 5 S

Test

1 1 i; 2f; 3h; 4b; 5a; 6d; 7e; 8 c; 9 g

2 1 Un café con leche y una tapa.
2 Un bocadillo de queso y una cerveza.
3 Un zumo de tomate y una ensalada.
4 Un café solo y un bocadillo de jamón.

3 1 ¿Es usted; 2 soy; 3 ¡Encantado! 4 ¡Mucho gusto! 5¿Cómo está (usted)? 6 Bien

4 1 ¿Es usted la Sra. Martín? 2 ¿Cómo está usted? 3 ¡Buenos días! 4 Esta es la Sra. Martín. 5 Quiero un café con leche.

5 1 Quiero un té con limón. 2 Sí. Quiero un bocadillo de jamón y una ensalada. 3 Nada más, gracias.

6 1 la señora; 2 la señorita; 3 el camarero; 4 la camarera; 5 el amigo

Summary 1

1 Buenos días, Buenas tardes, Buenas noches. *2* ¿Cómo está usted? *3* ¿Cómo estás? ¿Qué tal estás? *4* Muy bien, gracias. *5* Esta es la Sra. Martín. *6* Encantado/Encantada/Mucho gusto. *7* Quiero un café con leche y un zumo de naranja, por favor. *8* Gracias.

Unit 2

2 *the cathedral*: in a square; 5 minutes away
Goya's house: in a village; 15 minutes away

6 1 T; 2 F: it's at the end of avenida Goya on the left; 3 F: it's the third house on the left; 4 T

7 1 d; 2 c; 3 a; 4 b

11 1 A supermarket; B bank; C restaurant; D hospital

12 1 e; 2 a; 3 d; 4 g; 5 f; 6 c; 7 h; 8 b

13 1 a ¿Hay un banco por aquí? b ¿Hay un hotel por aquí? c ¿Hay un supermercado por aquí? 2 ¿Dónde está la estación? ¿Dónde está el restaurante?

16 2 Basílica del Pilar: 17th and 18th centuries. 3 Museo Pablo Gargallo/Palacio de los Argillo: no century given. 4 Palacio de Sástago: 16th century. 5 Casino Mercantil: 20th century.

17 1 Siga recto por la calle Alfonso. Está al final de la calle. 2 La primera a la izquierda y la segunda a la izquierda. Está al final de la calle. 3. Siga recto por la Plaza del Pilar.

18 1 Basilica del Pilar; 2 El Casino Mercantil; 3 Museo Pablo Gargallo/Palacio de los Argillo

19 3, 1, 4, 6, 2, 5

20 1 F: el hotel está cerca; 2 V; 3 V; 4 F: la biblioteca está cerca de la casa de María; 5 V

21 1 ¿Hay periódicos antiguos? Sí. 2 ¿Cómo se llama? Se llama el hotel de la Estación. 3 ¿Hay una sección de periódicos? Sí, hay. 4 ¿Hay un hotel por aquí? Sí, hay un hotel muy cerca. 5 ¿Dónde está la biblioteca municipal? Está cerca de la casa de María. 6 Usted conoce a María, ¿no? No. 7 ¿Dónde está? Está aquí. A la derecha. 8 ¿Aquí? Sí, aquí, enfrente de la oficina.

Test

1 1 g; 2 h; 3 e; 4 b; 5 c; 6 f; 7 d; 8 a

2 1 La segunda a la derecha y todo recto al final de la calle. 2 La tercera calle a la izquierda y está a la derecha. 3 Todo recto al final de la calle, a la izquierda y está a la izquierda. 4 La primera a la derecha, la segunda a la izquierda y está a la derecha.

3 1 favor; 2 ¿Hay; 3 aquí; 4 final; 5 primera/segunda/tercera; 6 ¿dónde; 7 lado; 8 Está; 9 a

4 1 dieciséis; 2 diecisiete; 3 siete; 4 veinte; 5 trece; 6 tres; 7 once; 8 doce; 9 cinco; 10 ocho

5 Está en la plaza de España.
   Está a cinco minutos en el autobús.
   Catorce./El número catorce.
   La primera (calle) a la izquierda.
6 1 las casas; 2 los melones; 3 los pasteles;
   4 los tomates; 5 las plazas

Summary 2

1 ¿Hay un museo por aquí? 2 ¿Dónde está
el banco? 3 ¿Dónde está la avenida Goya?
4 La catedral está a diez minutos. 5 Bilbao
está en el norte de España. 6 Es la segunda
(calle) a la izquierda. 7 Todo recto al final
de la calle. 8 El hotel está enfrente de la
estación.

Unit 3

2 potatoes – a kilo; onions – two kilos;
   tomatoes – half a kilo; cheese – 100
   grammes; oil – a litre; wine – 2 bottles
3 tomates – lata; cebollas – kilo; queso – cien
   gramos; zumo de naranja – botella;
   patatas fritas – paquete; aceite – litro
7 1 F: it costs 70 cents; 2 T; 3 F: he buys a
   large envelope; 4 T; 5 T
8 1 grande; 2 más; 3 cuesta; 4 para; 5 Deme;
   6 cuánto; 7 Son; 8 mandar
12 1 un melón; 2 una piña; 3 dos piñas; 4 la
   sandía
13 1 **Las patatas fritas. Las** quiero; *or* Un
   paquete de patatas fritas. Lo quiero.
   2 **Una lata de sardinas. La** quiero. 3 **Un
   litro de aceite. Lo** quiero. 4 **Dos botellas de
   vino. Las** quiero. 5 **Jamón. Lo** quiero.
   6 **Sellos. Los** quiero.
16 *la carnicería*: **la carne,** meat; **las salchichas,**
   sausages; **el cordero,** lamb; **el cerdo,** pork
   la frutería: **la fruta,** fruit; **las naranjas,**
   oranges; **las fresas,** strawberries; **los
   melones,** melons
   la verdulería: **la verdura,** vegetables; **las
   patatas,** potatoes; **las cebollas,** onions; **las
   zanahorias,** carrots
   la charcutería: **el jamón serrano,** smoked
   ham; **el chorizo,** spicy sausage
   la pastelería and la panadería: **los
   pasteles,** cakes; **las galletas,** biscuits; **el
   pan,** bread
   la pescadería: **el pescado,** fish; **las sardinas,**
   sardines; **la merluza,** hake
17 **Across:** 1 SALCHICHAS, 2 CARNICERIA, 3
   PUESTO, 4 SAL, 5 ACEITE, 6 AZUCAR
   Down: 1 PAN, 2 MERLUZA, 3 VINO, 4
   CORDERO, 5 PANADERIA, 6 PASTEL
18 1 María; 2 María; 3 the stranger; 4 the
   stranger; 5 the stranger knows María;
   6 the stranger
19 1 M; 2 F; 3 M; 4 F; 5 S; 6 P
20 1 ¿Qué tal? 2 ¿Qué quería? 3 ¿Quiere algo
   más? 4 ¿Me conoce? 5 ¿Cuánto cuesta?

Test

1 1 g; 2 c; 3 f; 4 a; 5 b; 6 g; 7 e; 8 d; 9 f; 10 a
2 1 Quiero dos kilos de patatas y medio kilo
   de cebollas. 2 Quiero un litro de vino y
   una lata de aceite. 3 Quiero cien gramos
   de jamón y doscientos gramos de queso.
   4 Quiero dos paquetes de patatas fritas y
   una caja de galletas. 5 Quiero cuatro
   postales y cinco sellos para el Reino Unido.
3 1 dieciocho; 2 veintisiete; 3 treinta y cinco;
   4 cincuenta y nueve; 5 cien; 6 doscientos
   cincuenta; 7 quinientos; 8 trescientos
   setenta; 9 cuatrocientos cuarenta; 10
   noventa y nueve
4 1 la charcutería, delicatessen; 2 la
   charcutería, delicatessen; 3 la carnicería,
   butcher's; 4 la frutería, fruit shop; 5 la
   verdulería, greengrocer's; 6 la pescadería,
   fishmonger's; 7 el puesto de comestibles,
   grocer's; 8 la frutería, fruit shop; 9 la
   pastelería, cake and pastry shop; 10 la
   panadería, baker's
5 ¿Cuánto valen las sandías?
   Quiero dos.
   No. Las quiero pequeñas.
   Nada más. ¿Cuánto es?
6 1 Deme; 2 Oiga; 3 Siga; 4 Tome; 5 Mire

Summary 3

1 Quiero medio kilo de fresas. 2 Quiero un
paquete de patatas. 3 Quiero un litro de
leche. 4 (No quiero) nada más. 5 Quiero
dos botellas de vino. 6 ¿Cuánto vale un
sello para Inglaterra? 7 Vale dos euros
cincuenta. 8 Quiero cinco sobres.
9 Tenga.

Review 1

1 a: 1, 2, 6, 8; b: 5; c: 1, 3; d: 4, 7
2 un café con leche; un té con limón; un
   zumo de naranja; un bocadillo de queso;
   una tarta de chocolate
3 1 c; 2 e; 3 a; 4 b; 5 d
4 1 ✓ 2 ✗ 3 ✓ 4 ✓ 5 ✗
5 1 A; 2 B; 3 A; 4 A; 5 B
6 1 está; 2 Deme; 3 a, de, al; 4 Hay; 5 cuesta;
   6 Las
7 1 para; 2 del; 3 Es; 4 soy; 5 es
8 1 10 minutes; 2 left; 3 55; 4 a market; 5 a
   bank
9 B: ¿Tiene latas de sardinas [tomates]?
   B: Sí. Quiero cinco [cuatro].
   B: Sí. Deme dos kilos [un kilo] de naranjas.
   A: Dos euros treinta. ¿Quiere una?
   [¿**Quiere?**]
   A: Son ocho euros sesenta [cuatro euros
   sesenta] pesetas.
11 Mucho gusto. Soy …
   Estoy muy bien. ¿Y usted?
   Sí, gracias. ¿Hay un bar por aquí?
   Está en el norte de Inglaterra.
   No. Está a trescientos kilómetros de
   Londres.

Unit 4

2

	¿De dónde es?	¿Dónde vive?
Pepe García	España	España (Barcelona)
Margarita Herrero	México	México
Jorge Martínez	Argentina	España (Barcelona)
El hermano de Pepe García	España	México

3 1 estamos; 2 está; 3 trabajo; 4 estudia; 5 viajamos; 6 están; 7 cenamos; 8 Hablamos

7 1 bilingual secretary; 2 Carmen Soto; 3 Javier Montero; 4 next to Javier Montero; 5 Ana Vázquez; 6 two

8 1 escribimos; 2 llaman; 3 Hablamos; 4 conduzco; 5 salgo; 6 sale; 7 viven; 8 salimos

12 1 the 3rd floor; 2 1975; 3 329 5568; 4 12; 5 17

13 1 dos cuatro seis, ochenta y cinco, ochenta y tres; 2 Calle Monzón, veintiséis; 3 cero cero cuarenta y cuatro noventa y uno, dos tres ocho, noventa y nueve sesenta y tres; 4 Avenida de la Independencia, treinta y cinco; 5 cero uno ocho uno, dos cuatro cinco, cincuenta y cuatro, veintiocho; 6 Paseo de Goya, ciento cincuenta y tres

16 1 four/**cuatro**; 2 Castilian or Spanish/**el castellano o español**, Catalan/**el catalán**, Galician/**el gallego**, Basque/**el euskera o vasco**; 3 Latin/**el latín**; 4 two/**dos**; 5 in Majorca/**en Mallorca** and in Valencia/**en Valencia**; 6 Basque/**el vasco**; 7 Castilian/**el castellano**

17 1 culturas; 2 oficiales; 3 origen; 4 diferente; 5 catalán

18

English	Catalan	Spanish
a building	el banc	**el banco**
a word for goodbye	adéu	**adiós**
a large town	la ciutat	**la ciudad**
a family member	el pare	**el padre**
a vegetable	el tomàquet	**el tomate**
a number	vint-i-quatre	**veinticuatro**
a drink	café amb llet	**café con leche**
a verb	treballar	**trabajar**

19 1 V; 2 V; 3 F; 4 V; 5 F; 6 F; 7 V; 8 V

20 1 ¿Qué tal **está**? (d); 2 Usted conoce a María, ¿**verdad**? (e); 3 ¿De **dónde** es usted? (b); 4 ¿**En qué** trabaja María? (c); 5 ¿Vive **cerca**? (a)

21 1 Sr. España; 2 Jorge Jimeno; 3 María; 4 María; 5 Jorge Jimeno; 6 Jorge Jimeno; 7 María; 8 María

Test

1 1 **Ésta es la** señora Campos. Es **española**.
2 **Éste es** Jorge Ballesteros. Es mexicano.

3 **Ésta es la** señorita Tomás. Es **argentina**.
4 **Ésta es la** señora Deschamps. Es **francesa**.
5 **Éste es** Dieter Müller. Es **alemán**.
6 **Éste es** Peter Jones y **éste es** Barry Wright. **Son ingleses**.

2 1 llamo; 2 soy; 3 Vivo; 4 Trabajamos; 5 trabajo; 6 soy; 7 es; 8 estamos; 9 comemos; 10 vivimos

3 1 El señor Rodríguez **es profesor**. 2 La señorita Martín **es estudiante**. 3 El señor Ortega y la señora Sánchez **son ingenieros**. 4 La señora Serrano y la señorita Moreno **son secretarias**. 5 El señor Carrasco **es recepcionista**.

4 1 La calle Santa Engracia veinticinco. Teléfono: noventa y uno, cinco tres tres, doce, treinta y siete. 2 Avenida Diagonal ciento cuarenta y tres. Teléfono: noventa y tres, cuatro uno ocho, noventa y cinco, cincuenta y ocho. 3 Paseo de la Independencia setenta y seis. Teléfono: noventa y seis, tres cuatro ocho, sesenta y ocho, noventa y cuatro. 4 Carretera Cariñena noventa y siete Tercero G. Teléfono: nueve siete seis, veintinueve, noventa y dos, setenta y ocho. 5 Plaza España quince. Teléfono: noventa y dos, cuatro cinco seis, treinta y dos, ochenta y cuatro.

5 Buenos días. Soy (add your name). Soy representante de ventas. No. Soy (add your nationality), pero vivo y trabajo en Madrid. Vivo en la calle Castellana. Número diecisiete.

6 1 Trabaj**amos** en un banco. 2 ¿Com**éis** en un restaurante? 3 Vivo en una plaza. 4 Mis padres llam**an** por teléfono. 5 Él no conoce a María.

Summary 4

1 Ésta es la señora Martínez. *2* ¿Es usted argentino? *3* Vivo en Barcelona. *4* ¿Trabajan en Francia? *5* Comemos en un restaurante. *6* Soy profesor/a. *7* ¿Son conductores? *8* Conozco a María. *9* Viven en la calle Rosas, número ochenta y seis. *10* Mi número de teléfono es tres uno ocho, sesenta y cinco, ochenta y tres.

Unit 5

2 Oscar es **el marido** de Margarita. Margarita es **la mujer** de Oscar. Pablo es **el hijo** de Margarita. **El padre** de Pepe es **el abuelo** de Carmen. Carmen es **la hermana** de José.

3 a cuántos; b cuántos; c cuántas; d Mi; e Su; f tu

7 1 M; 2 P; 3 M; 4 M; 5 P; 6 P

8 1 pequeño; 2 moderno; 3 bonitas; 4 ancha; 5 antiguos

12 1 V; 2 F: es para tres noches; 3 V; 4 V; 5 F: está en el segundo piso

13 a el treinta y uno de marzo. b el tres de junio. c el diez de noviembre. d el doce de diciembre. e el veintitrés de mayo. f el cinco de septiembre
16 a 5; b 8; c 4; d 1; e 2; f 3; g 7; h 6
17 1 He's looking for an article about María. 2 He asks her for a photocopy of the article. 3 His friend is staying at another hotel. 4 Because it is quiet. 5 Because he wants to see the street. 6 He can see María's house.
18 5, 4, 3, 1, 2
19 1 V; 2 F; 3 F: dos o tres noches; 4 V; 5 F; 6 V; 7 F

Test

1 1 Tengo tres hermanos y una hermana. 2 Tengo dos hijos, un niño de ocho años y una niña de seis años. 3 Mi padre tiene sesenta años y mi madre tiene cincuenta y ocho años. 4 Estoy casado y mi mujer se llama Josefina./Estoy casada y mi marido se llama José.
2 1 e; 2 d; 3 a; 4 b; 5 c
3 1 el abuelo; 2 el tío; 3 el hermano; 4 el hijo; 5 la hermana; 6 el padre; 7 la madre; 8 la abuela
4 1 para; 2 por; 3 por; 4 por; 5 para; 6 por
5 1 Una habitación doble para tres noches. 2 Quiero una habitación para el catorce de febrero. 3 ¿Cuánto es? 4 ¿Está en el tercer piso? 5 Tengo equipaje.
6 1 el veintitrés de junio; 2 el trece de febrero; 3 el diecinueve de septiembre; 4 el treinta de julio; 5 el uno/el primero de mayo

Summary 5

1 ¿Está usted casada? *2* Tengo tres hijos. *3* ¡Qué guapa! *4* Tiene tres años. *5* María es la hermana de José. *6* ¿Cuántos años tiene María? *7* ¿Cómo es su piso? *8* Es un piso/un apartamento grande en el centro de la ciudad. *9* Tiene una vista muy bonita. *10* Quiero una habitación doble para tres noches.

Unit 6

2 1 accountant; 2 furniture shop; 3 5 p.m.; 4 2 hours
3 1 a Son las diez. b Son las once y media. c Son las tres. d Son las seis y media. 2 a Soy representante de ventas. b Trabajo en una empresa de muebles. c Soy jefe de personal. d Trabajo en una tienda de comestibles. 3 a de diez a una y de cuatro a siete; b de nueve a cinco; c de nueve a una y de cuatro a ocho; d de dos a diez
7 1 a las siete de la mañana; 2 a las ocho de la mañana; 3 a las ocho y media 4 a las ocho de la tarde; 5 a las nueve y media; 6 a las doce menos cuarto de la noche o a las once y media

8 Pepe se levanta a las siete y trabaja de las nueve y cuarto a la una y cuarto. Come a las dos y vuelve a trabajar a las cuatro. Trabaja hasta las ocho menos cuarto. Se acuesta a las once y media.
12 a La película empieza a las siete y cuarto. b La película termina a las nueve. c El museo abre a las diez de la mañana.
13 *Suggested answers*: 1 La Máscara del Zorro empieza a las cinco/las siete y media/las diez. La Máscara del Zorro termina a las siete/las nueve y media/las doce. La Máscara del Zorro dura dos horas. 2 La pastelería abre a las nueve y media. La pastelería cierra a la una y media. La pastelería abre a las cuatro y media de la tarde. La pastelería cierra a las ocho de la tarde. 3 El museo está cerrado los lunes. El museo abre a las diez. El museo cierra a las siete. El museo abre a las once los domingos. El museo cierra a las cinco los domingos.
14 A: ¿Quieres ir al cine esta tarde? B: ¿A qué hora empieza la película? A: Empieza a las siete y termina a las nueve. B: Cenamos después.
17 1 Se levanta a las seis y media. 2 Toma un café. 3 Come en casa. 4 Cena a las nueve y media. 5 Da un paseo. Come con la familia.
19 *Horizontal*: TORTILLA, MAGDALENA, ZUMO, SOBREMESA *Vertical*: ALMUERZO, PASTEL, APERITIVO *Diagonal*: TOSTADA
20 1 Jorge offers María a drink; 2 Jorge; 3 María; 4 María; 5 María; 6 Jorge invites María to dinner; 7 María; 8 María
21 1 c; 2 a; 3 b; 4 e; 5 d
22 *Sample answer*: María trabaja de nueve a una y media y de cuatro y media a ocho. Trabaja en una oficina. No es muy interesante pero el sueldo es bueno. Jorge no tiene horario fijo pero trabaja muchas horas. Está de viaje.

Test

1 1 Son las siete y cuarto de la mañana. 2 Es la una y media de la tarde. 3 Son las seis y media de la tarde. 4 Son las once de la noche. 5 Son las cinco menos cuarto de la tarde.
2 1 Jaime trabaja desde las nueve hasta la una (por la mañana) y desde las cuatro hasta las ocho (por la tarde). 2 Carmen trabaja desde las ocho y media hasta la una y media y desde las cuatro y media hasta las siete y media. 3 Jorge trabaja desde las ocho de la tarde hasta las seis de la mañana. 4 Puri trabaja desde las ocho hasta las cinco. 5 Alfonso trabaja desde las tres menos cuarto hasta las ocho y media de la tarde.

3 Me levanto a las ... Desayuno a las ...
Salgo de casa a las ... Llego (a mi trabajo)
a las ... Como a las ... Termino (mi trabajo)
a las ... Vuelvo a mi casa a las ... Ceno a
las ... Y me acuesto a las ...

4 1 cierra; 2 dura; 3 cierra; 4 empieza,
termina; 5 abre

5 No, no quiero ir al cine.
Quiero cenar en un restaurante.
Quedamos a las siete y media en el
restaurante.

6 1 salgo; 2 vuelve; 3 tengo; 4 quieren; 5
conozco

7 1 Quiero **cenar**. 2 Quiero **salir**. 3 Quiero
visitar a mis padres. 4 Quiero **ir a casa**.
Note that **querer** *is followed by the
infinitive.*

8 1 Me levanto a las siete; 2 Ceno a las
nueve de la noche. 3 Me acuesto a las
once. 4 Me ducho por la mañana. 5
Descanso después de comer. 6 Salgo a las
ocho.

Summary 6

1 ¿Qué hora es? *2* Son las nueve menos
cuarto de la mañana. *3* Yo trabajo en una
tienda y él trabaja en una oficina.
4 Trabajo de nueve a cinco./Trabajo desde
las nueve hasta las cinco. *5* Se levantan a
las siete de la mañana y se acuestan a las
once. *6* La película empieza a las cinco y
termina a las siete. *7* La tienda abre a las
diez y cierra a las seis. *8* Quiere comer.
9 Quedamos en el restaurante a las ocho.
10 Trabajo los lunes.

Unit 7

2 *Primer plato*: sopa, ensalada; *Segundo
plato*: pescado, cordero, cocido; *Postre*:
flan, fruta; *Bebidas*: agua, vino

3 1 De primero; 2 empezar; 3 Cómo; 4 Qué;
5 Quiero; 6 beber

7 1 Carmen; 2 Alfonso; 3 Carmen; 4 Alfonso

8 1 ¿Qué hay de postre? 2 Falta un tenedor.
3 ¿Puede traer un café? 4 Ahora traen la
cuenta. 5 No puedo terminar mi postre.
6 Se come frío.

12 1 The table is dirty. 2 The soup is cold.
3 The fish is burnt. 4 The bill is wrong.
5 The restaurant is very bad.

13 El restaurante Cuatro Estaciones **es** muy
bueno. **Está** enfrente del cine Cervantes.
La comida **es buena** también. Pero hoy hay
un problema. Hay dos camareros **nuevos**.
Son malos. La sopa **está fría** y la carne **está
quemada**. Los clientes **están enfadados**. La
señora Martínez **es** una persona muy
importante. Ella **está enfadada**. La comida
es mala y su cuenta **está equivocada**.

14 1 ¿Puede cambiar**la**? 2 ¿Puede cambiar**lo**?
3 ¿Puede cambiar**las**? 4 ¿Puede cambiar**los**,

por favor? 5 ¿Puede cambiar**lo**? 6 ¿Puede
mirar**la**? 7 ¿Puede limpiar**la**?

17 1 calamares a la romana; 2 gazpacho; 3
tortilla de patata; 4 paella; 5 cocido; 6
tortilla de patata; 7 gazpacho; 8 cocido

18 1 Tiene pimiento, cebolla, tomate, aceite,
vinagre y sal. 2 Se cortan todos los
ingredientes y se añade agua. 3 La paella.
4 La tortilla de patata. 5 La tortilla y los
calamares. 6 Tiene carne, verdura, chorizo
y garbanzos. 7 Se hierve con agua.

19 *Sample answer*: Se reboza el pescado con
harina y huevo. Se cortan las patatas. Se
calienta el aceite. Se fríen las patatas y el
pescado. Se sirve con salsa.

21 1 F: no termina el pollo porque no tiene
hambre; 2 F: 3 F: quiere pedir la cuenta;
4 V; 5 V; 6 F: María sale primero

22 d, f, e, h, b, a, c, i, g, j

23 1 están; 2 come; 3 tiene; 4 quiere;
5 Quiere; 6 tiene; 7 conoce; 8 puede;
9 entiende; 10 se va

Test

1 1 el primer plato; 2 la sopa, la ensalada, la
verdura; 3 el segundo plato; 4 pescado,
carne: cordero, cocido; 5 el postre; 6 flan,
fruta, helado; 7 la cuenta

2 1 ¿Qué hay? 2 ¿Cómo es? 3 ¿Qué es?

3 A: ¿Qué **vas** a tomar de primero? B: Para
empezar quiero la sopa. A: Yo **quiero** la
ensalada. B: ¿Y de **segundo**? A: El cordero,
por favor. B: **Para** mí, el pollo. ¿Y para
beber? A: Agua mineral. A: ¿Qué **hay** de
postre? B: El helado es **bueno**. ¿Y para
usted? A: No quiero **nada**. **Estoy** lleno.

4 1 Falta un cuchillo. 2 Falta una cuchara.
3 Falta una copa. 4 Faltan (los) vasos.
5 Faltan (los) platos. 6 Falta un tenedor.

5 ¿Puede traer la sopa?
El pollo está frío.
¿Puede cambiarlo?
¿Puede traer la cuenta?
La cuenta está equivocada.

6 1 es 2 es 3 está 4 está

7 1 El pollo está quemado. ¿Puede **cambiarlo**,
por favor? 2 La sopa está fría. ¿Puede
calentarla, por favor? 3 Las copas están
sucias. ¿Puede **cambiarlas**, por favor? 4 La
mesa está sucia. ¿Puede **limpiarla**, por
favor? 5 Faltan dos cafés. ¿Puede **traerlos**,
por favor? 6 Falta un plato. ¿Puede **traerlo**,
por favor? 7 La cuenta está equivocada
¿Puede **mirarla**, por favor? 8 Quiero la
carne con patatas, no con ensalada. ¿Puede
traerla/cambiarla, por favor?

Summary 7

1 De primero quiero ensalada. *2* Para
empezar quiero sopa. *3* El pescado está
quemado. ¿Puede cambiarlo? *4* Faltan dos
cuchillos *5* ¿Puede traerlos? *6* ¿Qué quiere

de postre? 7 El restaurante es malo.
8 ¿Puede traer la cuenta, por favor?

Review 2

1   1 una francesa; 2 un alemán; 3 dos
    escocesas; 4 dos mexicanos; 5 un
    canadiense
2   1 José es periodista. 2 María es profesora.
    3 La señora Gil es contable. 4 Gustavo y
    Javier son ingenieros. 5 Alicia y Celia son
    recepcionistas. 6 Alfonso es secretario.
3   el padre; el marido; la madre; la hermana,
    el hermano; hijos; hijo; hija
4   entrada; cocina; dormitorio; salón;
    comedor
5   me levanto; me ducho; desayuno; salgo de;
    llego a; termino; vuelvo a; ceno; descanso;
    me acuesto
6   1 éste; 2 éstos; 3 ésta; 4 éste; 5 éstas
7   1 trabajamos; 2 vive; 3 comen; 4 viajo; 5
    escribes; 6 quiero; 7 tienes
8   1 Nos levantamos a las siete. 2 Se acuesta a
    las once. 3 Se viste a las ocho. 4 ¿Te duchas
    a las siete?
9   1 limpiar; 2 calentar; 3 traer; 4 traer
10 1 ¿Puede limpiarla? 2 ¿Puede limpiarlo? 3
    ¿Puede limpiarlos? 4 ¿Puede limpiarlas?
11 1 es; 2 está; 3 es; 4 está; 5 es
12

12	Message 1	Message 2	Message 3
Time	7.00, 7.45, 10.00	8.00, 9.30, 12.00	1.30, 5.00, 8.00
Information	have a drink before	have supper before	have supper after

13 1 V; 2 F: it comes with potatoes; 3 V; 4 F:
    the woman wants water; 5 F: the knife is
    dirty; 6 V; 7 F: she asks for it to be changed
14 Sí, estoy casado/a y tengo dos niños/chicos
    y una niña/chica.
    La chica tiene doce y los chicos tienen ocho
    y seis.
    Soy ingeniero/a.
    Soy inglés/inglesa. ¿De dónde es usted?
    Tengo un tío en España. Vive en Valencia.
15 De primero quiero sopa, de segundo
    quiero pollo. Para beber quiero cerveza.
    Quiero un helado. Me falta una cuchara.
    ¿Puede traer una?
    Quiero un café solo. Éste es café con leche.
    ¿Puede cambiarlo?
    (¿Me trae la cuenta? La cuenta está
    equivocada.)

Unit 8

2   1 F: lleva veinte minutos de retraso; 2 V;
    3 F; 4 F: el tren sale de la vía dos
3   1 A; 2 a; 3 para; 4 de; 5 de
7

7	Advantages	Disadvantages
Car	It's quicker. They can use it in Madrid.	He doesn't want to drive. It's a long way.
	They can leave luggage in it.	You have to eat in motorway service stations.
Bus	They can read and relax. It's more comfortable. It's cheaper.	They can't take much luggage.

8   1 ¿A cuántos kilómetros está Sevilla?
    2 Tarda media hora en autobús. 3 Tardo
    quince minutos a pie. 4 Madrid está a
    trescientos kilómetros.
12 1 C; 2 J; 3 J; 4 C; 5 J
13 1 B: **Tienen que hacer** los deberes.
    2 B: **Tengo que visitar** a mi abuela.
    3 B: No. **Tengo que comer** en casa.
    4 A: ¿**Tenéis que ir**?
16 1 Saturdays, Sundays, and public holidays
    between 10 a.m. and 4 p.m. 2 yes; 3 no; 4
    yes; 5 if there are too many people; 6 two;
    7 the service might continue; 8 telephone
    91/552 59 09
17 1 No puedes; 2 Hay que; 3 Hay que; 4 No
    pueden; 5 puede; 6 Hay que; 7 Hay que
18 1 Los suyos viven en Guatemala. 2 El suyo
    es nuevo. 3 El mío es interesante también.
    4 La vuestra es mala. 5 Los nuestros son
    pequeños.
19 1 Sí, vive sola en un pueblo cerca de
    Toledo. 2 Voy en tren hasta Toledo. 3 Sí,
    bastante. 4 Voy desde el viernes hasta el
    lunes. 5 Sí, señor. Tengo un problema.
    Tengo que hablar urgentemente con mi
    madre.
20 1 María; 2 María; 3 la madre de María; 4 la
    madre de María; 5 la madre de María;
    6 María; 7 Jorge; 8 María
21 1 V; 2 V; 3 F: there's a bus to a nearby
    village; 4 F; 5 V

Test

1   1 ¿A qué hora sale el próximo tren para
    Madrid? 2 ¿Puedo comprar un billete de
    ida y vuelta? 3 ¿A qué hora llega? 4 ¿Lleva
    retraso? 5 ¿De qué vía sale?
2   El **próximo** tren para Madrid sale de la **vía**
    dos **dentro** de diez minutos. Lleva cinco
    minutos de **retraso**. ¿Usted quiere **comprar**
    un billete de **ida** y **vuelta**? Es un viaje muy
    rápido y el tren es muy **cómodo**. ¿Tiene
    mucho **equipaje**?
3   1 Madrid está a seiscientos veintiún
    kilómetros de Barcelona. 2 Zaragoza está a
    trescientos kilómetros de Barcelona.
    3 Madrid está a quinientos cuarenta y dos
    kilómetros de Sevilla. 4 Zaragoza está a
    doscientos noventa kilómetros de Bilbao.
    5 Barcelona está a doscientos setenta
    kilómetros de Valencia.
4   1 Voy en motocicleta. A veces voy a pie.
    2 Voy en tren y luego en autobús. 3 Voy
    en coche pero a veces voy a pie. 4 Voy en

metro y autobús. 5 Voy a pie a la parada de autobús y luego en autobús.

5 No puedo porque tengo que trabajar en casa.
No puedo. Tengo que visitar a mi madre.
No puedo. Tengo que llevar el coche al garaje.
Lo siento. Tengo que limpiar la casa.
No puedo. Tengo que ir a mi trabajo.

6 1 Los míos son mayores. 2 El nuestro es nuevo. 3 Los suyos son muy interesantes. 4 Las mías son buenas. ¿Cómo son las tuyas? 5 ¿Son vuestros? 6 La suya es bonita. 7 Los tuyos son pequeños. 8 El nuestro es muy bonito. 9 Los tuyos son buenos. 10 El tuyo es nuevo.

Summary 8

1 ¿A qué hora sale el próximo tren para Madrid? 2 ¿Puedo comprar un billete de ida y vuelta? 3 El tren lleva veinte minutos de retraso. 4 ¿De qué vía sale el tren? 5 ¿A qué hora llegamos a Barcelona? 6 El autobús sale dentro de cinco minutos. 7 Tengo que trabajar. 8 ¿A cuántos kilómetros está Madrid de Barcelona? 9 Tardo media hora en llegar a mi trabajo en autobús.

Unit 9

2 *Carmen*: tall, slim, fair; *José*: short, plump, dark; *María José*: dark; *Pablo*: tall, dark; *Patricia* dark

3 1 baja; 2 gordo; 3 morenos; 4 altas; 5 rubia; 6 delgados; 7 son; 8 es; 9 somos; 10 soy, es

7 1 V; 2 V; 3 F; 4 V; 5 V

8 *Sample answers:* 1 Raúl es simpático, generoso, sincero. 2 Alicia es trabajadora, tranquila, seria. 3 Él y su mujer son honrados, abiertos, sinceros. 4 Él es nervioso, antipático, perezoso.

12 1 Antonio; 2 una blusa; 3 un vestido; 4 unos pantalones; 5 Beatriz; 6 un vestido

13 1 Es más grande / más pequeña / mejor / peor que esta casa.
2 Es la más grande / la más pequeña / la mejor / la peor casa de la calle.

16 1 ELECTRÓNICA. T.V. Vídeo, Sonido, Telefonía, Informática; 2 PERFUMERÍA; 3 DEPORTES; 4 Moda Joven EL Y ELLA; 5 Moda Joven EL Y ELLA; 6 JOYERÍA; 7 JOYERÍA; 8 ELECTRÓNICA. T.V. Vídeo, Sonido, Telefonía, Informática; 9 FOTOGRAFÍA; 10 PAPELERÍA; 11 ELECTRÓNICA. T.V. Vídeo, Sonido, Telefonía, Informática; 12 Moda Sport, Zapatería

17 1 centre/meeting/modern/variety/article/object/generally/difference/air conditioning. 2 No. Van a encontrar a los amigos. 3 Sí. Hay restaurantes y cafeterías.

4 la 3ª planta (chaquetas/vestidos, etc.); la 2ª planta (ropa sport); la 4ª planta (camping); la 5ª (vídeos, ordenadores, etc.); la 1ª (discos, libros). 5 Los grandes almacenes no cierran a mediodía. 6 El aire acondicionado.

18 1 delgado – Jorge; 2 extraño – Jorge; 3 fuerte – la tía; 4 generosa – la vecina; 5 gorda – la tía; 6 guapo – Jorge; 7 inteligente – Julia; 8 mayor – Jorge; 9 misterioso – Jorge; 10 moreno – Jorge; 11 perezoso – Tomás; 12 preocupada – la madre de Tomás y Julia; 13 simpática – la vecina; 14 trabajadora – Julia

19 1 the neighbour; 2 Tomás; 3 María's mother; 4 the neighbour; 5 María; 6 María's mother; 7 the neighbour; 8 Julia

Test

1 1 Es alto, delgado y muy guapo. 2 Es baja y tiene pelo largo y rubio. 3 Los hermanos son morenos, fuertes y bajos. 4 Las hermanas son delgadas y rubias. 5 El hombre es mayor; es moreno y alto.

2 1 trabajador; 2 simpáticos; 3 inteligente; 4 sincero; 5 nervioso

3 1 Es nerviosa. 2 Es bueno. 3 Es inteligente. 4 Tiene la personalidad adecuada. 5 Es simpático.

4 1 chaqueta; 2 camisa; 3 pantalón; 4 blusa; 5 vestido; 6 falda; 7 zapatos; 8 jersey

5 1 La pulsera es para mi madre. 2 El collar es para mi hermana. 3 El anillo es para mi abuela. 4 El libro es para mi hermano. 5 La blusa es para mi amiga. 6 El disco compacto es para mi padre. 7 El vídeo es para mi amigo. 8 El jersey es para mi tía.

6 1 No quiero esa falda. Quiero aquélla. 2 No quiero esta pulsera. Quiero ésta. 3 No quiero este vestido. Quiero éste. 4 No quiero este jersey. Quiero aquél. 5 No quiero aquel anillo. Quiero ése. 6 No quiero estos pendientes. Quiero éstos.

7 1 Ésa es más grande. 2 Ése es más nuevo. 3 Ése es mejor. 4 Ésa es peor. 5 Ése es más interesante.

Summary 9

1 Es muy alto. 2 Son muy morenos. 3 Creo que Juan es sincero. 4 Tengo que comprar un regalo para mi padre. 5 Quiero esta pulsera. 6 No quiero éste, quiero ése. 7 Mi casa es más grande que la suya. 8 Esta película es mejor que la otra.

Unit 10

2 1 Margarita's husband; 2 Pepe; 3 Margarita; 4 Pepe; 5 Margarita

3 Te gusta; me; le gusta; Le gusta; les gusta; les gustan

7 Bernardo went dancing until **one in the morning**; his **mother** woke him up at **eight**;

219

Bernardo went to play football with his friends. After the match, they went to a bar to have a drink. Elena is angry that he went out without her and that now he is too tired to go out. They go out together.

8 1 cenaron; 2 salí; 3 bailamos; 4 fuiste; 5 compró; 6 hiciste

12 1 Bernardo; 2 Elena; 3 Bernardo; 4 Elena; 5 Elena; 6 Bernardo

13 1 Fuimos al cine ayer. 2 La película fue buena. 3 Ayer fue el cumpleaños de mi padre. 4 Fueron a Perú de vacaciones. 5 ¿Fuisteis a la fiesta? 6 ¿Fuiste tú quien llamó?

16 1 a, New Year's Day; 2 f, Twelfth Night/Epiphany; 3 d, Easter; 4 e, National Holiday; 5 c, All Saints'; 6 j, Constitution Day; 7 g, Christmas Eve; 8 i, Christmas Day; 9 b, New Year's Eve; 10 h, Labour Day

17 1 Semana Santa; 2 Noche Buena; 3 Día del trabajo; 4 Noche Vieja; 5 Día de Navidad; 6 Día de la Constitución; 7 Los Reyes Magos; 8 Año Nuevo; 9 Todos los Santos; 10 Fiesta Nacional: la Virgen del Pilar

18 *Sample answers*: 1 Salí a las calles para ver las procesiones. 2 Descansamos en casa. Hice una cena especial. 3 Dormí. 4 Visité el cementerio. 5 Celebré la fiesta con los niños.

19 *Across*: Semana Santa; Reyes magos; Noche Buena; Noche Vieja
Down: Constitución; Año Nuevo; Navidad; Pascua

20 1 V; 2 F: tiene mucho trabajo; 3 F: vive sola y tiene amigos; 4 V; 5 V; 6 F: es de hace mucho tiempo; 7 F: es una foto de María, su madre y un señor; 8 V; 9 F

21 1 Sí, pero prefiere vivir sola. 2 Tiene muchos amigos. 3 Come bien, no se preocupe. 4 Está muy bien, tiene una vida muy buena. 5 Hace muchas cosas, pero no demasiadas.

Test

1 *Sample answers*: Me gusta/No me gusta el cine/el teatro/la televisión/la música/la fruta/la verdura/la carne/el chocolate
Me gustan/No me gustan las películas/los periódicos/los libros/los dibujos animados

2 Me gusta/No me gusta bailar/leer/trabajar/escuchar música

3 1 A él le gustan; 2 A nosotros nos gusta; 3 A ellos les gusta; 4 A vosotros os gustan; 5 A mí me gusta; 6 A ti te gusta; 7 A ellas les gusta

4 Lo siento mucho. No me gusta nada la música clásica.
No me gusta mucho. No me gusta la música. Prefiero el cine. ¿Te gusta el cine? No. No me gusta.
A mí me gusta ir al cine una vez al mes, pero prefiero estar en casa y leer un libro.

5 me levanté; fuimos; compré; compró; Comimos; fuimos; fueron; visité; fui; Salí; encontré; tomamos

6 1 ¿Qué hizo usted ayer? 2 ¿Dónde fue usted anoche? 3 ¿Qué hiciste la semana pasada? 4 ¿Dónde fuiste el mes pasado? 5 ¿Dónde fueron ustedes ayer?

7 1 dos veces a la semana; 2 tres veces a la semana; 3 una vez al mes; 4 tres veces al año; 5 dos veces al día; 6 todas las semanas

Summary 10

1 Me gusta la música clásica. *2* ¿Le gusta el cine? *3* ¿Te gusta bailar? *4* No me gusta nada. *5* ¿Qué hiciste anoche? *6* ¿Adónde fuiste la semana pasada? *7* Ayer fue mi cumpleaños. *8* Mi cumpleaños es el mes que viene. *9* Mis padres me visitaron la semana pasada. *10* Nado tres veces a la semana.

Review 3

1 1 tren; 2 vía; 3 lleva; 4 retraso; 5 billetes; 6 ida; 7 ida y vuelta; 8 reserva

2 1 alto, moreno y delgado; largo y liso; 2 baja, rubia y gorda; corto y rizado; 3 los ojos azules

3 1 Roberto es sincero. 2 Juana es honrada. 3 Los hermanos son inteligentes. 4 Mi padre es tranquilo. 5 Mi madre es nerviosa. 6 Las hermanas son serias. 7 Javier es simpático. 8 Carmen es antipática. 9 Los niños son felices. 10 Mi abuelo es generoso.

4 1 para; 2 a; 3 para; 4 a

5 1 Quiero comprar un billete de ida y vuelta. 2 ¿Se puede tomar un café en la sala de espera? 3 Necesitan comprar un billete. 4 Deseamos cambiar de habitación. 5 Tengo que viajar a Sevilla.

6 1 ¿Cuánto cuesta llegar al trabajo? 2 ¿Cuánto tardas en llegar al trabajo en autobús? 3 ¿A cuántos kilómetros está tu trabajo?

7 1 Éste, ése, aquél; 2 Aquéllas, éstas, ésas; 3 Ésa, aquélla, ésta; 4 Éstos, Ésos, aquéllos

8 1 Estos zapatos son mejores que aquéllos/ésos. 2 Mi trabajo es peor que el tuyo. 3 Su coche es más grande que el mío/mi coche. 4 Su coche es mejor que el mío/mi coche. 5 La película es menos interesante que el libro.

9 1 Me gusta el cine. 2 Me gusta jugar al fútbol. 3 Les gustan los coches rápidos. 4 Nos gustan los dibujos animados 5 ¿Te gusta escuchar la música? 6 No me gusta el teatro nada.

10 1 fue; 2 me levanté; 3 Desayuné; 4 salí; 5 llegó; 6 llegué; 7 gustó; 8 Terminé; 9 fui; 10 entré; 11 llamaste

11 1 Jorge; 2 Juan; 3 Juana; 4 Javier; 5 Ana (la hermana de Juan); 6 Ana (la hermana de Javier)

12 *Josefina*: música clásica, baile, cine bar, restaurante
María: música rock, baile, cine, bar, restaurante
Gustavo: música rock, cine, restaurante
13 Quiero un billete para Barcelona.
De ida y vuelta.
Quiero ir mañana y volver el diecisiete.
¿Cuánto tarda?
De segunda.
14 Fui al centro con mi amigo/a. Compré unos zapatos. Comí en un restaurante. Fui a casa. Estudié. Me llamaron mis amigos. Fuimos al bar. Fuimos al cine. Fui a casa en autobús a las once.

Unit 11

2 1 porque ayer volvió de sus vacaciones; 2 Beatriz estuvo en un apartamento y Antonio estuvo en un hotel; 3 hace dos años; 4 con sus padres. 5 Windsor
3 1 Estuve en un buen hotel. 2 Fui a la playa de vacaciones. 3 Volvieron ayer. 4 Volvimos hace tres días. 5 Llovió mucho. 6 Hizo mal tiempo. 7 Vieron el Támesis. 8 Vi a Juan hace una hora.
7 1 B; 2 A; 3 A; 4 A; 5 B
8 1 era; 2 trabajaba; 3 comprábamos; 4 visitábamos; 5 estábamos
12 1 V; 2 V; 3 F: en un piso pequeño; 4 V; 5 F: pasaba el verano en el centro de Madrid
13 Cuando era joven vivía en la ciudad pero cada verano iba a la casa de mis abuelos con mis dos hermanos. Mis abuelos tenían un coche viejo y grande y me acuerdo que una vez, mi abuelo nos llevó a las montañas. Mi padre trabajaba mucho y no tenía vacaciones largas, pero todos los fines de semana venía a vernos y nos daba regalos.
17 1 bulls, music, dance, wine, fireworks, childrens' games, noise, no sleep (five of these); 2 stay awake; 3 sleep; 4 San Fermín, Pamplona, because it was immortalized by Ernest Hemingway; 5 the fiesta in Valencia in which huge cardboard statues are burned and there are impressive firework displays
18 1 Fui a la fiesta de un pueblo. 2 Bailé hasta las cuatro de la mañana. 3 Vi los fuegos artificiales. 4 Corrí delante de los toros. 5 No dormí en toda la noche.
19 1 F: a su casa; 2 F: María se comportó mal; 3 V; 4 V; 5 V; 6 V; 7 F; 8 F: el viernes
20 Fui a ver a unos amigos.
Lo siento – no puedo ir.
Está bastante cerca de Toledo.
Se llama Las Fuentes.
Sí, sí. Podemos cenar en mi casa.
21 1 a; 2 a; 3 le; 4 le; 5 a; 6 a; 7 mi; 8 la; 9 me; 10 de

Test
1 1 volví; 2 fuiste; 3 fuimos; 4 hicimos; 5 estuvimos; 6 Vimos; 7 me bañé; 8 visitamos
2 1 se bañó; 2 se levantaron; 3 divertirme; 4 me acuerdo; 5 se aburren
3 1 Ayer fui al pueblo. 2 Estuvieron en Madrid. 3 Fue un coche grande. 4 Fuimos a un castillo. 5 Fue una buena película.
4 1 Llueve. 2 Hace sol. 3 Hace frío. 4 Hace calor. 5 Hace buen tiempo.
5 1 Fui hace dos años. 2 Le vi hace cinco minutos. 3 Tomé café hace poco. 4 Fui a Madrid hace mucho. 5 Lo compré hace dos años.
6 1 They lived on the coast for many years. 2 I used to work for a furniture company. 3 We went to see the football match on Sunday. 4 We used to go to watch football on Sundays. 5 My father used to drive badly. 6 He/She was in the disco. 7 You always used to be in the cinema. 8 Yesterday I bought a present for my friend.
7 *Sample answer*: Paseé por las Ramblas. Visité el Tibidabo. Compré cosas en los grandes almacenes. Comí en buenos restaurantes. Me bañé en el Mediterráneo. Bailé en las discotecas. Vi la arquitectura de Gaudí.

Summary 11
1 ¿Dónde fuiste de vacaciones? *2* Fui a Inglaterra. *3* Estuvimos en un hotel. *4* Hace buen tiempo. *5* Hace frío. *6* Fui a Australia hace tres años. *7* Vi a Juan hace poco. *8* Vivía en una casa grande cuando era joven. *9* Visitaba a mis abuelos. *10* No me gusta la playa.

Unit 12

2 1 voy al campo; 2 vale la pena; 3 podemos hacer una barbacoa; 4 no podemos ir; 5 no puedo ir el domingo
3 1 No van; 2 No vais; 3 Vas; 4 Va; 5 Voy; 6 No vas; 7 Va
7 1 Bernardo y los niños; 2 Bernardo y Alfonso; 3 Los niños; 4 Clara; 5 Bernardo y Alfonso; 6 Bernardo
8 Iremos pronto/temprano por la mañana el sábado que viene. Llegaremos a la casa a las diez. Los niños jugarán en el jardín y se bañarán en la piscina mientras preparo la comida. Podremos pasear por la tarde y visitaremos el pueblo. Vendrás por la tarde y cenaremos juntos. Tendremos que acostarnos temprano porque volveremos/vamos a volver a Madrid temprano por la mañana. Llegaremos a Madrid a mediodía y llamaré a mi madre. Por la tarde descansaremos y veremos la televisión.

12 False statements are 5 and 8.
1 Elisa no podrá ir al cine esta noche.
2 Está ocupada. 3 Se quedará en casa.
4 Puede ir el domingo. 6 Harán otra cosa esta noche. 7 Elisa llamará a las cinco y media. 9 Decidirán más tarde.

13 1 Estoy cansado/a. 2 Estoy enfermo/a.
3 Estoy ocupado/a. 4 Tengo que visitar a mi madre. 5 Tengo que preparar la comida. 6 Tengo que ir a Barcelona mañana.

14 1 Yo comeré en el restaurante Bella Vista.
2 Yo voy a visitar a mis tíos en México.
3 Nosotros trabajaremos toda la semana.
4 No, van a salir a las ocho. 5 No, vosotros llegaréis a las once.

17 1 V; 2 V; 3 F; 4 V; 5 F: en muchas ciudades hay por lo menos un teatro; 6 V

18 1 3; 2 City of Angels; 3 Avenida Cesar Augusto; 4 no; 5 976 445 011; 6 Club Náutico

19 1 a; 2 b; 3 c; 4 b; 5 a; 6 a

20 ¿Qué tal el viaje? Y este señor de la foto eres tú, ¿verdad? ¿Cuándo te enteraste? ¿Por qué no volviste? ¿Por qué vuelve?

Test

1 1 Roberto va (a ir) al cine. 2 Elisa va (a ir) a una boda. 3 Nosotros vamos a bailar.
4 Ellos van a visitar a unos amigos. 5 Tú vas a estudiar. 6 Vosotros vais a preparar la cena. 7 Yo voy a comprar un coche nuevo.
8 Mis hermanos van a jugar al fútbol. 9 Tú y yo vamos a ver una película. 10 Yo voy a terminar el libro.

2 1 ¿Te gustaría ir al cine? 2 ¿Quieres venir al cine? 3 ¿Vamos al cine?

3 1 iré; 2 Empezaré; 3 Estaré; 4 Saldré;
5 vendrá; 6 haré; 7 comerán; 8 tendremos;
9 tendrá; 10 prepararé

4 1 Estoy ocupada. 2 Tengo que trabajar.
3 Tengo un examen. 4 Estoy cansado/a.
5 Tengo que visitar a un amigo.

5 1 ¡Qué suerte! 2 Vale la pena. 3 ¡Qué lástima! 4 ¿Qué te parece? 5 ¡Estupendo!
6 La semana que viene. 7 Lo siento. 8 No importa. 9 De acuerdo. 10 ¿Qué (te) pasa?

6 *Across*: estaré, jugaremos, irá, podré, llamará, iréis
Down: estarán, harán, cenaré, descansará

Summary 12

1 Voy a estudiar esta noche. *2* Van a ver una película mañana. *3* ¿Te gustaría salir?
4 Lo siento pero no puedo. *5* Estoy cansada/Estoy cansado. *6* Iré mañana.
7 Vendrá la semana que viene. *8* Me quedaré en casa. *9* Vale la pena. *10* ¿Qué te parece?

Unit 13

2 1 a Sr. García is in a meeting; b Bernardo is going away; c he's travelling; 2 she can make a new appointment for him

3 Recepcionista: ¿Dígame?
You: ¿Puedo hablar con la señora Blasco, por favor?
Recepcionista: Sí. ¿De parte de quién? ... Perdone. La señora Blasco está reunida/en una reunión.
You: No podré asistir a la entrevista del lunes próximo. Quisiera cambiarla.
Recepcionista: Yo puedo cambiar la fecha. ¿Puede venir el miércoles por la tarde?
You: Perfecto.
Recepcionista: ¿Podría pasar por la oficina a las dos?
You: De acuerdo. Gracias.
Recepcionista: De nada. Hasta el miércoles.

7 3, 4, 5

8 1 Vivo; 2 estoy viviendo; 3 tengo; 4 voy;
5 compro; 6 leo; 7 estoy buscando; 8 encuentro; 9 volveré; 10 estoy estudiando;
11 Quiero

12 1a We can communicate more rapidly and with more information than ever. b We can see the latest information without waiting and can send messages to our colleagues in a second. c We can attend meetings without leaving the office. 2a How can we manage this information explosion? b Do we need it? c Do we want it?

14 1 del; 2 de los; de; 3 de las; 4 de la
1 Visité a mi familia sin ver a mi hermana.
2 Trabajé todo el día sin comer. 3 Hice los examenes sin estudiar. 4 Estoy en la oficina todo el día sin salir.

17 1 Director Hotel; 2 Ingeniero mecánico sénior/Ingeniero técnico industrial;
3 Programadores; 4 Jefe de ventas para España; 5 Director Hotel, Ingeniero mecánico sénior, Ingeniero técnico industrial; 6 Programadores sénior; 7 Jefe de ventas para España, Director Hotel;
8 Director Hotel

18 1 **filial**, subsidiary; **estrellas**, stars; **amplia**, wide; **dominio**, fluency; **edificación**, building; **líder**, leader; **licenciado**, graduate; se **requiere/requisitos**, requirements

2 2 Important Company Group requires:
HOTEL MANAGER
for a four-star hotel in Extremadura
Requirements: wide experience; ability to manage teams; written and spoken English.

3 Multinational Engineering , Building, and Maintenance Company requires: SENIOR MECHANICAL ENGINEER 10 years' experience, fluency in English
4 Independent Organization for Quality Control in the Building Industry requires for its area of installation: INDUSTRIAL TECHNICAL ENGINEER
• minimum of two years' experience in quality control of building installations
• knowledge of English

19 1 He wants to be with his family and he wants to open a new branch of his company. 2 Jorge wants to employ her in his company. 3 He is the boss of his own company. 4 He has a very good manager there who will take over. 5 Someone who knows Madrid and who is well-qualified, with experience, initiative, and motivation. 6 Call her mother.

20 Questions from the conversation and responses:
1 María. Voy a quedarme aquí.
2 María. Quiero estar cerca de mi familia.
5 María. Tengo un jefe muy bueno allí.
6 Jorge. ¡Yo! Pues sí, me gustaría mucho.
7 Jorge. Pronto.

21 *María*: Jorge va a quedarse aquí. Quiere estar cerca de su familia. En Granada tiene su propia empresa. Tiene bastante dinero. Está buscando un sitio para abrir una sucursal. Tiene un jefe muy bueno allí. Él se queda aquí. Necesita un jefe de personal para la compañía. Yo soy la persona adecuada.

Test

1 A: ¿Dígame? B: ¿Puedo hablar con la señora Gil por favor? A: ¿De parte de quién? B: Daniel Jiménez. A: Un momento, por favor, ahora se pone. B: Gracias. A: De nada.

2 1 ¿Puedo hablar con el Sr. García, por favor? 2 ¿Puede llamar más tarde? 3 ¿Puedo dejar un recado? 4 Quisiera cambiar la (hora de la) entrevista. 5 ¿Puede pasar por la oficina mañana?

3 1 Dígame. 2 Oiga, por favor. 3 Mire. 4 Tenga. 5 Pase por aquí. 6 Perdone.

4 1 el encargado/la encargada; 2 una empresa; 3 puesto; 4 las cualidades; 5 una entrevista; 6 una reunión; 7 un recado

5 1 estoy trabajando; 2 Termino; 3 estás haciendo; 4 llama; 5 descanso; 6 está jugando ; 7 llega

6 1 Trabajo todo el día sin parar. 2 Voy a hacer los exámenes sin estudiar. 3 Fui de compras ayer sin comer. 4 Estuve en casa el fin de semana sin salir.

Summary 13
1 ¿Dígame? 2 ¿Puedo hablar con el señor García? 3 ¿Podría llamarle más tarde? 4 ¿Puedo dejar un recado? 5 Quisiera cambiar el día de la entrevista. 6 Pase por aquí, por favor. 7 ¿Qué estás haciendo? 8 Hola. Soy ____, Trabajo para Nexus. Soy ____. 9 Asisto a reuniones sin salir de la oficina.

Unit 14

2 fiebre ✓ (empezó el lunes), gripe ✓, dolor de garganta ✓ (empezó el miércoles), inflamación de la garganta ✓

3 1 he trabajado; 2 ha viajado; 3 has cenado; 4 has estado

7 1 V; 2 F; 3 V; 4 F: he's twisted his ankle; 5 F: she tells him to put his leg on a chair

8 He tenido un día muy malo. Me he torcido el tobillo jugando al fútbol en la playa, me he quemado, me duele la cabeza y tengo la garganta inflamada. El médico me ha dicho que tengo que quedarme en el apartamento durante el resto de las vacaciones y no jugar al fútbol más en la playa. Quiero volver a casa.

12 1 no; 2 sí; 3 sí; 4 no; 5 sí; 6 no; 7 no

13 1 c; 2d; 3a; 4b; 5e

14 *Sample answers:* Bebo demasiado. Como demasiadas patatas. Fumo. No hago ejercicio. No como fruta. No descanso. He dejado de fumar. He dejado de comer patatas. He dejado de beber tanta cerveza.

17 1 frisbee: **disco volador**; kite: **cometa**; hiking: **excursionismo**; beach tennis: **palas**; pedal boat: **patinete de playa**; beach volleyball: **voleiplaya**
2 a los beneficios: benefits; b volar: to fly; c los reflejos: reflexes; d fortalecer: to strengthen; e el brazo: arm; f las lesiones: injuries; g el codo: elbow; h la muñeca: wrist; i la mano: hand; j el estrés: stress; k la torcedura: sprain; l la ampolla: blister
3 1 disco volador, cometas, palas; 2 el excursionismo; 3 disco volador, palas, voleiplaya; 4 patinete de playa; 5 voleiplaya; 6 cometas

18 1 Porque están juntos. 2 En casa de María. 3 Porque no debe vivir sola en el pueblo. 4 Dos. 5 Porque María ganará más dinero en su nuevo puesto. 6 Un edificio muy bueno para la empresa y un apartamento. 7 Dentro de seis meses. 8 Las echaba de menos pero no podía volver.

19 Quiero estar con mi familia. Sí, tengo dos dormitorios. He encontrado un apartamento muy cerca de aquí. Yo creo que podremos empezar dentro de seis meses.

20 9, 6, (3), 1, 2, 4, 8, 7, 5 (No. 3 is the perfect and does not refer to a specific time in the past)

21 Ayer Jorge encontró un edificio muy bueno para la empresa. Dentro de seis meses podrán empezar el trabajo. María tendrá que hablar con su jefe pronto. Hace muchos años Jorge dejó a su familia. Ahora están aquí. Hoy ha sido un día muy especial.

Test

1 1 Me duele la cabeza/Tengo dolor de cabeza. 2 Tengo fiebre. 3 Me duelen los ojos. 4 Me duele el pecho/Tengo dolor de pecho. 5 Me duele la garganta/Tengo dolor de garganta. 6 Tengo tos. 7 Me duelen los brazos. 8 Me duele la espalda/Tengo dolor de espalda.

2 Me encuentro … 1 bien; 2 mal(a); 3 muy bien; 4 mal(a), enfermo/a; 5 muy mal(a)

3 1 Tengo que ponerme una pomada. 2 Tengo que tomar unas pastillas. 3 Tengo que tomar aspirina. 4 Tengo que tomar un jarabe.

4 1 Trabajé, he trabajado; 2 He viajado, viajé; 3 He vivido; 4 ha llegado, llegó; 5 He perdido

5 1 Me he torcido el tobillo. 2 Me he hecho daño en la rodilla. 3 Se ha roto la pierna. 4 Se ha hecho daño en la cabeza. 5 Se ha quemado.

6 1 Pasa; 2 Abre; 3 Haz; 4 pon
1 Pase; 2 Levante; 3 Venga; 4 Siga

7 1 demasiado; 2 demasiado; 3 demasiado; 4 demasiado; 5 demasiados; 6 demasiada; 7 demasiado; 8 demasiadas

8 1 Debes trabajar menos. 2 Debe beber menos. 3 Debe ver menos televisión. 4 Debe hacer ejercicio. 5 Debe dejar de fumar. 6 Debe comer más verdura. 7 Debe comer menos. 8 Debes comer menos patatas.

Summary 14

1 ¿Qué le pasa? *2* Tengo fiebre. *3* Me duele la cabeza. *4* Me siento muy mal. *5* He estado enfermo. *6* He trabajado mucho esta semana. *7* Me he hecho daño en el pie. *8* Abre la puerta. *9* No debe fumar. *10* He dejado de fumar.

Review 4

1 1 cansarse; 2 bañarse; 3 aburrirse; 4 quemarse; 5 acordarse; 6 preocuparse; 7 divertirse; 8 quedarse; 9 sentirse; 10 hacerse daño

2 1 camping; 2 costa; 3 barco; 4 barbacoa; 5 jardín; 6 estupenda

3 1 b; 2 a; 3 c

4 1 Tienes razón. 2 Echar de menos (a alguien). 3 Vale la pena. 4 Para empezar.

5 1 Volví. 2 Estuvo en Alicante. 3 ¿Qué hicieron? 4 Fuimos a la playa. 5 Compraron una casa en la ciudad.

6 1 Hace buen tiempo. 2 Hace sol. 3 Hace calor. 4 Llueve. 5 Hace frío. 6 Hace mal tiempo.

7 Personalized answers using this model: Hace _____ horas/días/semanas/años, etc.

8 1 Jugaba; 2 Compré; 3 era; viajaba; 4 vivimos/vivíamos; 5 Tuve

9 1 Pase; 2 Abre; 3 Poned; 4 levanta; 5 Dígame

10 1 estoy estudiando; 2 están comiendo; 3 estamos viajando; 4 estáis terminando; 5 estás viviendo

11 1 Me he torcido el tobillo. 2 Me he hecho daño en el pie. 3 Me he roto el brazo. 4 Me he quemado la espalda.

12 1 A is going shopping; B is going to the cinema; 2 they're going to meet up in a bar; 3 they're going to dinner at A's uncle and aunt's house; 4 B is going to Venezuela

13 1 Srta. Vázquez; 2 the person trying to reach Beatriz Herrero; 3 Sr. Solano; 4 Beatriz Herrero; 5 Sr. López; 6 Eduardo Sanz – he can't attend the meeting tomorrow.

14 He estado de vacaciones. Fui a Alicante. Estuve en el apartamento de mis padres. Fui con unos amigos. Sí, me gusta bañarme pero también me gusta visitar las ciudades y los pueblos. Hacía sol todos los días, pero llovió el domingo todo el día. Bailé y me divertí.

16 ¿Puedo hablar con el sr. Solano, por favor? ¿Cuándo estará de vuelto? ¿Puedo dejarle un recado? Que he llamado pero no podré asistir a la reunión el viernes. ¿Puedo cambiarla? El próximo martes. A las diez. Hasta el martes.

Grammar summary

Nouns

Gender

In Spanish, all nouns are identified as either masculine or feminine. Gender can be identified by the form of the definite article – **el, los** (masculine) and **la, las** (feminine) – or the indefinite article – **un, unos** (masculine) and **una, unas** (feminine).

As a general rule, nouns ending in -o are usually masculine and nouns ending in -a are usually feminine:

    el zapato shoe   **la camisa** shirt

There are a few exceptions to this rule, for example:

    el día day   **la mano** hand

For nouns ending in other letters, the gender has to be learned in each case:

    el coche car   **la noche** night

Plurals

For nouns ending in a vowel, add -s:

el helado ice cream	**los helados** ice creams
la casa house	**las casas** houses
el billete ticket	**los billetes** tickets

For nouns ending in a consonant add -es:

    el hospital hospital   **los hospitales** hospitals

The definite article

The form is determined by the number and gender of the noun that follows.

	sing.	*pl.*
masc.	**el** coche	**los** coches
fem.	**la** casa	**las** casas

The masculine definite article is contracted when it is preceded by the preposition **a** or **de**:

a + el = **al**	Voy **al** cine. I'm going to the cinema.
de + el = **del**	el coche **del** camarero the waiter's car

The indefinite article

The form is determined by the number and gender of the noun that follows.

	sing.	pl.
masc.	**un** coche	**unos** coches
fem.	**una** casa	**unas** casas

The indefinite article is not used when stating someone's job.

Miguel es **profesor**. Miguel is a teacher.

Adjectives

Agreement

Adjectives agree in number and gender with the noun they describe. Adjectives ending in **-o** change as follows:

	sing.	pl.
masc.	el restaurante bueno	los restaurantes **buenos**
fem.	la casa buena	las casas **buenas**

With the exception of nationalities, most adjectives ending in **-e** or a consonant have the same form in the singular. In the plural, an **-s** is added to those ending in **-e** and **-es** to those ending in a consonant.

	sing.	pl.
masc. & fem.	inteligente	inteligentes
masc. & fem.	hábil	hábiles

Adjectives of nationality ending in a consonant change as follows:

	sing.	pl.
masc.	el señor francés	los señores franceses
fem.	la señora francesa	las señoras francesas

Position

Adjectives usually follow the noun:

> una vista **bonita** a pretty view
> un apartamento **grande** a big apartment

However, some adjectives precede the noun. The most common are: **bueno** ('good'), **malo** ('bad'), **otro** ('other'), **poco** ('little'/'few'). **bueno** and **malo** change form when they precede the noun:

bueno – buen   Hace buen tiempo. It's good weather.
malo – mal   Hace mal día. It's a bad day.

Comparatives and superlatives

Comparatives

The comparative of adjectives and adverbs is formed as follows:

(1) adjectives: **más** + adjective + **que** or **menos** + adjective + **que**
The adjective agrees in number and gender with the noun to which it refers.

> Este libro es **más** interesante **que** el otro. This book is more interesting than the other one.

(2) adverbs: verb/adverb + **más que** or **menos que**

Mi hermano trabaja **menos que** sus compañeros. My brother works less than his colleagues.
Este coche **va más** rápido que el otro. This car goes faster than the other.

Irregular comparative forms
A number of adjectives have irregular comparative forms:

bueno – mejor (better)   **grande – mayor** (bigger)
malo – peor (worse)   **pequeño – menor** (smaller)

Superlatives
The superlative of adjectives and adverbs is formed as follows:

(1) adjectives: **el/la … más** + adjective or **el/la … menos** + adjective
The adjective agrees in number and gender with the noun to which it refers:

El restaurante **más/menos** caro de la ciudad. The most/least expensive restaurant in the city.

(2) adverb: **el/la … que** + verb + **más/menos**

El que trabaja **más/menos** en la oficina es mi hermano. The one who works most/least in the office is my brother.

Subject pronouns

person	sing.		pl.	
	masc.	fem.	masc.	fem.
1st I/we	**yo**	**yo**	**nosotros**	**nosotras**
2nd (informal) you	**tú**	**tú**	**vosotros**	**vosotras**
2nd (formal) you	**usted**	**usted**	**ustedes**	**ustedes**
	(Ud/Vd)	**(Ud/Vd)**	**(Uds/Vds)**	**(Uds/Vds)**
3rd he/she/they	**él**	**ella**	**ellos**	**ellas**

Note: **Ud/Vd, Uds/Vds** are the written abbreviations of **Usted/ Ustedes**.

Yo soy mexicano. I'm Mexican.
Ellas son de Barcelona. They [*fem.*] are from Barcelona.

Subject pronouns are generally omitted in conversation.

Object pronouns

Direct object pronouns

person	sing.		pl.	
	masc.	fem.	masc.	fem.
1st (I; we)	**me**	**me**	**nos**	**nos**
2nd (you)	**te**	**te**	**os**	**os**
3rd (him/her/it; they)	**le/lo**	**la**	**les/los**	**las**

Lo vi en la tienda. I saw it in the shop.
La carne. ¿**La** quiere? The meat. Do you want it?

Indirect object pronouns

person	sing.		pl.	
	masc.	fem.	masc.	fem.
1st (I; we)	me	me	nos	nos
2nd (you)	te	te	os	os
3rd (him/her/it; they)	le/se	le/se	les/se	les/se

Mi madre **nos** dará café. My mother will give us coffee.
Te daré este libro. I'll give you this book.

Position of object pronouns
Object pronouns are usually placed immediately before the verb:

> Carmen **me** invitó a su boda. Carmen invited me to her
> wedding.

When the verb is in the infinitive, imperative, or gerund ('-ing')
form, the object pronoun is attached to the end of the verb:

> Quiero **comprarlo**. I want to buy it.   **Cómpralo**. Buy it.
> Está **comprándolo**. He's buying it.

Disjunctive pronouns

sing.	pl.
mí	nosotros
ti	vosotros
él/ella	ellos/ellas

A disjunctive pronoun is an emphatic form of pronoun used in
certain situations, which include:
(1) after a preposition:

> Para **mí**, la sopa. The soup for me.
> Voy sin **vosotros**. I'm going without you.

(2) for emphasis with the verb **gustar**:

> Le gusta a **él**. He (in particular) likes it.

Note that the pronouns **mí** and **ti** change when used with **con**:

> **conmigo** with me   **contigo** with you

Demonstrative adjectives and pronouns

	sing.	pl.
masc.	este anillo	estos pendientes
fem.	esta blusa	estas chaquetas

Two other kinds of demonstrative adjectives are used to indicate
comparative distance of objects. For something that is not very far
away: **ese** / **esa** / **esos** / **esas**:

Quiero **ese** anillo. I want that ring [*e.g. just there*].

For something at a greater distance: **aquel** / **aquella** / **aquellos** / **aquellas**:

Vivo en **aquella** casa. I live in that house (over there).

In the pronoun form an accent is added:

Quiero **éste**. I want this one.

Possessive adjectives and pronouns

Possessive adjectives ('my', 'your', etc.) and pronouns ('mine', 'yours', etc.) agree in number and gender with the noun to which they refer, rather than with the possessor.

Possessive adjectives

	sing.	pl.
my	**mi**	**mis**
your [*sing.*]	**tu**	**tus**
his/her/its/your [*formal sing.*]	**su**	**sus**
our	**nuestro/a**	**nuestros/as**
your [*pl.*]	**vuestro/a**	**vuestros/as**
their/your [*formal pl.*]	**su**	**sus**

Mi trabajo está cerca de **mi** casa. My work is near my house.
Nuestros padres están en Madrid. Our parents are in Madrid.

Possessive pronouns

	sing.	pl.
mine	**mío/a**	**míos/as**
yours [*sing.*]	**tuyo/a**	**tuyos/as**
his/hers/its/yours [*formal sing.*]	**suyo/a**	**suyos/as**
ours	**nuestro/a**	**nuestros/as**
yours [*pl.*]	**vuestro/a**	**vuestros/as**
theirs/yours [*formal pl.*]	**suyo/a**	**suyos/as**

Mi trabajo está cerca de mi casa. My work is near my house.
El mío está lejos de mi casa. Mine is a long way from my house.

Questions and exclamations

Questions are indicated by an inverted question mark at the beginning and a normal question mark at the end: ¿ ... ?

Questions are formed in three ways:
(1) by using the same word order as a sentence but with a rising intonation:

¿María trabaja en el centro de la ciudad? Does María work in the centre of town?

(2) by inverting the subject and verb in the sentence:

¿Estudia Juan todas las noches? Does Juan study every night?

(3) by using a question word:

¿Cuándo vas a visitar a tu madre? When are you going to visit your mother?

Numbers

0 cero	16 dieciséis	32 treinta y dos	600 seiscientos/as
1 uno/una	17 diecisiete	33 treinta y tres	700 setecientos/as
2 dos	18 dieciocho	40 cuarenta	800 ochocientos/as
3 tres	19 diecinueve	50 cincuenta	900 novecientos/as
4 cuatro	20 veinte	60 sesenta	
5 cinco	21 veintiuno	70 setenta	
6 seis	22 veintidós	80 ochenta	
7 siete	23 veintitrés	90 noventa	
8 ocho	24 veinticuatro	100 cien	
9 nueve	25 veinticinco	101 ciento uno/a	
10 diez	26 veintiséis	111 ciento once	
11 once	27 veintisiete	125 ciento veinticinco	
12 doce	28 veintiocho	200 doscientos/as	
13 trece	29 veintinueve	300 trescientos/as	
14 catorce	30 treinta	400 cuatrocientos/as	
15 quince	31 treinta y uno	500 quinientos/as	

Ordinal numbers

el primero/la primera	first	el sexto/la sexta	sixth
el segundo/la segunda	second	el séptimo/la séptima	seventh
el tercero/la tercera	third	el octavo/la octava	eighth
el cuarto/la cuarta	fourth	el noveno/la novena	ninth
el quinto/la quinta	fifth	el décimo/la décima	tenth

Ordinals are normally placed before the noun.

Viven en el cuarto piso. They live on the fourth floor.

Two ordinal numbers, **primero** and **tercero**, modify their form when they appear before a masculine noun:

el primer piso the first floor   **el tercer piso** the third floor

Adverbs

Most adverbs are formed by adding **-mente** to the feminine form of the adjective.

rápida – rápidamente   quickly

The following adverbs are irregular:

bastante	quite, enough	**menos**	less
bien	well	**mucho**	a lot, much
demasiado	too much	**muy**	very
mal	badly	**poco**	a little
más	more		

Verbs

The infinitive
The infinitive is the basic form of the verb found in the dictionary. In Spanish, the infinitive has one of three possible endings: **-ar**, **-er**, or **-ir**. Examples of regular verbs are: **trabajar** ('to work'), **comer** ('to eat'), **vivir** ('to live').

Regular verbs within each group take the same endings.

The present tense
The infinitive endings are replaced as follows:

trabajar		**comer**		**vivir**	
trabajo	trabaj**amos**	como	com**emos**	vivo	viv**imos**
trabaj**as**	trabaj**áis**	com**es**	com**éis**	viv**es**	viv**ís**
trabaj**a**	trabaj**an**	come	com**en**	vive	viv**en**

Radical-changing verbs
Radical-changing verbs are verbs which are regular in their endings (taking the endings of **-ar**, **-er**, or **-ir** verbs as appropriate), but which undergo a change in the stem in certain persons of the verb.

• Verbs that undergo a vowel change:

e – ie = querer ('to want') – **quiero**
Verbs that follow this pattern are: **cerrar** ('to close'), **empezar** ('to begin'), **pensar** ('to think'), **comenzar** ('to begin'), **divertir** ('to enjoy'), **preferir** ('to prefer').

o – ue = volver ('to return') – **vuelvo**
Verbs that follow this pattern are: **costar** ('to cost'), **poder** ('to be able'), **doler** ('to hurt'), **dormir** ('to sleep').

u – ue = jugar ('to play') – **juego**

e – i = vestir ('to dress') – **visto**
Verbs that follow this pattern are **seguir** ('to follow'), **repetir** ('to repeat').

• Verbs that undergo a consonant change in the first person singular:

c – zc = conducir ('to drive'): **conduzco, conduces**
Verbs that follow this pattern are: **parecer** ('to appear'), **ofrecer** ('to offer')

c – g = hacer ('to make, to do'): **hago, haces**
l – lg = salir ('to leave'): **salgo, sales**
n – ng = poner ('to put'): **pongo, pones**

• Irregular changes to spelling:

Verbs that change by adding **g** to the first person only, and change a vowel in the second and third person singular and third person plural:

tener ('to have')		venir ('to come')	
tengo	tenemos	vengo	venimos
tienes	tenéis	vienes	venís
tiene	tienen	viene	vienen

Verbs that change in the first person singular: e – **ig**:

traer ('to bring')	
traigo	traemos
traes	traéis
trae	traen

Some verbs are completely irregular in all persons:

ir ('to go')		ser ('to be')		estar ('to be')	
voy	vamos	soy	somos	estoy	estamos
vas	vais	eres	sois	estás	estáis
va	van	es	son	está	están

Reflexive verbs

A reflexive verb is one whose subject performs the action of the verb upon himself, herself or itself. In Spanish this idea is conveyed by the use of a reflexive pronoun ('myself', 'yourself', etc.), although the pronoun is not normally used in English, e.g. **levantarse**, 'to get up' [*literally* 'to raise oneself']:

Reflexive verbs take the endings of the relevant verb group (**-ar**, **-er**, or **-ir**).

(yo) **me** levant**o**   (nosotros/as) **nos** levant**amos**
(tú) **te** levant**as**   (vosotros/as) **os** levant**áis**
(él/ella/usted) **se** levant**a**   (ellos/as/ustedes) **se** levant**an**

In the infinitive (**levantarse**) and the imperative (**levántate**), the reflexive pronoun is added to the end of the verb.

Other reflexive verbs: **acostarse** ('to go to bed'), **ducharse** ('to have a shower'), **peinarse** ('to comb one's hair'), **vestirse** ('to get dressed'), **lavarse** ('to have a wash').

Use of the present tense

The present tense can express an action that is happening at the moment, or habitual actions:

> **Voy a la oficina.** I'm going to the office.
> **Voy a la playa los veranos.** I go to the beach in the summer.

The present continuous

The present continuous describes an action taking place at the moment of speaking. It is formed with the present tense of the verb **estar** + a verb in the gerund. The gerund is made up of the stem of the verb + the endings -**ando** for -**ar** verbs, and -**iendo** for -**er** and -**ir** verbs.

> **Estoy trabajando.** I'm working.
> **¿Estás comiendo?** Are you eating?
> **Está viviendo en Madrid.** He's living in Madrid.

The present continuous can also be used to describe an event in the present which continues over a period of time.

Mi hermana **está estudiando** en la universidad. My sister is studying at university.

The future tense

The future tense expresses an action that will happen in the future.

Jugaré al fútbol mañana. I'll play/I'm going to play football tomorrow.

Regular verbs are formed by adding the appropriate future suffix to the infinitive, as follows:

trabajar	**comer**	**vivir**
trabajar**é**	comer**é**	vivir**é**
trabajar**ás**	comer**ás**	vivir**ás**
trabajar**á**	comer**á**	vivir**á**
trabajar**emos**	comer**emos**	vivir**emos**
trabajar**éis**	comer**éis**	vivir**éis**
trabajar**án**	comer**án**	vivir**án**

The following verbs are irregular:

- Verbs that change the stem by adding **d**:

  tener: tendré, tendrás, tendrá, tendremos, tendréis, tendrán

Other verbs that follow this pattern are: **venir (vendré)**, **poner (pondré)**, **salir (saldré)**.

- Verbs that drop the e from the stem:

  saber ('to know'): sabré, sabrás, sabrá, sabremos, sabréis, sabrán

poder ('to be able') also follows this pattern: **podré**, **podrás**, etc.

- Verbs with irregular forms:

decir ('to say')		**hacer**		**querer**	
diré	diremos	haré	haremos	querré	querremos
dirás	diréis	harás	haréis	querrás	querréis
dirá	dirán	hará	harán	querrá	querrán

The construction **ir + a** + infinitive can also be used to talk about the future, in much the same way as the English construction ('going to').

Voy a jugar al fútbol mañana. I'm going to play football tomorrow.

The simple past

The simple past is used to describe finished or completed actions that happened in the past:

¿Adónde fuiste ayer? Where did you go yesterday?
¿Qué hiciste anoche? What did you do last night?
Bailé. I danced.

The simple past tense is formed as follows:

bailar ('to dance')		comer		salir	
bailé	bailamos	comí	comimos	salí	salimos
bailaste	bailasteis	comiste	comisteis	saliste	salisteis
bailó	bailaron	comió	comieron	salió	salieron

Note that -er and -ir verbs are formed in exactly the same way.
Note also that the first person plural in -ar and -ir verb types is the
same as for the simple present.

The following are irregular in all persons.

- Verbs that change the stem vowel to **u**:

  poder: pude, pudiste, pudo
  saber: supe
  poner: puse

- Verbs that change the stem vowel to **i**:

  decir: dije, dijiste, dijo
  hacer: hice
  querer: quise
  venir: vine

- Verbs that add the consonant **j**:

  traer: traje, trajiste, trajo
  decir: dije
  conducir: conduje

dar ('to give')		ser		estar	
di	dimos	fui	fuimos	estuve	estuvimos
diste	disteis	fuiste	fuisteis	estuviste	estuvisteis
dio	dieron	fue	fueron	estuvo	estuvieron

The imperfect
The imperfect tense is used to describe:

- things that used to happen:

  Cuando **era** pequeña **vivía** en el campo. When I was young I
  used to live in the country.

- places, objects, and people in the past:

  Era alta y delgada. She was tall and slim.

- background information that is secondary to the main action:

  Preparaba la cena cuando llegó mi tío. I was preparing dinner
  when my uncle arrived.

The imperfect tense is formed as follows:

bailar		comer		salir	
bailaba	bailábamos	comía	comíamos	salía	salíamos
bailabas	bailabais	comías	comíais	salías	salíais
bailaba	bailaban	comía	comían	salía	salían

Irregular verbs in the imperfect:

ser		ir	
era	éramos	iba	íbamos
eras	erais	ibas	ibais
era	eran	iba	iban

Perfect

The perfect tense is used to describe events in the recent past, in much the same way as the English perfect tense ('I have finished', etc.):

He trabajado mucho esta semana. I've worked a lot this week.
No he jugado al fútbol este año. I haven't played football this year.

The perfect is formed using the present of **haber** ('to have') + the past participle of the verb. The past participle is made up of the stem of the verb + the endings **-ado** for **-ar** verbs, and **-ido** for **-er** and **-ir** verbs. The participle does not vary in gender or number.

bailar		comer	
he bailado	hemos bailado	he comido	hemos comido
has bailado	habéis bailado	has comido	habéis comido
ha bailado	han bailado	ha comido	han comido
salir			
he salido	hemos salido		
has salido	habéis salido		
ha salido	han salido		

Many verbs have an irregular past participle, e.g.:

abrir ('to open'): **abierto**   hacer ('to make, to do'): **hecho**
escribir ('to write'): **escrito**   poner ('to put'): **puesto**
volver ('to return'): **vuelto**

The imperative

The imperative is used to tell or order someone to do something. There are two forms of the imperative: informal [*sing. and pl.*] and formal [*sing. and pl.*]:

	tú [*informal sing.*]	vosotros [*informal pl.*]	usted [*formal pl.*]	ustedes [*formal sing.*]	
hablar	habla	hablad	hable	hablen	speak
comer	come	comed	coma	coman	eat
escribir	escribe	escribid	escriba	escriban	write

Habla más despacio. Speak more quietly.

The formal 'you' form (**usted, ustedes**) is used in polite conversation in shops and other formal situations:

Deme dos kilos, por favor. Give me/Could you give me two kilos, please.
Siga esta calle. Follow this street.

ser and estar
Spanish has two verbs meaning 'to be': **ser** and **estar**.

ser is used:
– to describe a permanent state:

> **Soy** profesora. I'm a teacher.
> La casa **es** grande. The house is big.
> Mi jefe **es** simpático. My boss is nice.

– to tell the time:

> **Son** las dos. It's two o'clock.

estar is used:
– to describe position or location, or a temporary state

> ¿Dónde **está** tu pueblo? Where is your town?
> **Estoy** enfermo. I'm ill.
> La casa **está** limpia. The house is clean.

See under the tenses in the verb section of the Grammar Summary for details of how **ser** and **estar** are formed.

Verbs followed by the infinitive
Certain verbs, such as **poder** ('to be able'), **querer** ('to want'), and **necesitar** ('to need'), are followed by the infinitive:

> ¿**Puede traer** la cuenta? Could you bring the bill?
> **Quiero salir** esta noche. I want to go out tonight.
> **Necesito cambiar** el billete. I need to change the ticket.

Note these other constructions which also take the infinitive:

> **Tengo que estudiar** esta noche. I have to study tonight.
> **Hay que limpiar** esta casa. This house has to be cleaned.
> **Fui a** bailar. I went dancing.

Other verb constructions

• **hacer**
  To describe the weather:

  > **Hace sol**. It's sunny.

  To describe when you did something:

  > Le vi **hace** cinco minutos. I saw him five minutes ago.

• **gustar** ('to like')
  The verb gustar is used with an indirect object pronoun:

  > **Me gusta** el cine. I like the cinema. [*literally* The cinema is pleasing to me.]

• **se** in passive constructions
  se is often used in passive constructions or where there is no specific subject. It is followed by a verb in the third person singular or plural:

  > **Se toma** con nata. You eat it [*literally* it is eaten] with cream.
  > **Se puede** comer frío. You can eat it/It can be eaten cold.
  > **Se cortan** los ingredientes. You slice the ingredients.

Vocabulary

A

	a la plancha	grilled
	a pie	on foot
	a veces	sometimes
	a ver	let's see
	abierto	open
	abril	April
	abrir	to open
la	abuela	grandmother
el	abuelo	grandfather
	aburrirse	to get bored
el	accidente	accident
el	aceite	oil
	acordarse	to remember
	acostarse	to go to bed
la	actitud	attitude
	actual	current
	acudir	to gather in a place
	adecuado	adequate, necessary, suitable
	adelgazar	to slim, to lose weight
	adiós	goodbye
	¿adónde?	where (to)?
las	afueras	outskirts (of a city)
la	agencia	agency
	agosto	August
el	agua [fem.]	water
	ahora mismo	right now
	ahora se pone	he/she is just coming [answering the telephone]
	alemán	German
	Alemania	Germany
	¿algo más?	anything else?
	alguien	someone
	allí	there
el	almíbar	syrup
el	almuerzo	mid-morning snack
	alto	tall
	América	America
el/la	amigo/a	friend
	añadir	to add
	ancho	wide
el	anillo	ring [jewellery]
el	año pasado	last year
	anoche	last night
	anteayer	the day before yesterday
	antiguo	old, antique
	antipático	unpleasant, unfriendly
	anular	to annul, cancel
el	anuncio	advertisement
el	aparcamiento	car park
	aparcar	to park
el	apartamento	apartment
	aquí	here
	Argentina	Argentina
	argentino	Argentinian
el	artículo	(newspaper) article
el	ascensor	lift
	asistir	to attend
	atrás	behind
	Australia	Australia
	australiano	Australian
el	autobús	bus
la	autopista	motorway
la	avenida	avenue
	ayudar	to help
el	azúcar	sugar
	azul	blue

B

	bailar	to dance
	bajo	short [stature]
	bañarse	to bathe
el	banco	bank
	barato	cheap
la	barbacoa	barbecue
el	barco	boat
la	barrera	barrier
	bastante	quite
la	bebida	drink
la	biblioteca	library
	bien	fine
	bilingüe	bilingual
el	billete	(travel) ticket
(el)	billete de) ida y vuelta	return (ticket)
	blanco	white
la	blusa	blouse
la	boca	mouth
el	bocadillo	baguette-type sandwich
la	boda	wedding
	bonito	pretty
el	bote	jar
la	botella	bottle
	buenas noches	good night
	buenas noticias	good news
	buenas tardes	good afternoon
	bueno	good
	buenos días	good morning
	buscar	to look for

C

el	caballero	gentleman
el	café con leche	white coffee
el	café sólo	black coffee
la	cafetería	cafeteria/bar
la	caja	box
los	calamares	squid
	calentar	to heat up
	calificado	qualified
la	cama	bed
	cambiar	to change
el	camión	lorry
la	camisa	shirt
el	campamento	young people's camping holiday
el	campo	countryside
	Canadá	Canada
	canadiense	Canadian
	cansado	tired
	cansarse	to get tired
la	carnicería	butcher's shop
	caro	expensive
el	carrete de fotos	roll of film
la	carta	letter, à la carte menu
la	cartera	wallet
la	casa	house
	casado	married
	casi nunca	hardly ever
la	catedral	cathedral
la	cebolla	onion
el	cementerio	cemetery
	cenar	to have supper, dinner
el	céntimo	cent
	cerca	near
el	cerdo	pork, pig
	cerrar	to close [shop, museum]
la	cerveza	beer
el	champán	champagne
el	champiñón	mushroom
la	chaqueta	jacket, cardigan
la	charcutería	delicatessen
la	chica	girl
el	chico	boy
	chino	Chinese
el	chocolate	chocolate
el	choque	collision, crash
el	chorizo	Spanish spicy sausage
la	chuleta	chop (of meat)
el/la	ciclista	cyclist
	cien	hundred
	cinco	five
	cincuenta	fifty
el	cine	cinema
la	ciudad	city, town
el	coche	car
el	cocido	stew [with meat and chickpeas]
la	cocina	kitchen, cooking

	coger	to catch
el	collar	necklace
	Colombia	Colombia
	colombiano	Colombian
el	comedor	dining room
	comer	to eat
la	comida fuerte	main meal
	como	like [similar to]
	¿cómo es?	what's it like? what does it consist of?
	¿cómo está usted?	how are you?
	¿cómo se llama?	what's your name?
el/la	compañero/a	colleague
	comportarse	to behave
	comprar	to shop, to buy
las	compras	shopping
la	comunidad	community
	con	with
el	concierto	concert
el	concurso	competition
el/la	conductor(a)	driver
el	conejo	rabbit
	conmigo	with me
	conocer	to know, to meet
el/la	contable	accountant
	contagiar	to pass on [germs, an illness]
	continuar	to continue
la	conversación	conversation
el	cordero	lamb
el/la	corredor(a)	runner
	correr	to run
el	cortado	coffee with a dash of milk
	cortar	to cut
	corto	short (hair)
la	costa	coast
	costar	to cost, to take (time)
	crecer	to grow
	creer	to think, to believe
el	cristal	glass
la	cualidad	(personal) quality
	¿cuánto cuesta?	how much does it cost? how long does it take?
	¿cuánto vale?	how much is it?
	¿cuántos años tienen?	how old are they?
	cuarenta	forty
el	(cuarto de) baño	bathroom
	cuatro	four
	cuatrocientos	four hundred
la	cuchara	spoon
el	cuchillo	knife
la	cuenta	bill
	cuidar	to look after
el	cumpleaños	birthday

D

dar a la calle	to face the street
de	from, of
de acuerdo	fine
de nada	that's OK, that's fine, it's a pleasure
debajo	underneath
decidir	to decide
decir	to say
dejar	to let, leave, give, lend
dejar de fumar	to give up smoking
delante de	in front of
delgado	thin, slim
demasiado	too much, too many
dentro de	within
el/la dependiente/a	shop assistant
los deportes	sports
derecha	right [*direction*]
el derecho	(legal) right
desayunar	to have breakfast
descansar	to relax
después	afterwards
detrás de	behind
el día	day
los dibujos animados	cartoons
diciembre	December
diez	ten
¿dígame?	hello? [*answering telephone*]
el dinero	money
dirigir	to direct, to manage
el disco compacto	compact disc
el/la diseñador/a	designer
el disquete	floppy disk
distinto	different
divertirse	to enjoy oneself
el documento	document
doler (me duele)	to hurt (it hurts)
el dolor	pain
domingo	Sunday
¿dónde?	where?
el dormitorio	bedroom
dos	two
doscientos	two hundred
ducharse	to have a shower
durante	during
durar	to last

E

echar de menos	to miss
el edificio	building
el efecto	effect
él	he, it
el/la	the
ella	she, it
ellos/ellas	they
empezar	to begin

el/la empleado/a	employee
la empresa	company
el/la empresario/a	company director
en	in
en seguida	immediately
encantado	pleased to meet you
encantar	to love
el/la encargado/a	person in charge
encima	above
encontrar	to find
encontrarse	to feel
la energía	energy
enero	January
enfadado	angry, annoyed
enfermo	ill, sick
enfrente de	opposite
la ensalada	salad
la ensaladilla rusa	Russian salad
enseñar	to show
entender	to understand
enterarse	to find out
entonces	then, in that case
la entrada	entrance hall
entre	between
entrenar	to train
la entrevista	interview
equilibrado	balanced
el equipaje	luggage
el equipo	team
equivocado	wrong, mistaken
escocés	Scottish
Escocia	Scotland
escribir	to write
el escritor	writer
los espaguetis	spaghetti
la espalda	back
España	Spain
español	Spanish
esperar	to wait
esta noche	tonight
esta	this [*fem.*]
ésta	this one [*fem.*]
la estación	station
el estanco	newsagent's stall
estar	to be
el este	east
este	this [*masc.*]
éste	this one [*masc.*]
estrecho	narrow
estudiar	to study
¡estupendo!	great! terrific!
el euro	euro
exactamente	exactly
el examen	exam
el excursionismo	walking, hiking
explicar	to explain

F

la	falda	skirt
	faltar	to lack, to be missing
la	familia	family
	febrero	February
la	fecha	date
	¡felicidades!	congratulations!
	feliz	happy
la	fiebre	temperature, fever
la	fiesta	party, festival
el	fin de semana	weekend
	físicamente	physically
el	flan	crème caramel
el	formulario	form
la	foto	photo
la	fotocopia	photocopy
el/la	fotógrafo/a	photographer
	francés	French
	Francia	France
	freír	to fry
la	fresa	strawberry
	frío	cold
la	fruta	fruit
la	fruta del tiempo	seasonal fruit
la	frutería	fruiterer's
los	fuegos artificiales	fireworks
	fuera	away, outside
	fuerte	strong
los	fumadores	smoking section
	fumar	to smoke
el/la	funcionario/a	clerk, civil servant

G

	Gales	Wales
	galés	Welsh
la	galleta	biscuit
	ganar	to earn, to win
el	garbanzo	chickpea
la	garganta	throat
	generoso	generous
la	gente	people
	gordo	fat, plump
	gracias	thank you
el	gramo	gramme
	grande	big
los	grandes almacenes	department store
	grave	serious
	gravemente	seriously
la	gripe	flu
	guapo	beautiful, attractive
	Guatemala	Guatemala
	gustar	to please

H

la	habitación doble	double room
	hablar	to speak
	hace buen tiempo	it's good weather
	hace bueno	it's a fine day
	hace calor	it's hot
	hace frío	it's cold
	hace mucho	a long time ago
	hace poco	recently, a short time ago
	hace sol	it's sunny
	hacer	to do, to make
	hacer camping	to go camping
	hacer ejercicio	to take exercise
	hacerse daño	to hurt oneself
la	hamburguesa	hamburger
la	harina	flour
	hasta	until
	hasta luego	see you later
	hay	there is, there are
	hay que …	it's necessary to …
el	helado	ice cream
	herido	injured
la	hermana	sister
el	hermano	brother
	hervir	to boil
el	hielo	ice
la	hija	daughter
el	hijo	son
	histórico	historic
	¡hola!	hello!
	honrado	honest
la	hora	hour
el	horario	timetable
el	hospital	hospital
el	hotel	hotel
	hoy	today

I

la	idea	idea
	importante	important
	incómodo	uncomfortable
	inflamado	swollen, inflamed
la	influencia	influence
la	información	information
la	informática	information technology
la	ingeniera	engineer [female]
el	ingeniero	engineer [male]
	Inglaterra	England
	inglés	English
la	iniciativa	initiative
la	instalación	installation
	inteligente	intelligent
la	interconexión	computer network
	interesante	interesting
	ir	to go
	ir bien	to go well
	Italia	Italy
	italiano	Italian
	izquierda	left [direction]

J

el	jamón	ham
el	jarabe	syrup [e.g.cough syrup]
el	jardín	garden
el/la	jefe/a	boss, head
el	jersey	sweater
la	joyería	jeweller's
las	judías	beans
el	jueves	Thursday
el/la	jugador/a	player
	jugar	to play [games, sport]
	julio	July
	junio	June
	junto	together
la	juventud	youth

K

el	kilo	kilo

L

	lado (al lado de)	next to
	largo	long
la	lata	tin, can
	lavarse	to have a wash
la	leche	milk
	leer	to read
	lejos	far away
	levantarse	to get up
la	ley	law
	libre	free [time]
	ligero	light [weight]
el	limón	lemon
	limpiar	to clean
la	línea	line
	liso	straight
el	litro	litre
	llamar	to call
la	llave	key
	llegar	to arrive
	lleno	full
	llevar	to take, to carry, to give a lift, to wear
	llevar a cabo	to carry out
	llevar retraso	to be delayed
	llover	to rain
	luego	then, afterwards
el	lugar	place, spot
el	lunes	Monday

M

la	madre	mother
la	magdalena	cupcake
	malo	bad
la	mañana	morning
	mandar	to send
	manejar	to manage, to handle, to operate

el	mantenimiento	maintenance
la	manzana	apple
el	mapa	map
el	marido	husband
los	mariscos	seafood
el	martes	Tuesday
	marzo	March
	más o menos	more or less
	mayo	May
	mayor	old [person], older
la	medianoche	midnight
	medio	half
el	mediodía	midday
	mejor	better
el	melocotón	peach
el	melón	melon
	menos	except, less
el	menú del día	menu of the day, set menu
el	mercado	market
la	merluza	hake
el	mes	month
el	mes que viene	next month
la	mesa	table
el	metro	underground
	mexicano	Mexican
	México	Mexico
la	mezcla	mixture
	mi	my
	mientras	while
el	miércoles	Wednesday
el	minuto	minute
	mirar	to look
	¡mire!	look!
	moderno	modern
el	momento	moment
la	montaña	mountain
	montar	to ride, to get on (a train, bus, etc.)
el	monumento	monument
	moreno	dark [complexion, hair]
el	motivo	reason, motive
	mucho	much, a lot
	mucho gusto	pleased to meet you
	muchos	many
los	muebles	furniture
	muerto	dead
la	muralla	wall
el	músculo	muscle
el	museo	museum
	muy	very
	muy bien	very well

N

la	nacionalidad	nationality
	nada más	nothing else
	nervioso	nervous, excited
la	niña	little girl

el niño	little boy
no importa	it's not important
la noche	night
las normas	regulations, rules
el norte	north
nosotros	we, us, ourselves
las noticias	news
la novela	soap opera
noventa	ninety
noviembre	November
nueve	nine
nuevo	new

O

obligado	obliged
ochenta	eighty
ocho	eight
octubre	October
ocupado	busy
ocurrir	to occur, to happen
el oeste	west
la oficina	office
la oficina de correos	post office
la oficina de empleo	job centre
ofrecer	to offer
¡oiga!	excuse me!
el ojo	eye
olvidar	to forget
otro	other, another

P

el padre	father
los padres	parents
el palacio	palace
el pan	bread
la panadería	baker's
el pantalón	trousers
los pantalones	trousers
el pañuelo	handkerchief
el paquete	parcel
para	for
para empezar	to start with
la parada de autobús	bus stop
parar	to stop
parecido	similar
el partido	(football) game, match
el pasaporte	passport
pasar	to spend, to pass (time)
pasear	to walk, to stroll
el paseo	walk, stroll
el pastel	cake
la pastelería	cake shop
la pastilla	pill, tablet
la patata	potato
las patatas fritas	crisps
el pecho	chest [body]
pedir	to ask for
peinarse	to comb one's hair

pelear(se)	to quarrel, to fight
la película	film
la película cómica	comedy film
peligroso	dangerous
el pelo	hair
pequeño	small
perder	to lose
perder peso	to lose weight
perdón	I'm sorry
perdone	excuse me
perezoso	lazy
el perfume	perfume
el periódico	newspaper
el/la periodista	journalist
permitir	to permit, allow
pero	but
la persona	person
personal	personnel
la personalidad	personality
pesar	to weigh
la pescadería	fishmonger's
el pescado	fish
el pie	foot
la pierna	leg
el pimiento	pepper [vegetable]
la piña	pineapple
pisar	to step on
el piso	apartment, floor (of a building)
la pizza	pizza
el plato	plate, dish, course
la playa	beach
la plaza	(town) square
pobre	poor
el pollo	chicken
la pomada	ointment
ponerse en contacto con	to get in touch with
por aquí	around here
por favor	please
por lo menos	at least
la postal	postcard
el postre	dessert
precioso	beautiful
preferir	to prefer
preguntar	to ask (a question)
el premio	prize
preocupado	worried
preocuparse	to worry
primero	first
el/la primo/a	cousin
el programa	television programme
prometer	to promise
pronto	early, soon
la propina	tip
próximo	next
el pueblo	town, village
la puerta	door

	pues	well
el	puesto	(work) position, (market) stall
la	pulsera	bracelet

Q

	que	which
	¡qué casualidad!	what a coincidence!
	¿qué desea?	what would you like?
	¡qué envidia!	I'm so envious/jealous!
	¡qué lástima!	what a pity!
	¿qué quería?	what would you like?
	¡qué suerte!	you lucky thing!
	¡qué susto!	what a shock!
	¿qué te parece?	what do you think?
	quedar	to arrange to meet
	quedarse	to stay
	quemado	burnt
	quemarse	to get sunburnt
	querer	to love, to want
el	queso	cheese
	quiero ...	I'd like ...
	quince	fifteen
	quinientos	five hundred
	quizás	perhaps, possibly

R

	rápido	fast
la	raqueta de tenis	tennis racquet
	raro	strange
	rebozar	to cover in batter
el	recado	message
	recetar	to prescribe
	recibir	to receive
	recomendar	to recommend
	recordar	to remember
el	recuerdo	memory
el	refresco	soft drink
el	regalo	gift
el	régimen	diet
el/la	representante de ventas	sales representative
	reservar	to reserve
el	restaurante	restaurant
el	retraso	delay
	rizado	curly
la	rodilla	knee
	romper	to break
la	ropa	clothes
	rosa	pink
	rubio	blond(e)
el	ruido	noise

S

la	sal	salt
la	sala de conciertos	concert hall
la	salchicha	sausage
	salir	to leave, go out
el	salón	lounge
	¡salud!	cheers!
los	saludos	greetings
las	sandalias	sandals
la	sandía	watermelon
la	sardina	sardine
la	sección	section
el/la	secretario/a	secretary
el	secreto	secret
	seguir	to follow
	segundo	second
los	seguros	insurance
	seis	six
el	sello	stamp
la	semana	week
	sencillo	simple
el	señor	Mr
la	señora	Mrs, Ms
la	señorita	Miss
	sentirse	to feel
	septiembre	September
	ser	to be
	serio	serious
el	servicio al cliente	customer service
	sesenta	sixty
la	sesión	performance
	setenta	seventy
	siete	seven
el	siglo	century
el	silencio	silence
la	silla	chair
	simpático	likeable, friendly, pleasant
	sincero	sincere
el	sitio	space, place
	sobre	about
el	sobre	envelope
la	sopa	soup
	sospechar	to suspect
	su	his, her
	sucio	dirty
la	sucursal	branch (of a company)
el	sueldo	salary
la	suerte	luck
el	supermercado	supermarket
el	sur	south

T

	también	as well, also
el	Támesis	Thames
la	tapa	bar snack
la	tarde	afternoon

243

la	tarta	cake, tart
el	té	tea
el	teatro	theatre
el	temperamento	temperament
la	temporada	(sports) season
	tener	to have
	tener hambre	to be hungry
	tener prisa	to be in a hurry
	tener razón	to be right
	tener sueño	to be sleepy
	tercero	third
	terminar	to finish
la	tía	aunt
la	tienda	shop
la	tienda de electrodomésticos	electrical appliance shop
el	tío	uncle
el	tobillo	ankle
	todo recto	straight ahead
	todos	all, every
	tomar	to have (food or drink)
los	tomates	tomatoes
	torcer	to twist
el	toro	bull
la	tostada	toast
	trabajador	hardworking
	trabajar	to work
el	trabajo	work
	traer	to bring
el	tráfico	traffic
el	traje	suit
	tranquilamente	quietly, without fuss
la	tranquilidad	calmness, peacefulness
	tranquilo	calm
	tranquilo	quiet, peaceful
	trasladar	to move house
el	trayecto	route
	treinta	thirty
el	tren	train
	tres	three
	trescientos	three hundred
	triste	sad
	tú	you [*informal*]

U

	último	last
la	universidad	university
	uno	one
	urgentemente	urgently
	usar	to use
	usted	you [*formal*]
	utilizar	to use
la	uva	grape

V

las	vacaciones	holidays
el	vagón	carriage (train)
	vale	OK
	vale la pena	it's worth it
	varios	several
el/la	vecino/a	neighbour
	veinte	twenty
	ver	to see
el	verano	summer
la	verdulería	greengrocer's
la	verdura	vegetables
el	vestido	dress
	vestirse	to get dressed
la	vía	platform
	viajar	to travel
el	viaje	journey
el	vídeo	video
	viejo	old
el	viernes	Friday
el	vino	wine
el	vino blanco	white wine
el	vino tinto	red wine
	violento	violent
	visitar	to visit
la	vista	view
	vivir	to live
	volver	to return
	vosotros	you [*informal pl.*]
la	vuelta	return (journey, ticket)

Y

	yo	I

Z

la	zanahoria	carrot
los	zapatos	shoes
el	zumo (de naranja)	(orange) juice

Glossary of grammatical terms

Adjective: A word used to give information about a noun.

una casa **grande** a big house
mi coche es **nuevo** my car is new

Adverb: A word used to give information about a verb.

Conduce **rápidamente**. He drives fast.
Estoy **bien**. I'm well.

Article: In English 'the' is the definite article (in Spanish **el/la/los/las**) and 'a' and 'an' are the indefinite articles (**un/una/unos/unas**). See *Definite article, Indefinite article*.

Comparative: The form of an adjective or adverb used to express higher or lower degree. See also *Superlative*.

El anillo es **más/menos caro** que el collar. The ring is more/less expensive than the necklace.

Conditional: A verb form often used to say what you would like to do or to give an invitation.

Me gustaría ir a Ibiza de vacaciones. I'd like to go to Ibiza for my holidays.

Definite article: In English, the definite article is 'the'. In Spanish, the definite articles are **el, la, los, las**.

Direct object: The noun, pronoun, or phrase directly affected by the action of the verb.

He comprado **una chaqueta**. I've bought a jacket.
Las quiero. I want them

Disjunctive pronoun: A form of pronoun used after a preposition or for emphasis.

Para **mí**, la sopa. The soup for me.
Le gusta **a él**. He (in particular) likes it.

Ending: A letter or letters added to the stem of the verb to show the tense, subject, and number; also to nouns and adjectives, to show the number and gender.

Trabajar**é** mañana. I'll work tomorrow.
las cas**as** grand**es** the big houses

Feminine: One of the two genders in Spanish. See *Gender*.

Future tense: The form of a verb used to express what will happen in the future.

El tren **llegará** pronto. The train will arrive soon.

Gender: In Spanish, all nouns have a gender, either masculine or feminine, although a very small number can have both. The gender of a noun is indicated by the form of the definite or indefinite article used (**el/la; un/una**). Gender also affects the form of accompanying words such as adjectives, possessive pronouns, etc.

masculine: **el coche, un pueblo bonito**
feminine: **la casa, una blusa roja**

Gerund: A form mainly used in the present or past continuous tense. It corresponds to the '-ing' form in English. See *Present continuous*.

Estoy **estudiando**. I'm studying.

Imperative: The form of a verb that is used to express orders or instructions, or to suggest that someone does something.

Pase por aquí, por favor. Please come this way. [*formal*]
Pasa por aquí. Come this way. [*informal*]

Imperfect tense: The form of a verb used to express a continuous or habitual action in the past.

Antes **vivía** en Barcelona. Previously, he used to live in Barcelona.

Indefinite article: In English, the indefinite articles are 'a' and 'an'. In Spanish they are **un, una**, and in the plural form **unos, unas**, the equivalent of 'some' in English.

Indirect object: The noun, pronoun, or phrase indirectly affected by the action of the verb.

Le voy a escribir. I'm going to write to him.

Infinitive: The basic form of a verb which does not indicate a particular tense or number or person.

trabajar, 'to work'
comer, 'to have dinner, to eat'
vivir, 'to live'

Intonation: The pattern of sounds made in a sentence as the speaker's voice rises and falls.

Irregular verb: A verb that does not follow one of the set patterns and has its own individual forms. Many common verbs such as **venir** ('to come'), **ser** ('to be'), and **ir** ('to go') are irregular.

Masculine: One of the two genders in Spanish. See *Gender*.

Noun: A word that identifies a person, thing, place, or concept.

hermano brother
Sr. García Sr. García
coche car
libro book
jardín garden
vida life

Number: Indicating whether a noun or pronoun is singular or plural. Number is one of the factors determining the form of accompanying words such as adjectives and possessive forms.

singular: **un hombre** a man
una mujer a woman
plural: **dos hombres** two men
dos mujeres two women
unos coches some cars

Cardinal numbers: numbers used to count – one, two, three/ **uno, dos, tres**, etc.
Ordinal numbers: numbers that show the position or order of something – first, second, third/**primero, segundo, tercero**, etc.

Object: The noun, pronoun, or phrase affected by the action of the verb.

See *Direct object, Indirect object.*

Past participle: The form of a verb used either on its own as an adjective:

Estoy **cansado**. I'm tired.

or in combination with the verb **haber** in the perfect tense:

He **hablado** con Miguel. I have spoken to Miguel.

Perfect tense: The form of a verb used to talk about the recent past, very like the English perfect tense (e.g. he has eaten).

He **terminado** mi trabajo. I've finished my work.

Person: A category used to distinguish between the 'I'/'we' (first person), 'you' (second person), and 'he'/'she'/'it'/'they' (third person) forms of the verb. The person is reflected in the verb and/or in the pronoun accompanying it, although in Spanish the pronoun is often omitted.

(**Yo**) hablo. (first person singular)
Ella trabaja. (third person singular)
Vosotros descansáis. (second person plural)

Plural: Denoting more than one. See *Number*.

Possessive forms: Adjectives and pronouns used to show belonging.

Él ha perdido **su** libro. He has lost his book.
Ese coche es **mío**. That car is mine.

Preposition: A word (e.g. 'at', 'by', 'from') or phrase (e.g. 'to the left of', 'next to') used before a noun or pronoun to show its relationship to the rest of the sentence.

Estaré **en** la escuela **a** las nueve. I'll be at school at nine.
Tus libros están **en** la mesa. Your books are on the table.
El hospital está **al lado del** hotel. The hospital is next to the hotel.

Present tense: The form of a verb used to express something that is happening or in existence now, or as a habitual occurrence.

Hablamos todos los días. We speak every day.
Tengo un trabajo bueno. I have a good job.

Pronoun: A word used to stand for a noun. Pronouns may refer to things or concepts ('it', 'them'), or people ('she', 'him'), and may be indefinite ('someone', 'something').

Yo creo que **tú** tienes razón. I think that you are right.
A mí me gusta **éste**. I like this one.
¿**Algo** más? Anything else?

Reflexive verb: A verb whose object refers to the same person as its subject. The verb form contains an pronoun to indicate this reflexive action:

Su madre **se levanta** a las siete. His mother gets [herself] up at seven.

Regular verb: A verb that follows a common set pattern.

Simple past tense: A tense used to describe an action which occurred once in the past at a defined moment and which is now complete:

Fui al cine ayer. I went to the cinema yesterday.

Singular: Denoting only one. See *Number*.

Stem: The part of a verb to which endings showing tense, number, and person are added.

hablar: (yo) **hablo**, (tú) **habl**as

Subject: The noun, pronoun, or phrase that performs the action indicated by the verb.

Mi madre está enferma. My mother is ill.
Ella tiene quince años. She's 15.

Subjunctive: A form of the verb used for formal imperatives or polite enquiries or requests.

Pase por aquí. Please come through.
Quisiera hablar con el Sr. García. I'd like to speak to Sr. García.

Superlative: The form of an adjective or adverb used to express the highest or lowest degree. See also *Comparative*.

Su coche es **el más rápido**. His car is the fastest.
Juan es **el mejor** de la clase. Juan is the best in the class.

Syllable: A unit of pronunciation which forms either the whole or part of a word.

sol (one syllable)
jar/dín (two syllables)
pis/ci/na (three syllables)

Tense: The form of a verb which indicates when the action takes place, i.e. in the past, present, or future.

Verb: A word or phrase used to express what is being done or what is happening. It may also express a state.

Miguel **está comiendo**. Miguel is eating.
El tren **ha salido**. The train has left.
Pablo **tiene** dos hermanos. Pablo has two brothers

Index

In addition to the Language Building pages listed below, see also the relevant section of the Grammar Summary.